Making Photographs

DEVELOPING A PERSONAL VISUAL WORKFLOW

Ibarionex Perello

rockynook

Making Photographs
Developing a Personal Visual Workflow

Ibarionex Perello
www.ibarionex.net

PROJECT EDITOR: Jocelyn Howell
PROJECT MANAGER: Lisa Brazieal
MARKETING COORDINATOR: Mercedes Murray
INTERIOR DESIGN: Andrew Massiatte López
INTERIOR LAYOUT: Kim Scott, Bumpy Design
COVER DESIGN: Andrew Massiatte López

ISBN: 978-1-68198-399-8

1st Edition (1st printing, December 2018)
© 2019 Ibarionex Perello
All images © Ibarionex Perello unless otherwise noted

Rocky Nook Inc.
1010 B Street, Suite 350
San Rafael, CA 94901
USA

www.rockynook.com

Distributed in the U.S. by Ingram Publisher Services
Distributed in the UK and Europe by Publishers Group UK

LIBRARY OF CONGRESS CONTROL NUMBER: 2018940619

Printed in Korea

Para Taisha. Tu fuerza y valor me inspiras.

About the Author

Ibarionex Perello is a photographer, writer, educator, and the host of *The Candid Frame* photography podcast. He has worked in the photography industry for over 25 years and is the author or coauthor of six books, including *Chasing the Light: Improving Your Photography Using Available Light* and *Adobe Master Class: Photoshop*. His photographs and articles have appeared in numerous publications and websites, including *Outdoor Photographer*, *Digital Photo Pro*, *Shutterbug*, *Rangefinder*, *Popular Photography*, and many more.

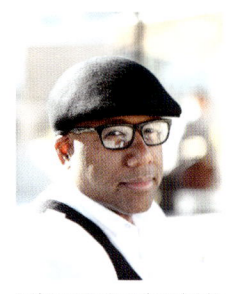

Author portrait: Neil Waybright

Ibarionex has served as an adjunct professor at ArtCenter College of Design and he teaches workshops through the Los Angeles Center of Photography. He has spoken at numerous photographic events in the Unites States and abroad. He lives in the Los Angeles area with his wife and their dog Zooey.

Website: ibarionex.net
Podcast: thecandidframe.com
Instagram: @Ibarionex

Table of Contents

Foreword

Ibarionex Perello's new book and photography course has a great advantage for its readers. Ibarionex is one of the best podcasters in the world of photography today. His insights and questions when he speaks with photographers are second to none; he probes and questions with intensity and love of the medium, and I know this from personal experience.

I have no doubt that he has learned and assimilated an enormous amount from the hundreds of artists he has spoken with, and this, combined with his own experiences as a photographer, adds to the depth of this new book. He has written a rich and provocative work of inspiration and instruction that will carry any open-minded enthusiast along on their trip toward personal discovery.

In today's world, where more than a billion people on the planet now have daily access to an image-making device, the cry for a reliable working method, and how to develop a personal point of view, seems universal. The guidelines and questions that this book puts into play will stimulate and educate anyone curious enough to take the time to enter *Making Photographs: Developing a Visual Workflow*.

I highly recommend taking the trip with Ibarionex and seeing how your understanding of your own work, and photography in general, comes into focus.

Joel Meyerowitz

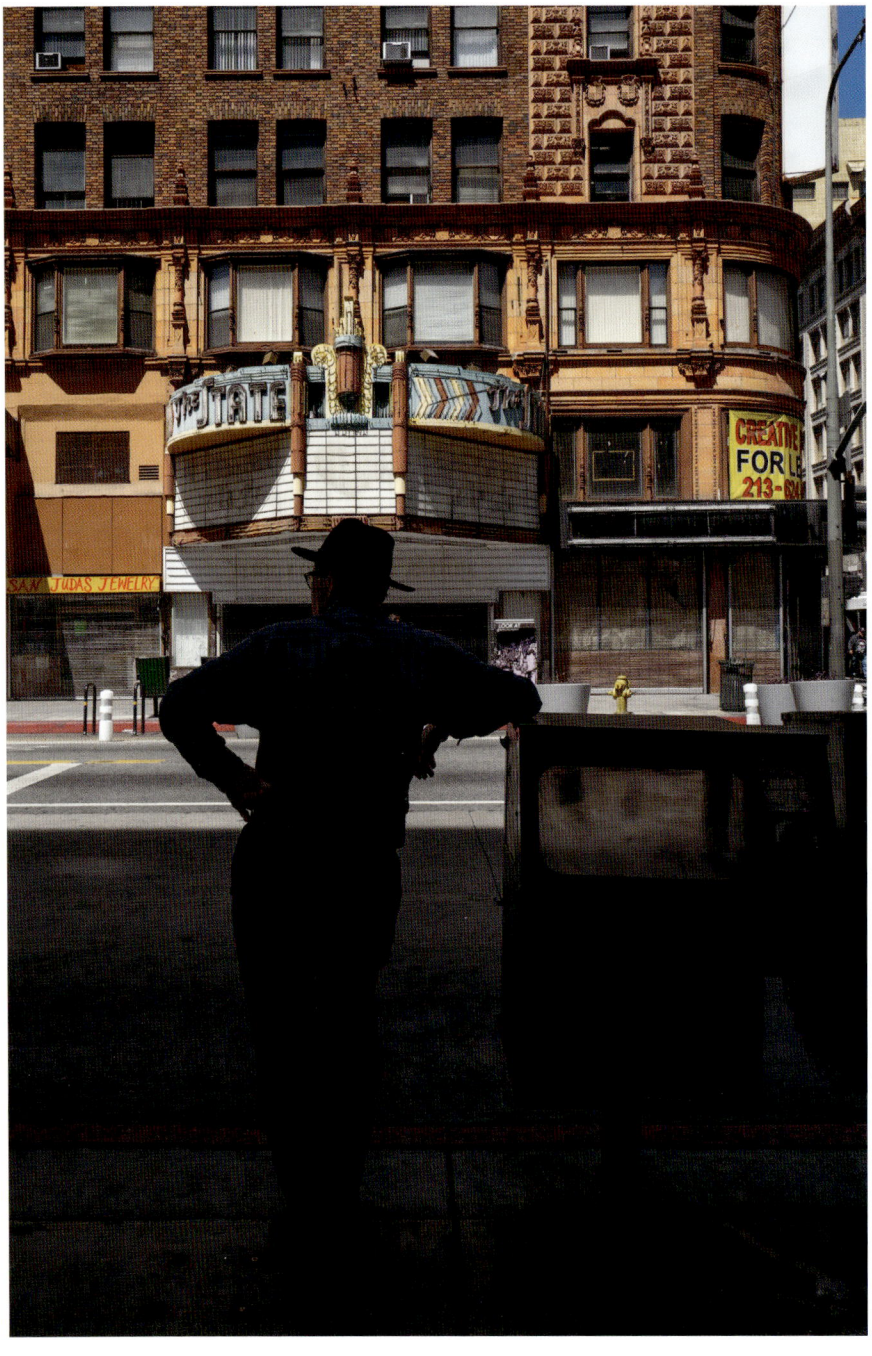

Introduction

I believe the thing that makes it difficult to improve your photography is the ease with which you are able to make photographs. Raise the camera to your eye, press the button, and there you have it: a photograph.

It is this very simplicity that leads you to pick up a camera rather than a guitar or a tennis racket. With today's technology, you can pick up almost any kind of camera and produce a picture that is both well exposed and in focus. If you are lucky, you produce an image that is visually pleasing and solicits the admiration of family and friends. If you try the same thing with a guitar, you succeed only in producing a noise that no one, except maybe your mother, describes as music.

Photography is the rare creative process that offers entry to virtually anyone. And its simplicity is enough to lure you into a lifelong passion.

However, there comes a time when photography becomes harder. Surprisingly, the difficulty does not lie in an inability to understand shutter speed and aperture, or ISO and exposure compensation. These technical matters are relatively easy to understand, if not to master. The real challenge lies in the ability to make good images consistently.

Anyone is capable of producing a really good image if they capture enough photographs. However, the challenge is being able to do so consistently, and more importantly, to understand how and why you were able to do it in the first place. Without that knowledge, your good photography relies more on luck than skill or talent.

With this book, I hope to remedy this issue by helping you to move beyond the technical side of photography to the world of seeing. It is the act of seeing that really provides photography its magic. It is the seeing that provides wonderful moments of discovery that inspire you to reach for the camera in the first place. It is the seeing that, when practiced and improved, allows you to reach your full potential as a photographer.

Throughout this book we are going to break down seeing into a visual workflow, with individual steps that will help you to not only make great photographs, but also gain a clearer understanding of what it takes to do so.

We will break down this visual workflow into four categories:

Light and shadow

Line and shape

Color

Gesture

You will discover how observing light and shadow helps you to make creative images of your subjects rather than simply document them. By observing line and shape, you will develop an understanding of framing and composition. You will see how color can help guide your eye to or away from your subject. And you will find how gesture transforms a good photograph into a great one.

By providing structure to your personal way of seeing, you will create a repeatable process that takes the guesswork out of a successful photograph. You will develop the skills needed to evaluate any subject and scene and transform it into a photograph that reflects both your vision and your unique way of seeing the world.

This visual workflow is not only important when you are making photographs, but is just as valuable when you are sorting through the hundreds of images you create during a shooting session. You will learn to use the very same principles of your new visual workflow to evaluate and compare images. You will confidently select your best photographs and understand why they are superior to others.

Along the way, I will share my own personal journey of seeing. I will share not only how it made a difference in my photography, but also how it taught me to enjoy and appreciate the visual feast that our world has to offer. I will be honest with those circumstances and thoughts that sometimes threaten my ability to be my best.

As you transform the way you see and capture the world, you will use photography to share how you, and only you, see what is around us. We will see the world through your eyes.

Let's go.

The Mindset

I vividly remember the moment I fell in love with photography. I was in the darkroom of the Boys Club of Hollywood that my brothers and I attended. I looked into a developing tray where I had just inserted a blank sheet of photographic paper. I rocked the tray back and forth, creating repeating waves over the white sheet. The room was quiet except for the steady slosh of chemicals in a white plastic tray. Slowly, from nothingness, an image appeared. At first, it was nothing more than splotches of gray, but within minutes I recognized it as the scene I had photographed just hours before. I had never seen anything so wondrous.

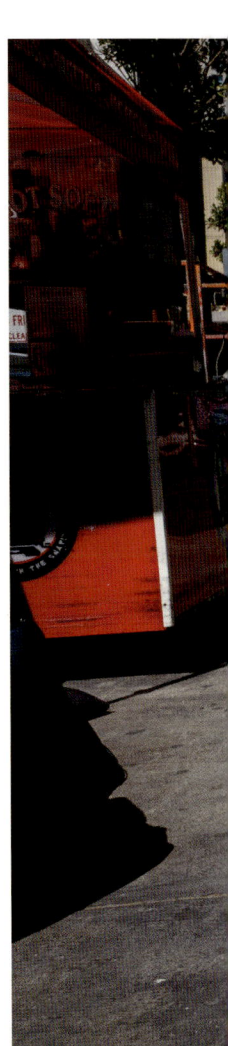

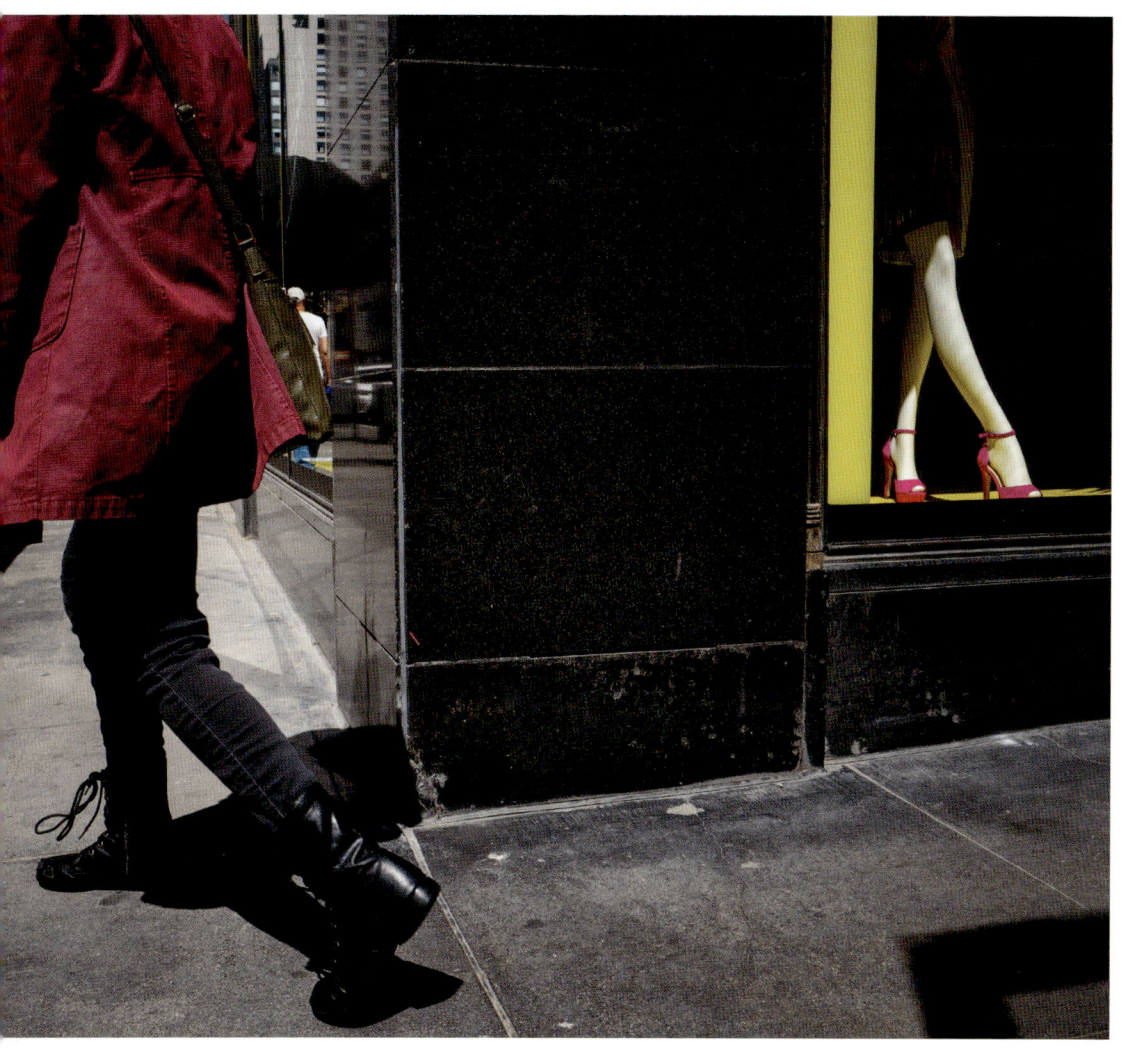

As I moved the print through the rest of the developing process I felt excitement and joy. The pride that I felt holding the finished print in my hands was unlike anything I had ever experienced before. I had made this, and it was beautiful.

I felt empowered in that moment, a feeling that had so often eluded me. I was a fat kid with a bad stutter who constantly feared failing at sports on the playground or sounding foolish in the classroom. I tried to be invisible, hoping to avoid the ridicule and the teasing of my classmates. The less I stood out, the better.

Though I did not know it at the time, that choice robbed me of the many joys we are meant to experience. By trying to hide, I was closing myself off from not only negative attention, but also the happiness that can be had by exploring the unfamiliar, taking risks, and discovering something new about the world and about myself.

I discovered just such a moment in the darkroom. It is a feeling that I have continued to pursue all these years later.

You have your own story of how you discovered that joy. Your story may be similar to mine, or it may not be. But what we have in common are those feelings of exhilaration, of discovery, of wonder that are derived from seeing our personal point of view made manifest in a photograph. Those feelings are not derived from merely documenting what is in front of us; rather, it is the pride and satisfaction that comes from creating an image that expresses something of ourselves to another human being. With a photograph, we are able to express and share something that we find difficult, if not impossible, to express in words.

Yet, despite the rich and powerful feelings that we often associate with photography, there are so many things that stand in the way of experiencing them. Sometimes the obstacles lie in a lack of technical knowledge. More often than not, it has nothing to do with the camera. The things that stand in the way of our creative selves are often our insecurities or the fear of failure. Frustration only grows as we struggle to consistently make a good photograph. Many times, we fail. And when we do succeed, we do not completely understand how we did it. The fulfillment that came so easily at first becomes painfully elusive.

Thankfully, I have found ways to negotiate around such obstacles. The approach that I share with you in the following chapters will help you to derive more joy from your passion and allow you to make the most of whatever time you dedicate to your photography.

A High Bar – Reasonable Perspective

I am a perfectionist and as such, I have a history of unreasonable expectations. I have often sat in judgment of my talent as a photographer based on the number of exceptional images that I could produce in a photo session. If I returned with half a dozen great images, I was a savant. If I returned with nothing, I was a boorish hack. There was no in-between.

What was lost in those extremes was a true understanding of the nature of creativity. Creativity is not measured solely by its successes, but also by its false starts, mistakes, and deviations. Creativity is as much about those moments of confusion and uncertainty as those times of confidence and clarity. When it comes to photography, creativity is rooted in those photographs that fall short of the mark as well as those that hit the bullseye.

It is important to set a high goal for yourself, a standard that will challenge you in any variety of ways. It is the effort involved in accomplishing such goals that allows you to learn and discover. But it has to be done with the understanding that there will be many missteps along the way, and for photographers that means a lot of bad photographs. But that is okay, because that is part of the creative process.

When I was photographing in San Francisco, I set a single goal for myself. I wanted to make a photograph in the city that I had not made before. I did not want to make a duplicate of a photograph that I had made in San Francisco or even in another city. I wanted to challenge myself to see just a little differently. I wanted to surprise myself.

When I saw the window display pictured in the chapter opening image, I was drawn to how the light illuminated the mannequin's pale legs and brightly colored heels. As I observed the rest of the scene, I saw a red food cart off to the left and a triangular shadow just below the window. I knew that I could use those elements for an interesting composition, but I also knew that I needed something else. I needed a human figure to help complete the scene.

For the next 20 minutes, I photographed different people as they walked past, constantly shifting my position in an effort to create a sense of symmetry and balance in the composition. Most of the frames were failures, either because the person was not right or my timing was off. I could feel frustration building, but I persisted, trusting the instincts that led me to the scene.

When a woman in a purple jacket and black boots walked by, I waited for the moment when her splayed legs mirrored those of the mannequin. It was a photograph that for me went beyond capturing someone walking down the street. It was a photograph that was built on my growing sensitivity to disparate elements in a scene that could only be connected within the context of a photographic composition.

Remember that a master photographer is often great in the eyes of others because they shared only their best work. They did not share the countless lesser images they made to get to those exceptional ones.

As the photographer, you see everything you produce, so your perception of yourself and your photography is highly skewed. Remember that each and every photograph you produce is just a single step in the journey. You will never arrive at your destination without taking them.

Staying Aware Through Journaling

Photography for me is more than just the act of making a photograph. It is the means by which I am able to avoid the many distractions that exist in my life. When I am out with my camera, I am present in my life and my existence in a way that I often find difficult during my day-to-day routine. I often describe it as a meditative process that allows me to shake away the voices in my head. I enjoy and appreciate what I am seeing in the moment. I am open to anything and everything. It is in this state of mind when I discover subjects and scenes that I never anticipated when I walked off my stoop, camera in hand.

However, these experiences do not always come easily, even with all my years of practice. Sometimes my mind and my feelings are caught up with anxiety about whether or not I will produce a good photograph. There are moments when I am filled with fear as I struggle to summon the courage to approach a stranger to make their portrait. Or I fall into depression when I compare myself and my work to another photographer and find myself lacking. It is in such moments when negative feelings overwhelm. The joy that inspired me to pick up the camera is no longer found.

Photography becomes a struggle and, on some days, even a chore. During such moments, it is hard to find the inspiration to pick up the camera, much less try to make photographs. Does that sound familiar?

I used to think that if I could only get rid of those thoughts and feelings, I would be more creative. I just needed to summon enough strength or force of will to regain my confidence and find inspiration. And when I was not able to do that, I was angry at myself for my weaknesses and lack of discipline.

When I shared this with a friend, he suggested I keep a journal dedicated to my creative process. In it I would write down not just what I did that day, but how I was feeling about the work itself. I would document both my successes and my failures. When I struggled, I would explore what feelings were at the heart of such moments. And when I succeeded, I would examine what I did to help me move past negative feelings and create.

Within a short period of time, I came to recognize that I felt those negative thoughts and feelings virtually any time I wanted to be creative. The intensity would vary, but they were always there. However, I found that when I made photographs, those feelings quickly diminished. They might not completely disappear, but they did not stand in my way of making the photographs.

As I dutifully wrote in my journal, I examined my own process of creativity and saw how my feelings and thoughts helped or hindered that process. Most importantly, I realized that the only solution for those negative feelings and thoughts was the physical act of being creative. I could not wait for inspiration to arrive and save me. I had to create my own inspiration by just taking action and making photographs.

Without journaling, I was trapped in my thoughts.

I was like a hamster on a treadmill, expending lots of energy but getting nowhere. I would think and think, believing that thinking alone would get me out of the rut, but it only led to endless procrastination and self-flagellation.

Each time I went out to photograph and logged it in my journal, I was able to reconnect myself with the positivity of photography. I linked photography more with joy and less with frustration, anxiety, and struggle.

By associating photography with those positive feelings of joy, achievement, and discovery, I moved past the many excuses that I used to not make time for photography. It challenged me to take risks and discover what I was capable of when I moved out of my comfort zone and explored the unfamiliar.

The moment of hesitation described in the journal entry on the following page is familiar to me. I am faced with it virtually every time I go out and make photographs of strangers. Back home, I am able to overcome it easily enough because there is no language barrier. Yet on that day in Paris I proved to myself that language was not the real obstacle; it was my own fear, particularly the fear of looking foolish, that was really holding me back.

Journal entries like the one on the following page helped me to understand both my strengths and weaknesses when it came to making photographs. As I thought of this particular encounter, I came to understand that it was less about the fear of rejection and more about looking foolish in someone else's eyes. Over time, these observations led me to taking more risks and reconsidering when and how to approach a subject or a scene.

▶ JOURNAL ENTRY | AUGUST 28, 2017

Today was our last day in Paris. While sitting in a café having breakfast, I caught sight of an amazing looking man with an impressive white beard. He was wearing dark shades, a straw hat, and denim jacket. The moment I caught sight of him, I knew I would love to photograph him, but I hesitated.

I pointed him out to Cynthia and she said I should ask him to make his photograph. I shook my head. I felt terribly insecure with my inability to speak French and to explain not only that I wanted to make his photograph, but why. He disappeared around the corner and I just counted it as yet another missed opportunity.

A few minutes later, he reappeared and walked past us. Cynthia repeated her suggestion, but again I chose not to get up and approach him. I felt frustrated and angry at myself. How many times had I planned to study conversational French for just such occasions? I had not, and this was the result, another great shot that would live only in my memory.

To my surprise, I saw him again walking in the opposite direction on the side of the street where we were having coffee. This time he caught my gaze and I smiled and shyly raised my camera up in a gesture suggesting that I wanted to make his photograph. He nodded and waved me over.

Without saying a word, I walked up to him and gestured to him to move to a location that provided a better quality of light and background. I moved in tight knowing that I wanted to emphasize his face and beard. He was smoking a cigarette and exhaled a cloud of smoke. I realized that I wanted to incorporate that into the shot. I pantomimed that I wanted him to do that again. I caught the moment when the smoke rose from the corner of his mouth and hung frozen in the air. I took several more frames and thanked him with the little French that I knew. He nodded and was back on his way.

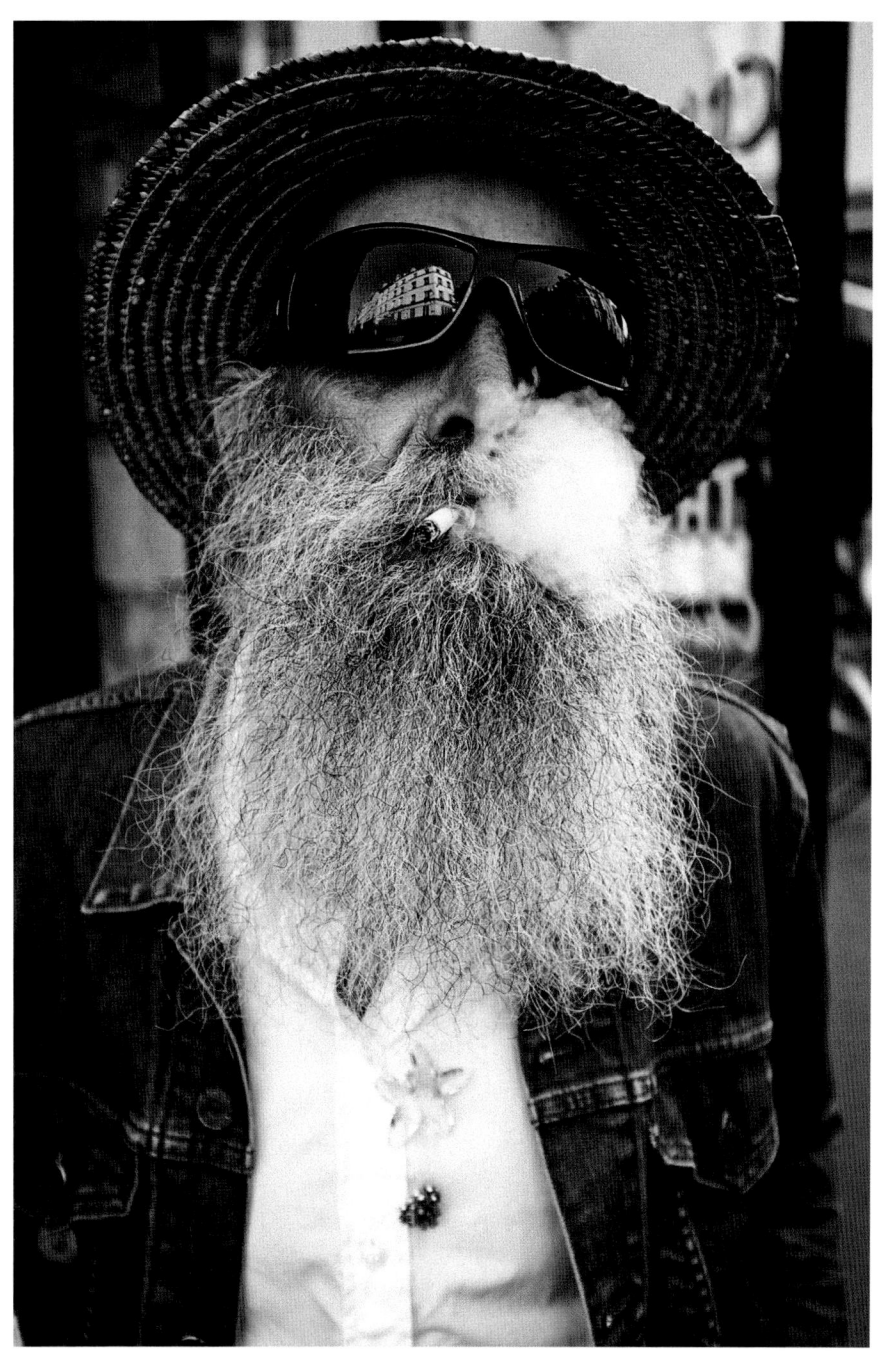

Your Journal

Your journal can be as simple as a spiral notebook or an app on your electronic device or computer. Regardless of format, you want to have it readily accessible. If you choose a physical notebook, choose one that is small enough to fit into your camera bag.

I use an app called Day One (www.dayoneapp.com), which I can access via my phone, tablet, or computer. I sync my photo journal between all those devices, making it completely accessible to me. The reason I prefer this is that I can easily include a photograph from that day's shooting session that I captured with or uploaded to my phone. It not only serves as a good reference tool when going through past posts, but it allows me to connect what I wrote with a specific photograph.

You should write in your journal soon after you have finished shooting. Do not wait for the next day to write about the experience. You want to write down your thoughts and feelings while they are still fresh. If you have a great day of photography, focus not only on what you saw and felt, but what specifically about the experience made it feel worthwhile. Ask yourself questions such as the following:

How present was I while I was shooting?

Did I feel challenged?

If I was feeling anxiety or fear, how did I move past it?

How did I feel when I was "in the zone?"

When was I at my happiest? My unhappiest?

How did I feel physically during the shoot? How did I feel before and after?

What was the easiest thing about today? What was the most difficult?

Did I allow fear and anxiety keep me from making a photograph?

Was I feeling physically uncomfortable, hungry, or tired?

What negative self-talk was I listening to? When have I heard this before?

Was I putting too much pressure on myself to perform?

Was I competing with or comparing myself with someone else?

I write in my journal before culling through the images on my computer. I do not want my judgment about the images to influence how I evaluate the shooting experience. I want each journal entry to be an honest expression of what I experienced while photographing.

When I make the mistake of looking at the images first, it shifts my perspective from how I felt while shooting to how I feel about the images themselves. If I am dissatisfied with the day's results, it inevitably impacts what I write down in the journal, which does me no good.

The journal creates an objective perspective on how I think and feel when I am shooting. When I later compare my notes on a session to another single shooting session, or several, this perspective allows me to learn about my process for creating images.

Gaining Perspective

Over the weeks and months of journaling, I saw patterns emerge. I was at my best when I kept my promise to myself to get out at a particular date and time to photograph. I was more productive when I was working alone, rather than with other photographers. I enjoyed the freedom I felt when I chose to work with only one camera and one lens. I felt less pressure when I went out with no expectation, no agenda in terms of what kind of photographs I intended to make. I discovered more interesting subject matter when I limited where I lingered, rather than endlessly walking.

I also realized how unproductive I was when I was hungry or thirsty. I was less interested in seeing when my legs and feet ached. My enthusiasm diminished when I reviewed the images on my LCD and found them lackluster. I was too preoccupied with settings and controls when using a new piece of kit. Sometimes I avoided making images when I anticipated a person's negative reaction.

Writing down and later reading these entries helped me to identify what to do and what to avoid in order to make the most of my time practicing photography. And when I evaluated my images alongside these journal entries, I saw how my photography benefited from my being in a positive and comfortable a mindset.

These regular entries identified the things that helped me to focus more on my process of seeing. When I focused on distractions, I lacked focus and intent. I would *take* photographs, but I was not seeing carefully enough to *make* photographs.

Meditation and Breathing

One of the discoveries I made through journaling was how much I would subject myself to negative self-talk before I exposed a single frame.

> *"I am not going to find anything good to shoot."*

> *"I'm not as talented as I think."*

> *"That person will probably punch me in the face if I try to take his photograph."*

> *"I'm not fooling anyone. I'm just a hack."*

> *"I'm not as good as the photographer I am out here with."*

> *"The light sucks. I won't be able to make anything work here."*

> *"I don't have the right equipment. If only I had (fill in the blank)."*

You probably have your own personal version of that voice. But regardless of what that voice says or sounds like for you, it is an obstacle that can stand in the way between you and your creativity. I know it often has for me.

My journal entries revealed that to me. Most importantly, they showed me that the more I tried to fight those feelings, the worse they became. I was having an argument with a reflection in a mirror and was frustrated that I could not win the debate.

The mistake I made was in believing that I had to find a way to get rid of those feelings in order to release my creativity. I falsely believed that other people, especially successful creative people, did not experience this. They simply picked up the camera, the pen, or the paintbrush and beauty and creativity flowed out of them like fresh spring water. They were special. They were talented. It just comes harder to someone like me.

My journal entries made me realize how wrong I was because I could see that there were many times when I was awash in creativity. There were moments when I was completely in the zone and enjoying every minute of the process. Though the images were not always exceptional, I could see myself stretching and experimenting and playing. Yes, there were times when the experience was difficult and challenging, but I began to understand what circumstances frequently led to those bad experiences, and that I could do something about them.

One of the biggest lessons I learned was the importance of establishing my mindset before I even raised the camera to my eye. That moment has become the most important time for any photography session, whether on the street or in the studio.

Each time I begin a shooting session, I make time to simply breathe. It can be anywhere—in my car, a corner in the studio, a bathroom stall—it does not matter. I just need to be free of any distractions as I focus on my breath going in and out of my body. I take a deep inhale and feel the air filling my lungs and expanding my chest. On the release, I feel the warmth of the air as it moves through my nostrils and how the muscles in my shoulders and back relax. The negative thoughts and voice may appear, but I simply acknowledge them and redirect my attention back to my breath.

At first, this was difficult to do and my thoughts kept interrupting, but over time it became easier. Increasingly, I kept the focus more on my breathing rather than the negative voices that invaded my thoughts. I did not linger on what might or might not happen in the next few minutes or hours. In that moment, all that I needed to do was focus on one thing, my breathing.

Taking this time to breathe has become a regular part of my photographic process. It sometimes takes just one or two minutes. Sometimes, I spend more time, especially if I am feeling anxious or antsy. The days when I am particularly impatient to begin shooting are the days I know I need to spend more time focusing on my breathing.

It is in that space of calmness that I am the most creative. It is in such moments that I am actively observing the world around me and am open to the subtle nuances of light, shadow, gesture, and color. Without the pressure to perform or the struggle to silence the voices in my head, I find the place where I can be my best.

My journaling revealed to me how often I felt rushed when making photographs. This feeling of not having enough time pervaded my thinking. I either never had enough time to shoot or, if I was in the midst of creating photographs, I did not have enough time to get it right. And the crazy thing was that there was rarely an external source for all this pressure. There was no boss or client breathing down my neck. It was all coming from me. Journaling helped me to recognize this in myself and led me to using the act of breathing to serve as a ready and simple remedy.

Create a photographic journal in which you will write anytime you go out and make photographs. Each time you complete a shoot, sit down and write about how you felt while producing photographs. If you need a prompt, use some of the questions found in this chapter to begin your evaluation of your shooting process. Remember to write down your feelings and experience before culling and editing your images.

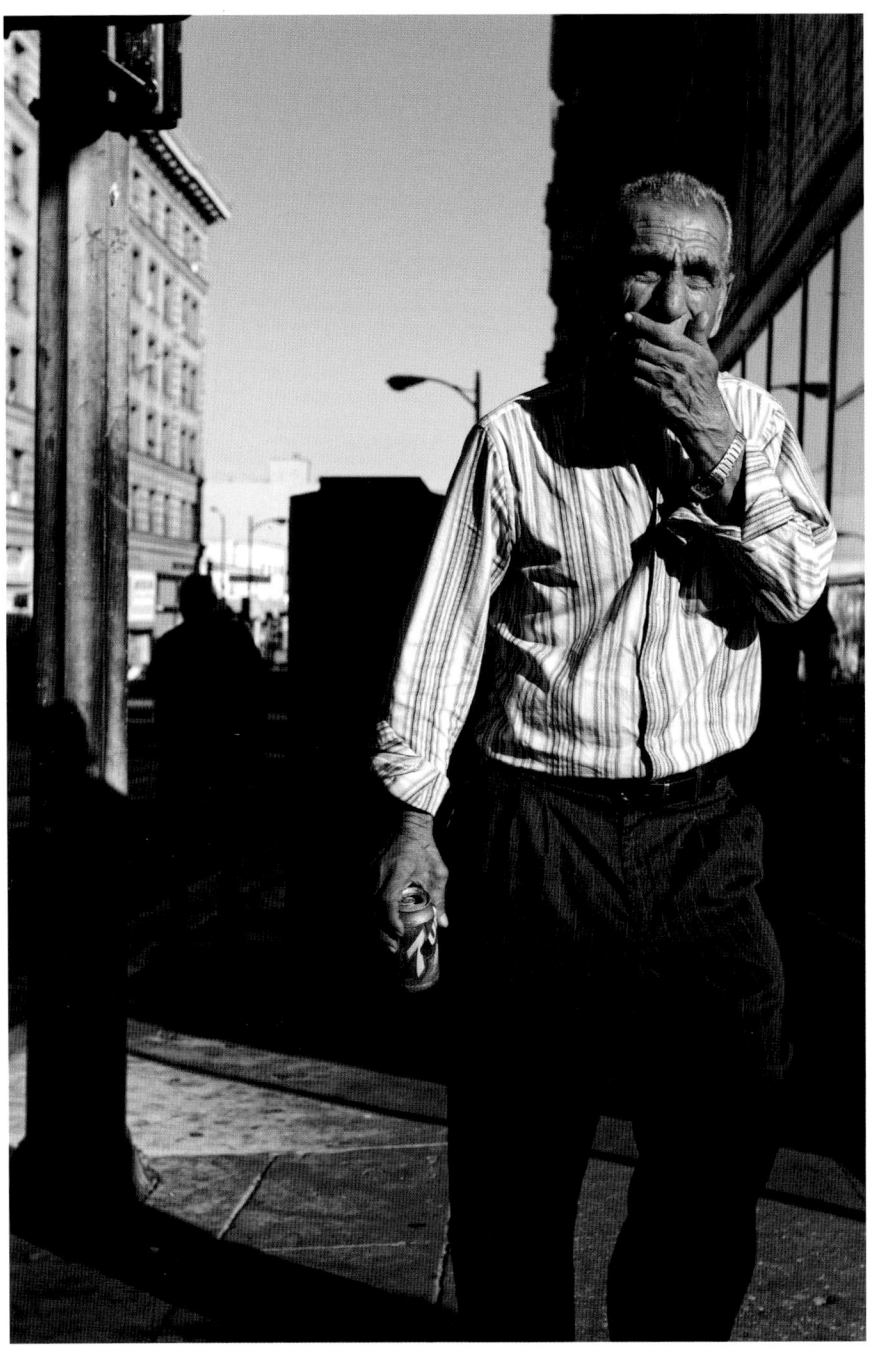

Preparation

I have been photographing in Downtown Los Angeles for over twenty-six years, but my affinity for the area began in childhood. As a kid, I loved being dropped off at one of the movie palaces that lined Broadway: the Orpheum, the Tower, the Million Dollar. While my parents shopped at one of the major department stores, my brothers and I enjoyed second-run horror films and kung fu movies.

Downtown was a city from another time. I knew nothing about its history as the former financial and artistic heart of Los Angeles, but I was enamored of the canyons of classic architecture, the majesty of the theaters, and the rush of people. This was a different world from my flat, residential neighborhood several miles south of Downtown.

It was these qualities that years later drew me back to Downtown Los Angeles. Soon after graduating college, I returned to Broadway with a camera and began to rediscover it with a photographer's eye.

As the years passed, I gained a reputation for my work among other photographers and I was asked by a trio of photographers if they could join me on an outing. I normally photographed by myself, but I welcomed their company.

After about a half an hour of photographing, one of the photographers approached me and asked, "What are you seeing?"

At first, I did not understand the question. He explained that they had observed me as I made photographs, but they did not understand what I was responding to and why.

It was a question that caught me by surprise. I explained to them that I was often lured to a certain scene because of the quality of the light or the presence of shadow. I shared how I would look not only at my subject, but also at what was in front of it, behind it, and alongside it. I explained how I quickly scanned the edges of my frame to determine what small elements I would include or exclude. I talked about how I waited for the telling gesture or flourish to help complete the shot.

In explaining my process, I realized that not everyone knew how to see this way. I had always assumed that everyone else already knew this, but obviously that was not the case.

As with the photograph of a man walking on a downtown street (previous page), I did not understand that I was seeing it differently than other people. What drew me to the street corner was the quality of the light and shadow. I was fascinated by how the late afternoon light cut through the street and illuminated the sidewalk and the building in the distance. The long shadows not only obscured some of the elements in the scene, but succeeded in creating a very moody and high-contrast setting.

I had no sooner discovered the scene than the man walked out of the shadows. I responded to the light illuminating him by quickly exposing a single frame. I captured him just as he raised a hand to his mouth, providing a wonderful gesture. It was only later that I saw the silhouetted figure of another man several feet behind him, which added a sense of mystery and tension to the frame.

Like with many of the photographs I make, I was drawn to a scene even though there was nothing of interest happening at the moment of discovery. Nevertheless, I sensed its potential. In this case it was the quality of light and shadow, and my awareness of those elements culminated in the moment that eventually played out in front of me, a moment I would have otherwise completely missed.

I began to understand how my careful observation of scenes allowed me to make photographs rather than take them. Other photographers were often acting on a reflex. They saw something of interest, raised a camera to their eye, and released the shutter, not really considering all the elements in the frame. I, on the other hand, was fully immersing myself into every aspect of the scene, both big and small, and considering how each aspect would influence the final photograph.

I should not have been surprised at this disparity in seeing considering that any time I sat down with other photographers the discussion inevitably gravitated toward gear rather than process. I was as guilty of it as the next person. If I was impressed by someone else's image, my first question would be about the camera and lens that they used. We all start this way. However, I found that my fixation on the camera and the technical aspects of the shot was a distraction. My fixation on sharpness or how a particular control was handled, while important, sometimes drew my focus away from

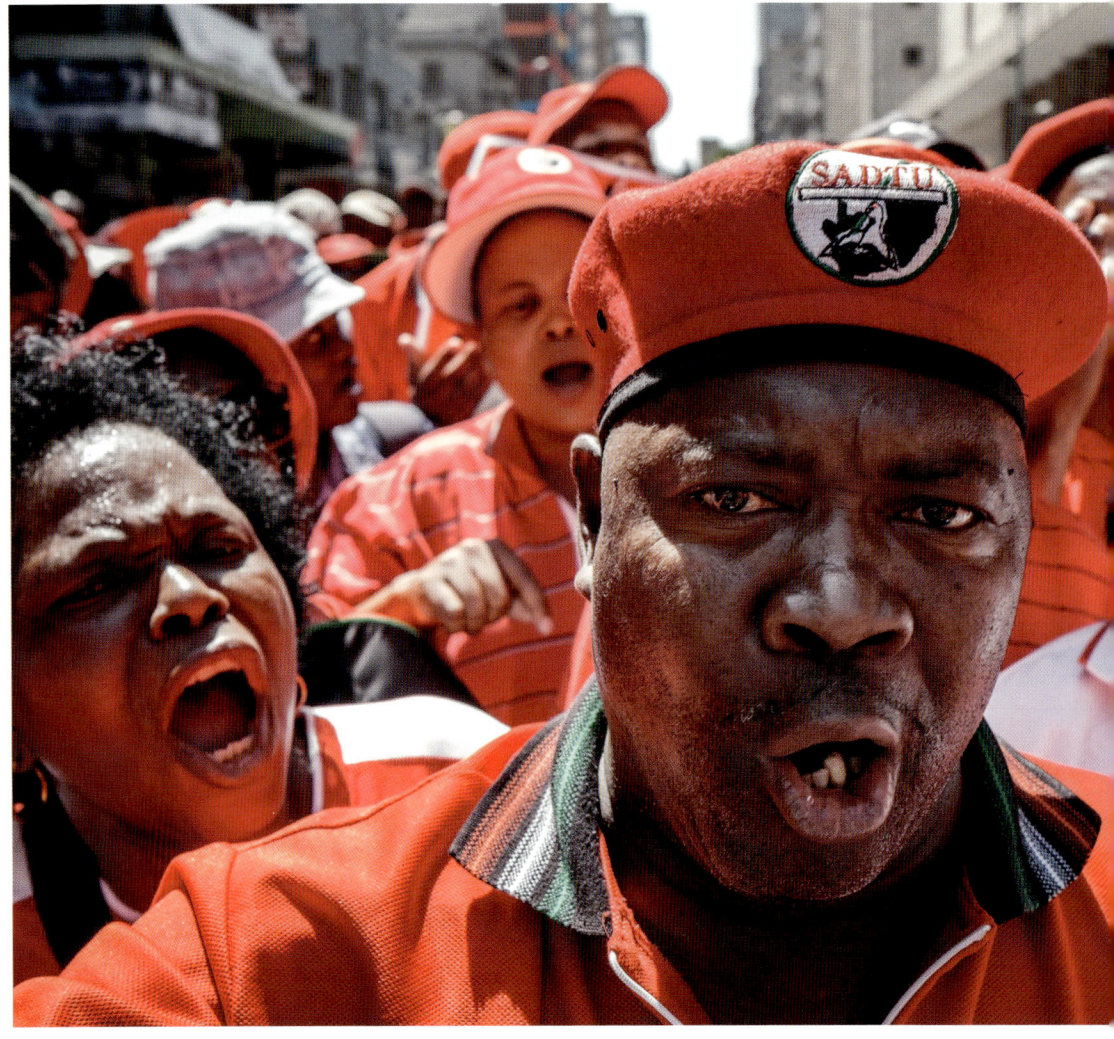

observing the world around me. It was much easier to evaluate the quality of bokeh balls in an out of focus area than to learn how the slightest of hand gestures made or broke a photograph.

Over time, I recognized the importance of understanding the technical side of photography, but not being a slave to it. The camera and the lens are the tools I need to master so that I can translate what I see into a photograph. It is the photograph and not the camera itself that matters.

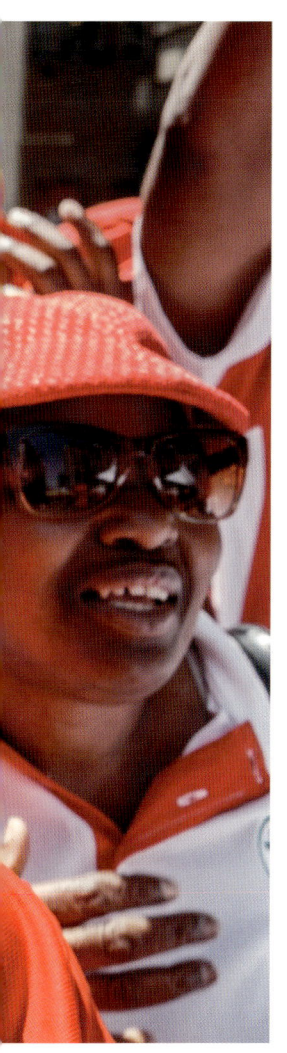

Seeing Beyond the Technical

While in South Africa, I was loaned a Fujifilm XT-2 by the South African Fuji rep. I appreciated the opportunity to use the camera, but I was faced with a bit of a learning curve. With my trusty x100s, I did not have to think about how to change any of my settings. I knew exactly where the controls were and how the menus were laid out. However, with the XT-2, I initially found myself missing some shots because certain controls were located on a different part of the camera body or functioned differently. The delay this caused was just a matter of seconds, but it was enough of a hiccup that I found myself focusing more on the camera than what I was seeing. Granted, the autofocus was much faster and more accurate than my x100s, but I was losing that advantage because the camera was not as intuitive for me.

I photographed a political demonstration several days after receiving the camera and it was the first time I was not distracted by the new body. I was finally becoming comfortable with its layout and functionality. As I weaved and dodged around the protesters, I was only concerned with adjusting my focus point as I selected individual faces in the crowd that I wanted to emphasize in the composition. When I shot slightly upward and included more of the bright sky, I easily applied exposure compensation without having to take my eye away from the viewfinder.

The sound of thousands of people yelling and chanting around me was intoxicating. Being in the middle of it all was an adrenaline rush. But in the midst of all that, I felt present and in the moment. I was making visual discoveries as the scene changed moment by moment. I saw with a preciseness what was only possible when I was free from distractions.

I easily would have missed special moments like this had I been too preoccupied with the camera. It was and is essential for me to make whatever camera I am using a natural extension of my eye and hand. It is only then that I am completely focused on my process of seeing and making photographs.

Be Prepared

Though it may be an oft-quoted cliché, you want the camera to be an extension of you, of both your hand and your eye. It is not about understanding every single control and feature of your camera; rather, it is understanding which features and controls most impact the look and feel of your photographs.

The camera features with which I concern myself are those that control ISO, exposure mode, shutter speed, aperture, white balance, and focus. The camera may possess other features and custom options, but I do not need most of them every time I make photographs. By focusing on the core features, I ensure that I get the picture to look just the way I intend it to.

As I discuss in detail in the next chapter, I set the key settings on my camera every day, even before walking out my front door for a shoot. This means that I set the ISO, choose an aperture of f/5.6, make sure that my white balance is set to Auto, and reset my AF point for the center focus point.

I do this not because I expect every scene to be properly captured with those settings, but because it creates a known starting point for all my key settings. I do not have to make the painful discovery that my first great shot of the day was ruined because of incorrect settings. I have plenty of stories where a shot was trashed because I was photographing with settings from another shoot that were completely inappropriate for what I was doing at the time.

When I have a fixed starting point for my settings, I know exactly how any given setting may need to be changed to accommodate a new shooting situation. If I want less depth of field, I turn my f-stop ring so many clicks to get to f/2.8. If I want to compose my photograph with my subject at the left edge of the frame, I can engage my AF control and move the active cursor in the correct direction. If I find myself moving into a scene that is appreciably darker, I can increase my ISO by the two, three, or four stops necessary to ensure not only a good exposure, but a fast-enough shutter speed to counter camera shake.

Knowing my camera and being able to quickly make adjustments provides me with a huge speed advantage over a photographer who is fumbling with their camera. I can go into a scene and immediately begin to make photographs because I have already made all my technical choices. I do not have to shoot, chimp, and make corrections for things I could have easily determined a couple of seconds before. This is an important skill to develop because it helps keep you focused on your seeing.

Because I use this approach, my process is one of discovery. By seeing rather than looking, I leap the chasm between taking photographs and making photographs.

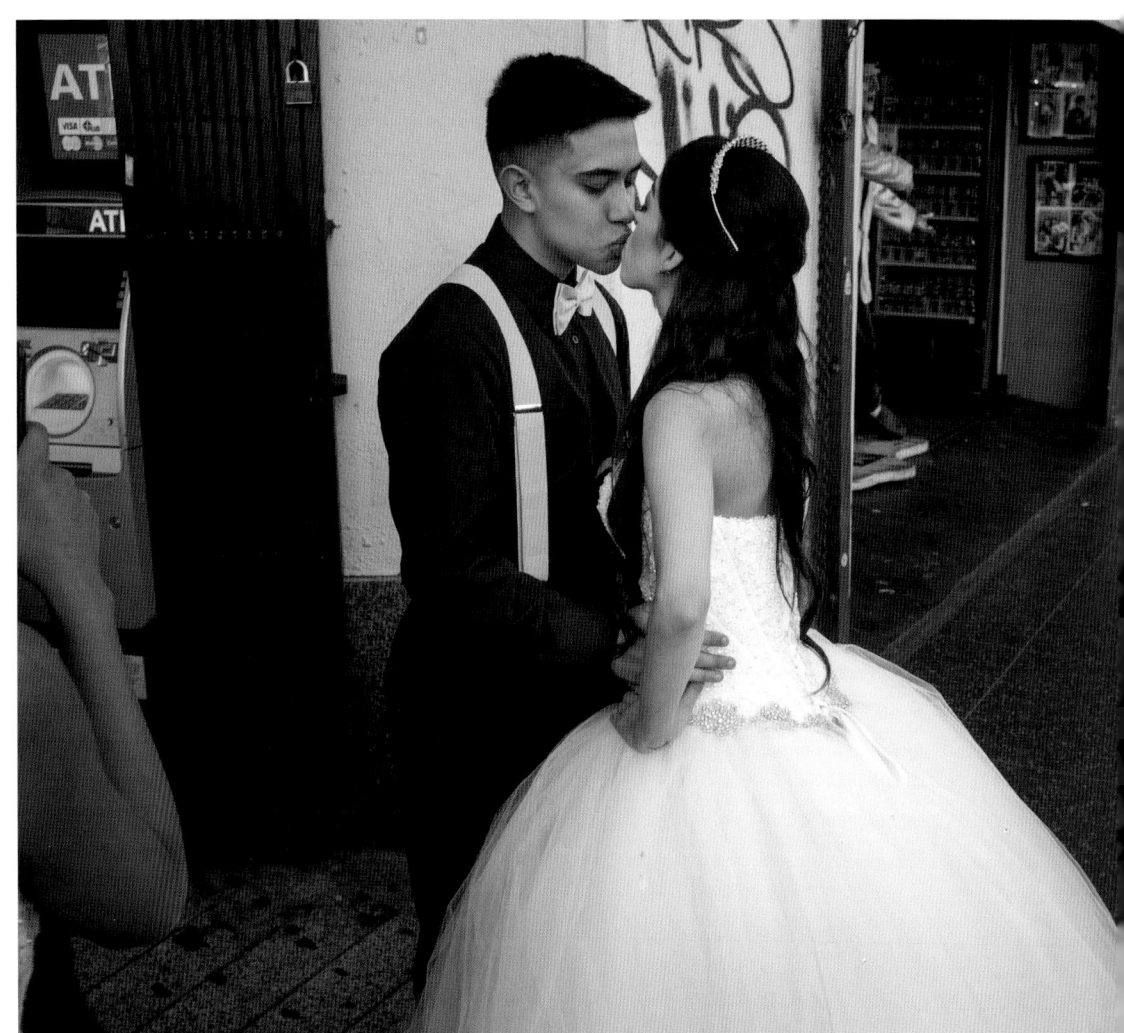

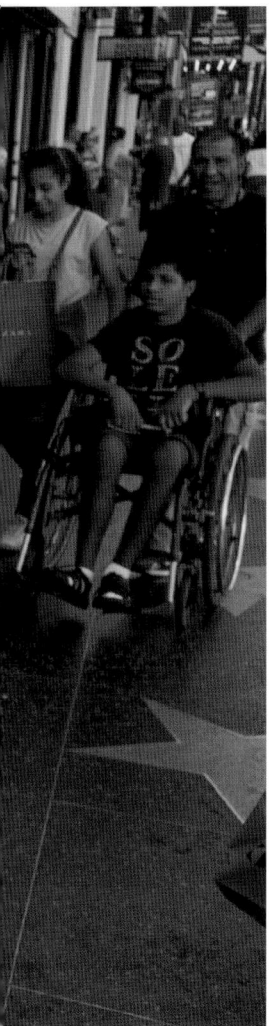

Reading a Scene

While teaching a photo workshop in Hollywood, I let my students loose on the chaos that is Hollywood and Highland. It is a street filled with endless tourists solicited for photographs by costumed superheroes and faux celebrities. Camera phones are in abundance, held by outstretched arms or selfie sticks. The area is awash with activity that resists focus or order.

On this outing I spotted a group of formally dressed teenagers across the street from where I stood. They were obviously dressed for a quinceañera. The contrast between them and the scene around them peaked my interest and I could not get across the street fast enough.

As I was crossing the street, I evaluated the scene that I was walking toward. The kids were in a shaded part of the corner resulting in a flat quality of light. I checked my settings and saw that my ISO was set for 400, which with an aperture of f/5.6, provided me with a shutter speed of 1/200 second—just enough to freeze action. The young people stood around as if waiting for something, so those settings would be more than sufficient. However, I made a note that if they became more active, I would raise my ISO to 800 and increase my shutter speed to 1/400 second to freeze their movement.

As I reached them, the couple posed for a friend's camera and kissed, but I did not get the shot. I was not in the right position. I was too far away to make them a more dominant element in the frame. I struggled as I moved through the crowd of people who were moving around me.

I did not give up. I lingered, making photographs. I held out hope that another kiss might happen again. I carefully refined my composition, paying careful attention to the edges of the frame. I tried minimizing distractions, which was difficult in such a fast-changing situation.

Their friend prompted them to kiss for a photograph again and I saw my lost opportunity return. I bobbed and weaved around the people who walked past me and I got a couple of frames of the couple sharing a gentle kiss.

As I made the exposures, I was aware of a family that included a boy in a wheelchair appearing at right edge of my frame. I saw a glimpse of an Elvis statue near the center of the composition. I saw the girl to my left holding her camera phone. I also saw the ATM machine, the presence of which I disliked, but which I could not eliminate in the seconds I had to compose the shot. And though I did not have control over those secondary elements, I was aware of each of them. I was not surprised to discover them later.

Even before opening this photograph in Adobe Lightroom, I knew I would render it in black and white. The girl's white dress and the way that it contrasted with the boy's dark clothing was a visual draw for me. I knew it would be the anchor of my image, especially when I converted the image to monochrome. This also helped eliminate some color distractions that existed in the background. I applied a subtle vignette to darken the edges of the frame and to emphasize the tonal contrast and the gesture of the kiss.

There were a myriad of choices I made in order to successfully capture this image. A few decisions revolved around camera settings, which I resolved even before I got into position to make a single frame. The majority of my choices were concerned with anticipating the moment, framing my composition, and hoping for a little bit of luck.

Great photographs are created by capturing fleeting moments of time, moments that can only be captured by a camera. But it is not the sophisticated technology of the camera alone that makes this possible. The key is you, the photographer, who when in control of the camera, captures that elusive and beautiful moment.

Read your camera
manual and practice
changing your settings
for ISO, shutter speed,
aperture, exposure
compensation, focus
points, and white
balance. Memorize not
only how to access these
controls, but also what
direction you need to
rotate a dial or move a
control to affect a certain
change, whether it is
to increase or decrease
shutter speed or aperture
or ISO. Discover how
to quickly return the
camera's AF point to its
center starting position.

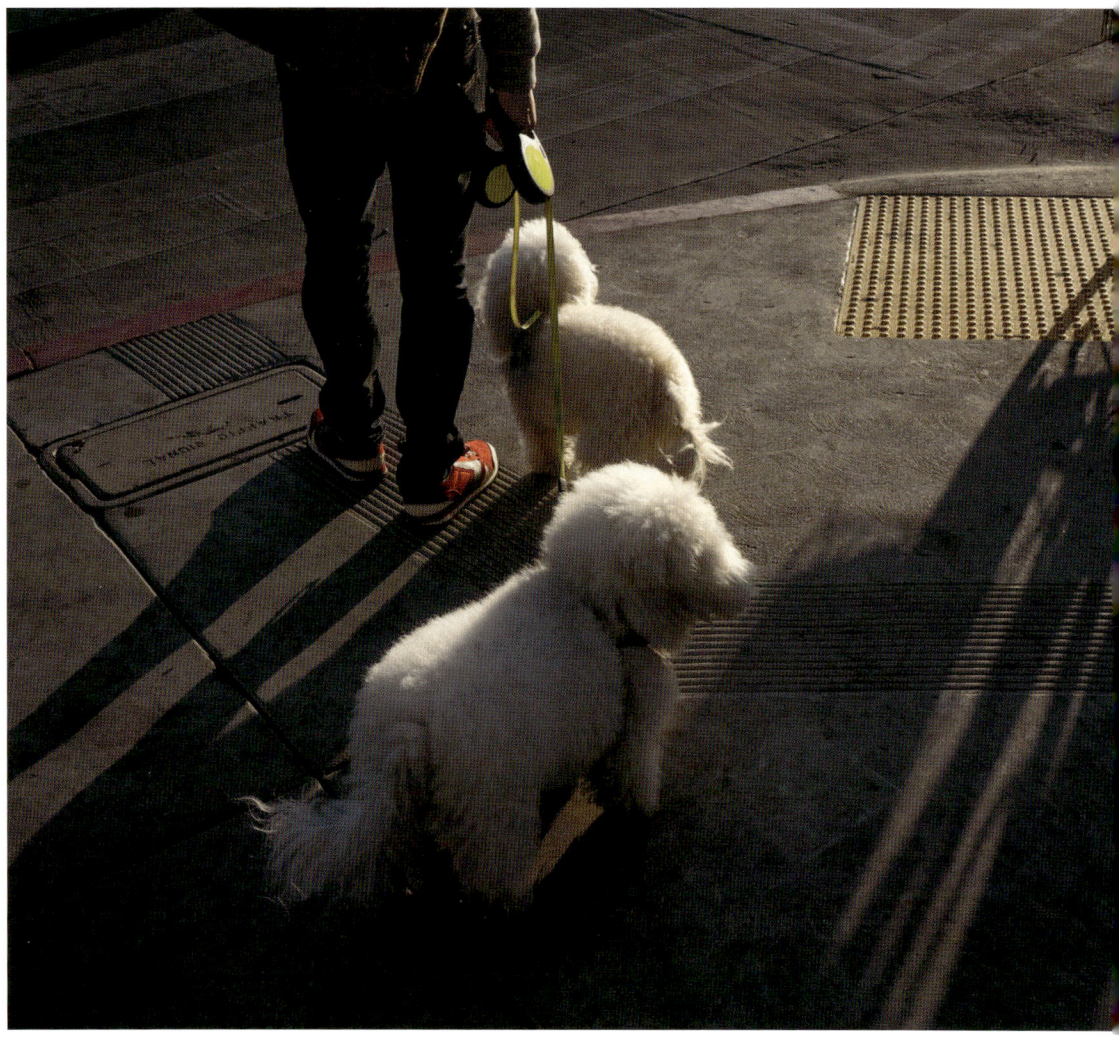

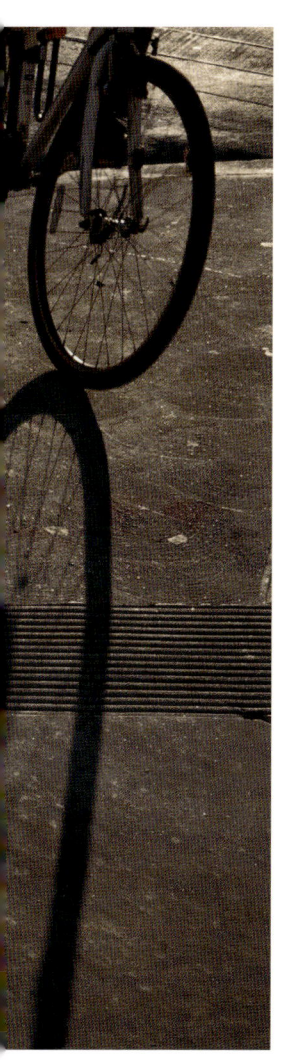

Core Settings

I was at a workshop at the Leica Gallery Los Angeles waiting for the late afternoon session to begin. As I waited I was tempted to sit down and browse through the many photography books on display. The range of photographers and styles was incredible and the collection offered a diversity I did not often see in a local bookstore. Yet I looked through the window and was seduced by the quality of the late afternoon light. The books would be here; the light would not. I grabbed the Leica M10 that had been loaned to me and walked outside.

The sun was moving toward the horizon. Its glow cast a warm yellow-orange color on the buildings and passing cars. Street signs and traffic signals cast elongated shadows that created unexpected patterns on the sidewalk. The texture of the street was revealed and included the truncated yellow domes that are a fixture of each sidewalk corner. The sunlight made the domes appear more saturated, drawing attention not only to them, but also to the curb's strip of peeling red paint.

The light was fading fast and I knew that I would not likely find a better stage for a moment to play itself out. There was not much foot traffic, which worried me, but experience had taught me that patience frequently pays off. As a few people walked through the scene, I made several exposures. They were tests that allowed me to experiment with exposure and composition. These were not captured at the right moment, but they provided me a sense of where I wanted to be when the right subject finally arrived.

When a man with two dogs crossed the street, I made several frames. The dogs possessed a fluffy white fur that glowed with sunlight. I stopped and asked the man about his dogs. We chatted for a moment and then he continued on.

After the man left, I did not stop making photographs. As much as I thought I might like one of the images I had just produced, I held out hope for something better. The light was still there and so was the potential for something else to happen.

I made more frames as other people walked through the scene, but nothing thrilled me. Then I noticed that the man and his dogs had returned and were waiting to cross the street to my left. It was then that a cyclist appeared and rode toward us. I could tell he was going to ride up onto the curb. From the previous photographs, I had become aware of the shadows cast by anyone who stepped onto the curb. I knew that the wheels of the bicycle would provide a great graphic element, especially when juxtaposed against the figures of the two dogs. I took a few steps back to ensure I included the dogs and the long stretch of shadow from the cyclist. I made just two frames and then the moment was gone.

I remained there until the light disappeared behind the buildings in the distance. It was only then that I played back the images on the camera's LCD screen and was rewarded for my patience. Now I could return to the books.

Our photographs are captured within fractions of a second. When we discuss our cameras, we talk about fast autofocus and fast lenses. This fixation can make it seem like great photography is dependent on speed and speed alone. Hence, a great photographer must have fast reflexes. This is only partly true.

Depressing the shutter release button is more than just a matter of good timing. It is the culmination of a series of choices. It is the choice to stop rather than continue walking. It is the decision to go horizontal rather than vertical. It is the decision to include certain elements in the foreground and background. It is the choice to go with a shallow depth of field rather than a deep one.

There are many times when all of these choices are made in a split second—a kind of practiced reflex. However, I contend that the majority of photographs can be made much more thoughtfully, even before all the elements of a scene have revealed themselves. For me, it begins well before I have even discovered my first subject of the day and have exposed a single frame.

Core Settings

The photograph that begins this chapter is a perfect example of a time when being prepared was key to getting the shot. When I decided to stop at the corner, I had no idea that a pair of dogs and a cyclist would converge at a precise moment in time. All

I had was an instinct that the quality of light and shadow, of line and shape, might offer me a setting where something interesting could occur. But to prepare myself for that opportunity, I made sure that my camera was ready to capture the moment when it was finally revealed to me.

The photograph was the culmination of a series of choices. And while there were several choices that were made at the moment of exposure, the majority of them were made before "the moment." Because such magical moments are so fleeting, so unpredictable, it is important to make as many choices as possible before the moment of exposure. Otherwise, making decisions becomes a distraction and robs you of the opportunity for a successful photograph. How many times have you missed a wonderful photograph because you were preoccupied with your camera settings? With this in mind, my essential choices begin with the camera's core settings.

My core settings include ISO, aperture, shutter speed, white balance, and focus. Each is established at the beginning of my shooting session. This prepares me to make images and provides a valuable and repeatable starting point for making any necessary changes.

ISO

The first setting I adjust is the ISO, which controls the sensitivity of the camera's sensor to light. ISO ranges will vary from camera to camera, starting as low as 50 and going up to an astronomically high 3,280,000. The higher the number, the more sensitive the sensor is to light—an important consideration when working with diminishing levels of illumination.

On a bright sunny day, I use an ISO of 100 or 200. On a day that is cloudy or heavily overcast, I set my ISO to 400 or 800. When photographing indoors under any variety of artificial light sources, I increase the ISO to 1600, 3200, or even higher. By increasing the ISO, I ensure that the camera delivers an accurate exposure. This also provides me more flexibility with respect to my choice of aperture and shutter speed.

When photographing for a local nonprofit organization that gives young girls opportunities to work with and care for horses, I was faced with difficult lighting conditions. Inside the barn, light levels were low and I needed to increase my camera's ISO to 3200 in order to achieve a reasonable shutter speed. Though the shutter speed was a stop slower than I normally felt comfortable shooting at, I was confident that I could still produce a sharp result without increasing the ISO further.

As you increase the ISO, it may introduce more noise to the image, but most modern cameras maintain excellent dynamic range and color accuracy with ISOs as high as 6400. I do not hesitate to increase the ISO as needed. I can often reduce the presence of noise in my final image in Lightroom or Photoshop.

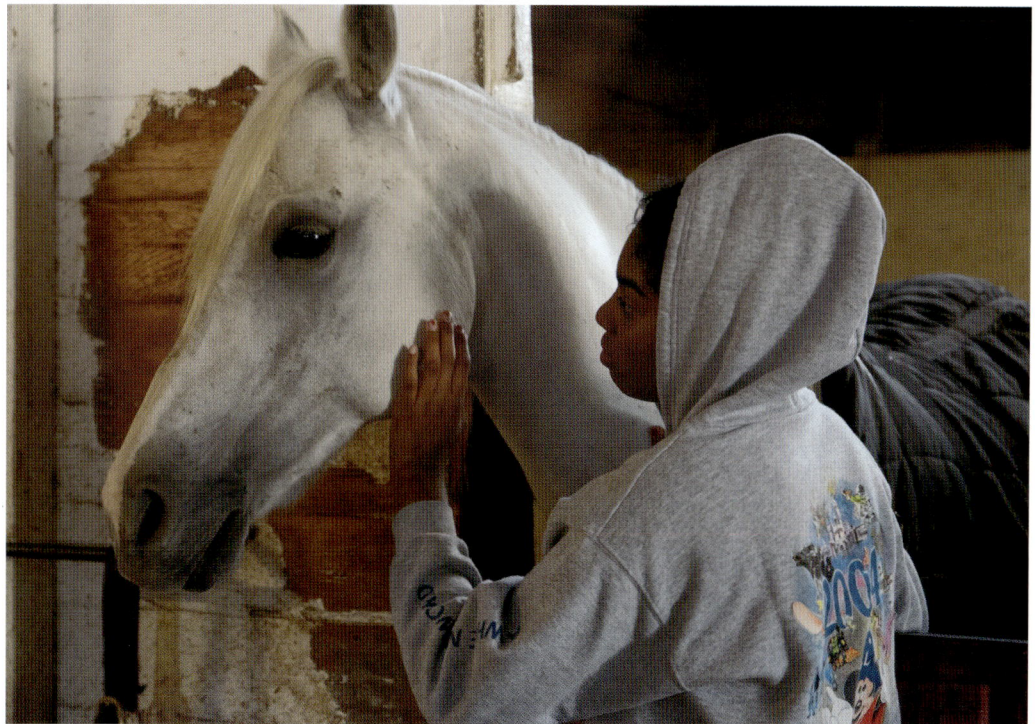

Digital cameras also possess an automatic ISO feature that dynamically controls the ISO based on light levels. I find this to be a valuable tool when I am faced with fast-changing lighting conditions or when setting the ISO manually proves to be time-consuming. However, I set the ISO manually whenever possible so that I produce consistent results and develop an awareness of the quantity and quality of the light.

Exposure Mode

For most shooting situations, I set my camera to aperture-priority mode. In this exposure mode, I set the camera's aperture, leaving the camera to choose the shutter speed based on the quantity of light. Having control over the aperture provides me important creative control to produce a deep or shallow depth of field.

My default aperture of choice is f/5.6, but this is not solely for aesthetic reasons. When I set my ISO correctly, this is an aperture that results in a shutter speed of around 1/200 second, which allows me to shoot handheld. I want to reduce any chance that my handling of the camera produces a soft image due to camera shake. Even though I might produce a sharp result with a shutter speed as low as 1/30 second, this normally requires me to be very conscious of how I handle the camera. Unfortunately, I cannot say that I am always so calm and steady. I would much rather use a shutter speed that counters my jittery eagerness to make the photograph.

If I am shooting on an overcast day and set my ISO to 400 (see chart A), I expect that the camera will select a shutter speed of 1/4000 second at an aperture of f/5.6. If I close down the aperture to f/16 to increase my depth of field, the shutter speed will likely be 1/500 second, well above my minimum requirement. This provides me with great flexibility.

ISO 400 sunny	ISO 800 cloudy
1/500 sec @ f/16	1/250 sec @ f/8
1/1000 sec @ f/11	**1/500 sec @ f/5.6**
1/2000 sec @ f/8	1/1000 sec @ f/4
1/4000 sec @ f/5.6	1/2000 sec @ f/2.8

chart A   *chart B*

If light levels decrease even more, I increase my ISO to 800 (see chart B), and with an aperture of f/5.6, the camera will choose a shutter speed of 1/500 second. If I set my aperture to f/8, the camera will change to 1/250 second. If I want a wide aperture of f/2.8, the shutter speed increases to around 1/2000 second. In any of these cases, I do not worry about producing a soft image because of camera shake.

By setting my aperture to f/5.6, I establish a consistent starting point. If I want to quickly change my aperture in any direction, I already know what aperture I am moving from. I can even adjust the aperture control simply by paying attention to the number of clicks in either direction. Most importantly, if I encounter a scene to which I have to react instantly, I can bring the camera to my eye and make a photograph with the reasonable expectation that the image will be both well-exposed and sharp.

If I do change the aperture for any reason, after I am done making my photograph, I return the aperture to f/5.6 in preparation for the next photo opportunity. As I said before, doing this ahead of time means there is one less choice to make at the time of exposure that could potentially distract me from making the photograph.

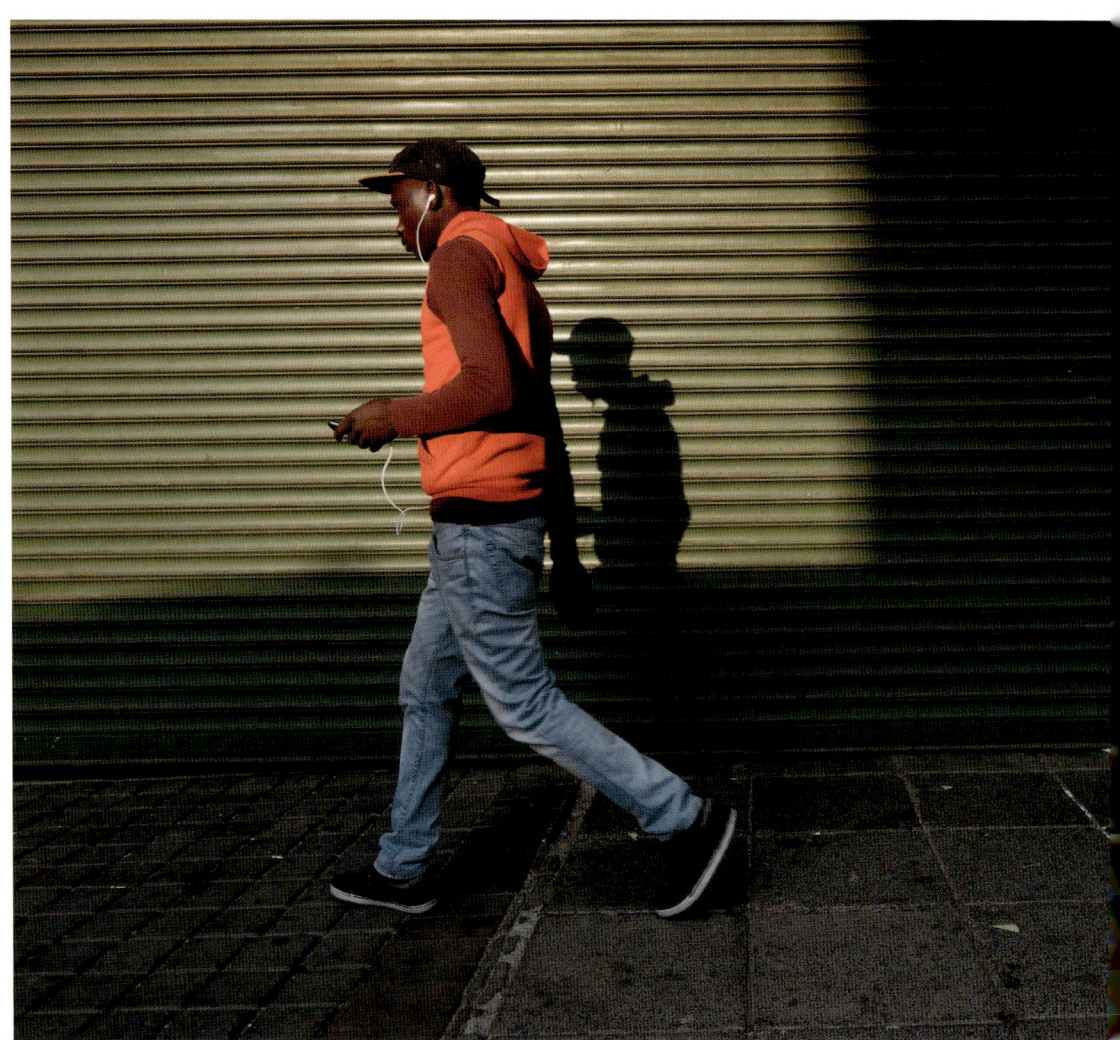

In aperture-priority mode, the camera's metering system will provide an "accurate exposure" for the scene, which retains detail in both the shadows and the highlights. This is what I want the majority of the time. However, there are times when the lighting can fool the camera, resulting in an exposure in which you lose detail in either the highlights or shadows. In a high-contrast scene, the exposure may be biased toward the shadows or highlights, and the camera's meter, while trying its best, may deliver an exposure that loses important details. Under such circumstances, I use manual exposure mode to lock in my exposure or to purposely bias the exposure toward the highlights.

When I was preparing to make this photograph in which a man is walking past a security gate, I knew that the camera's meter would choose an exposure that would open up the shadows dominating the scene. I knew from experience that this would result in an overexposure in the highlight area, which is where I wanted to position a subject. So I set my camera to manual exposure mode and chose an aperture and shutter speed combination that biased the exposure toward the highlights and allowed the shadows to be rendered darker. I knew I would lose some details in the shadow areas, but I was okay with that because those elements were not as important to me. I also knew that I could recover some shadow detail during post-processing if I needed to. When the man in the red hoodie walked through the scene, I had complete confidence that he would be well-exposed.

In this situation, I also had the option to remain in aperture-priority mode and use the camera's exposure compensation mode. (Exposure compensation allows you to bias the exposure of the camera in increments of 1/3 stop, up to plus or minus three to five stops, depending on your camera.) However, I wanted to make sure that all the photographs in the sequence were consistently exposed. Otherwise, subjects wearing light or dark clothing could have influenced the exposure in unpredictable ways.

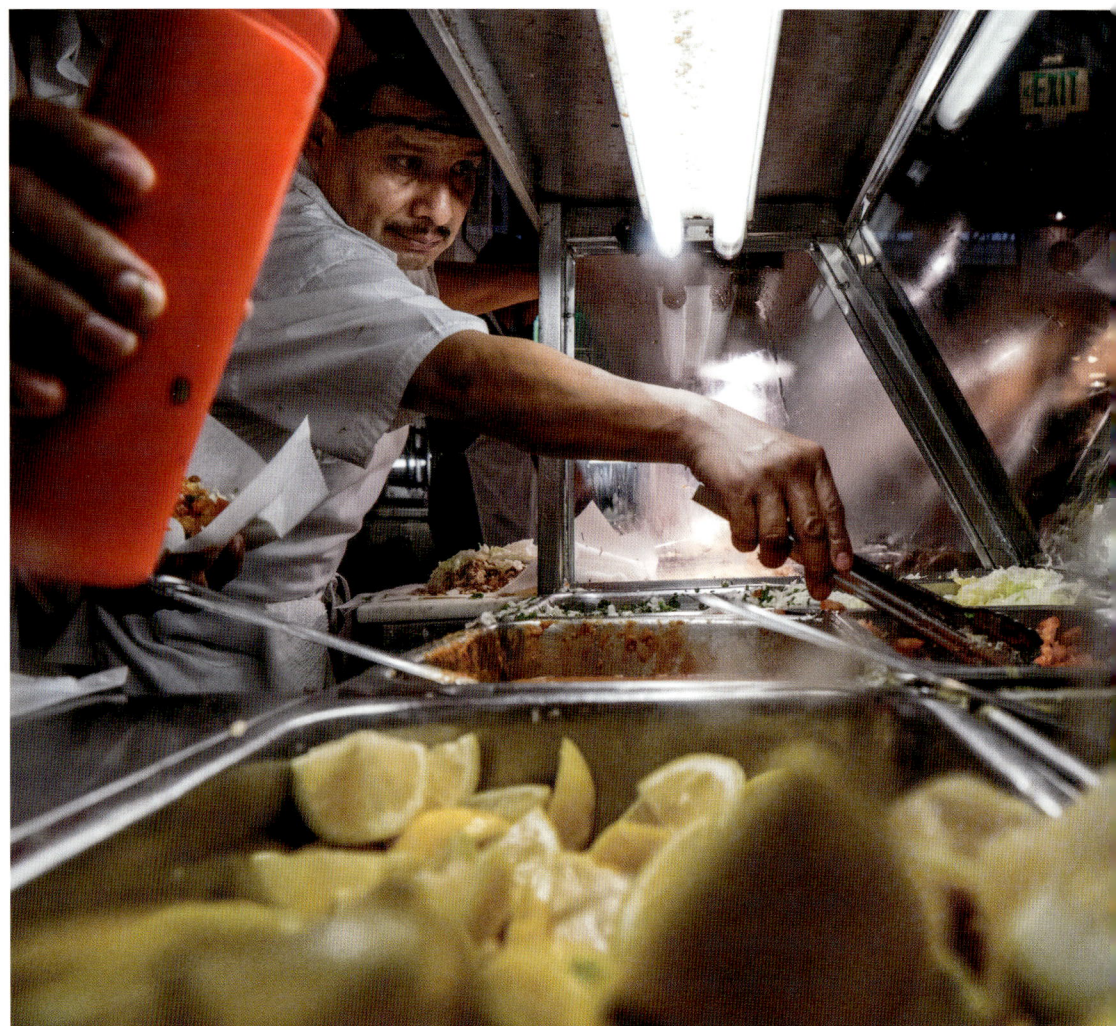

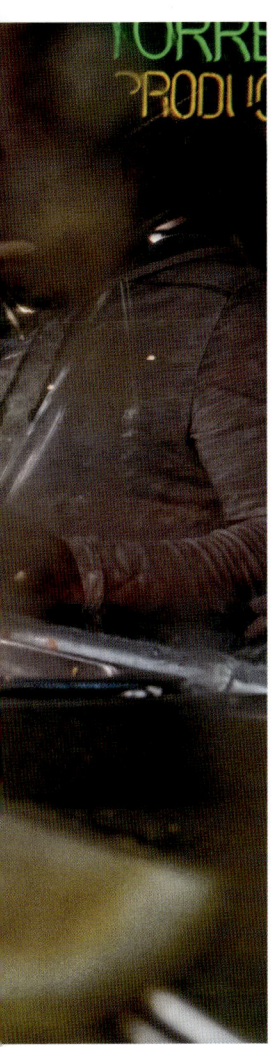

White Balance

White balance controls how the camera renders color. Because different light sources (e.g., sunlight, tungsten, fluorescent, LED, halogen) produce light at different color temperatures, it is important that the camera is prepared to produce images illuminated by those light sources.

By default, a digital camera is set for automatic white balance. In this mode, the camera evaluates the light coming through the lens and, to the best of its ability, discerns what kind of lighting you are shooting under. This often produces reasonable results and is a good choice if the scene is illuminated by one or more different light sources.

I prefer to set the white balance manually. I find that the presets provide greater color accuracy than the automatic white balance. Using presets also ensures that all the shots made during a particular session are consistent in terms of color. Using auto white balance, which adjusts white balance and color dynamically, can result in photographs that are not consistent from one shot to the next, which can make editing large numbers of images difficult.

When I shot the photograph of the taqueria, I was keenly aware of the unpredictability of my camera's auto white balance feature under fluorescent lights. Not only are there warm and cool fluorescent lights, but even within these categories, the color temperature can vary greatly. I set the color temperature manually to achieve the most accurate color possible. Though I did not completely nail the white balance, it was close enough that I only needed to make a slight adjustment for it in Lightroom.

If you shoot raw images rather than jpegs, you can adjust your white balance after the fact in your raw converter. However, I prefer to get it right in-camera and eliminate an additional step in my post-processing workflow.

—

"Depressing the shutter release button is more than just a matter of good timing. It is the culmination of a series of choices."

Focus

One of the greatest advances in camera technology is autofocus. It not only helps to produce in-focus photographs, but it does so in conditions under which it would be difficult to focus manually. These systems are fast and accurate and work wonderfully even under difficult lighting conditions.

But just because the word "auto" proceeds the word "focus" does not mean that it is a control you can ignore; quite the contrary. Your camera likely has multiple autofocus sensors, ranging from dozens to hundreds, each of which is used by the camera to detect focus on your subject. The area of coverage will vary from camera to camera, but you can choose whether to use all or some of those sensors for focus detection.

By default, the camera will use all of the sensors to determine focus on your subject, whether the subject stands in the middle of the frame or is slightly off-center. You depress the shutter release button halfway, and the camera quickly detects focus. Then the photograph can be made. It works beautifully most of the time.

However, there are times when the autofocus is fooled, particularly when there are multiple elements within the scene, such as an object in front of your subject. In such a situation the camera targets something other than your subject. You might encounter this, for example, when shooting a sporting event with multiple athletes on the field.

Rather than allowing the camera to choose the point of focus using all the autofocus sensors, I will select a focus setting where only a small group of sensors or even a single sensor is used for focus detection. I will also choose a focus mode that allows me to move the target area around to prioritize my subject wherever they are located in the frame. This eliminates the possibility that a secondary element will be in focus. This is

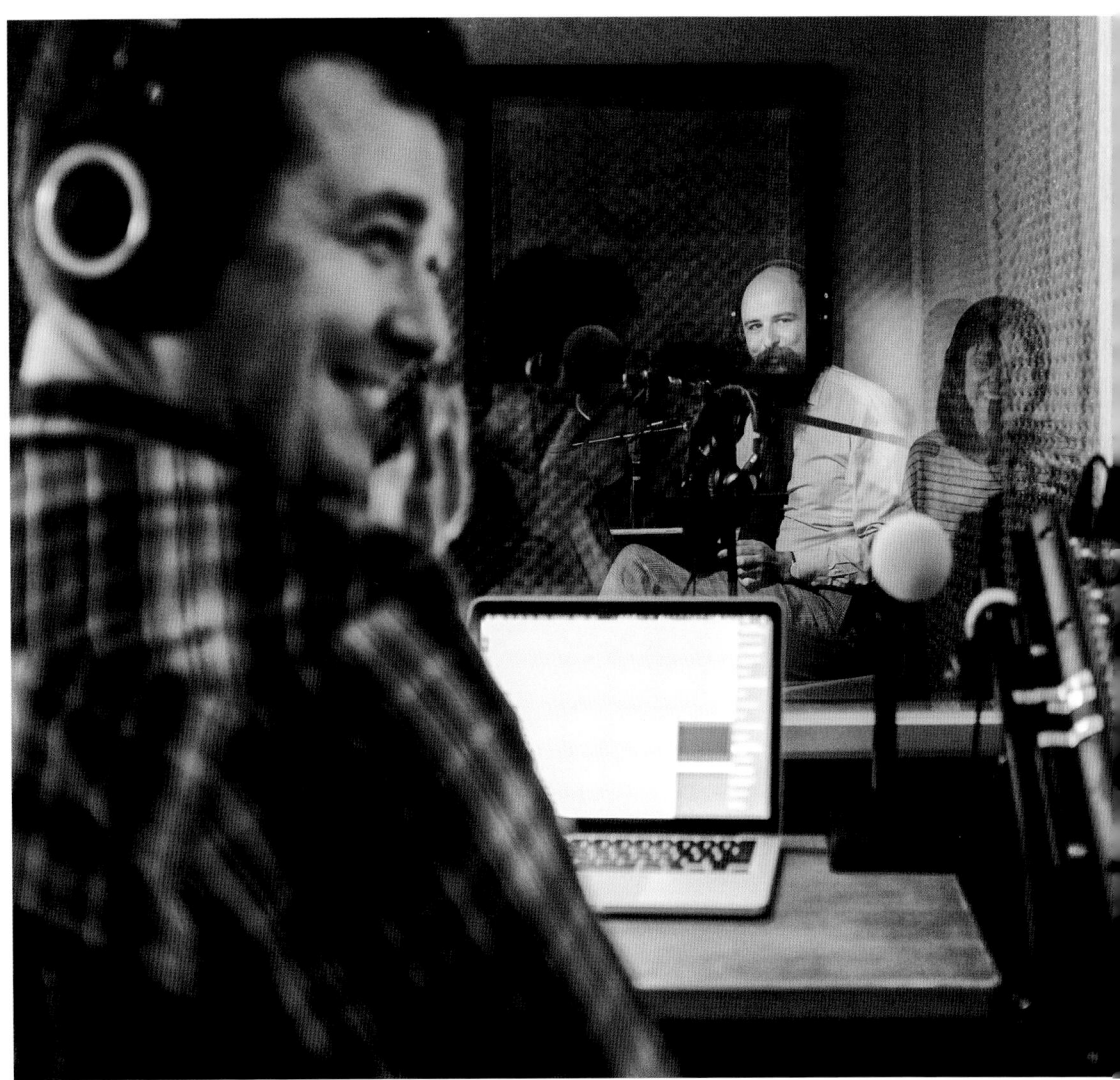

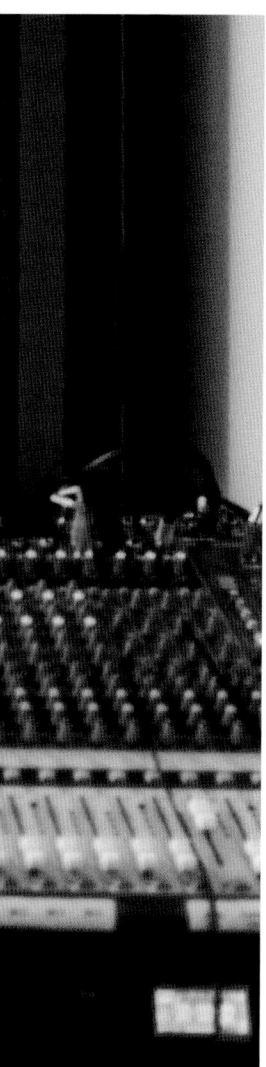

especially important when shooting with a wide aperture, such as f/2, which produces a very shallow depth of field, or when producing a portrait in which I want to nail focus on the eyes.

I set my AF sensors to the center area by default. This prepares me for the majority of images in which my subject is likely to be at or close to the center of the frame. However, if they are not, I can quickly move the AF target area to anywhere in the screen.

For this photograph of NPR host Jesse Thorn in his studio, I knew that the camera might experience difficulty nailing focus on him. The light levels were low and there were different elements in the booth and in the reflection that could confuse the camera's autofocus system, resulting in a soft image. So I chose a single AF point for focus detection and targeted Jesse's eye to ensure that he was rendered sharp in the composition.

Raw versus Jpeg

The photographs that you create can be saved in at least two different file formats: raw and jpeg. With jpegs, the captured image gains the benefit of the camera's onboard processing with adjustments to contrast, sharpness, and color. This usually produces an image that does not require much post-processing and that you could immediately print or share on your social networks. Jpeg files can be opened by virtually any device or software. The files are compressed, allowing you to save more images to a memory card than you can with raw files, which are uncompressed.

Raw files do not have the benefit of any in-camera processing. A raw file contains the unprocessed data that was captured by the sensor and is saved to the memory card using the camera manufacturer's own codec. These files require post-processing using a raw converter like the one available in Adobe Lightroom or Photoshop. Unlike jpegs, these files cannot be immediately shared and must be processed and converted into another file format for e-mailing or printing.

The great advantage of raw files is that they contain the full dynamic range captured by the sensor. This gives you full control over the tonality, color, contrast, and sharpness of the image. With raw files, you have the freedom to interpret the images in any way you choose, whereas jpegs are processed for you, leaving less latitude for further refinement.

Most professional photographers prefer to shoot raw files because of the control that it gives them. On the other hand, jpegs can save you time and effort because you don't have to process each image.

If you are new to photography, you may prefer to set your camera to raw + jpeg, which will save both the raw and jpeg files to your memory card. This gives you jpeg files that you can immediately print and share, and you can later work with the raw files as you gain experience working in your photo-editing software of choice. Just make sure that you use a large-capacity card to accommodate the increased number of files.

A Consistent Starting Point

By always setting my ISO, exposure mode, aperture, white balance, and focus to the same default settings, I establish a starting point for all my photography. I avoid the experience of my first images of the day being ruined because they were made with settings from a shoot that occurred days or weeks before. I always start from exactly the same place.

When a scene demands a change, I do not have to adjust each and every setting. At most, I normally adjust one or two. If the light changes, I increase or decrease my ISO and adjust my white balance accordingly. Because I have my aperture set to f/5.6, I quickly check my shutter speed to ensure that I am shooting at 1/200 second or faster. If not, I increase my ISO further. After that, I focus entirely on composition.

As I was talking to a man on the street, I noticed the cigarette in his hand. I quickly adjusted my aperture to f/2.5 because I knew that I wanted to render the tip of his cigarette with a very shallow depth of field. I did not have to worry about shutter speed, as I knew that it would be significantly higher than my base minimum of 1/200 second. All I needed to do was focus on the tip of the cigarette, compose the shot, and make the photograph.

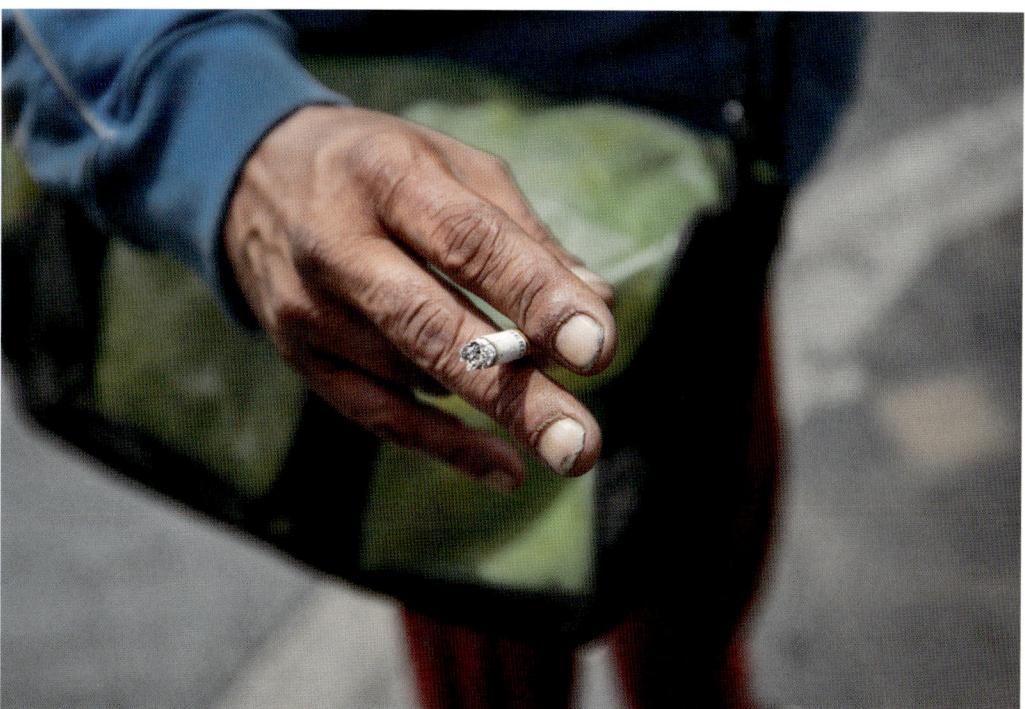

I can make whatever changes I need to even before I have discovered my first subject if I make it a point to evaluate the conditions under which I will be shooting, whether it is a bright sunny day at a music festival or dim evening inside a restaurant. By making any necessary adjustments before the moment is revealed to me, I minimize technical distractions that stand in the way of my making a photograph.

Familiarize yourself with your camera's controls for adjusting ISO, exposure mode, aperture, white balance, and focus. Set your core settings and make photographs under different lighting conditions, noting the shutter speed the camera is choosing for you. Remember to set your white balance for the light source that you are shooting under.

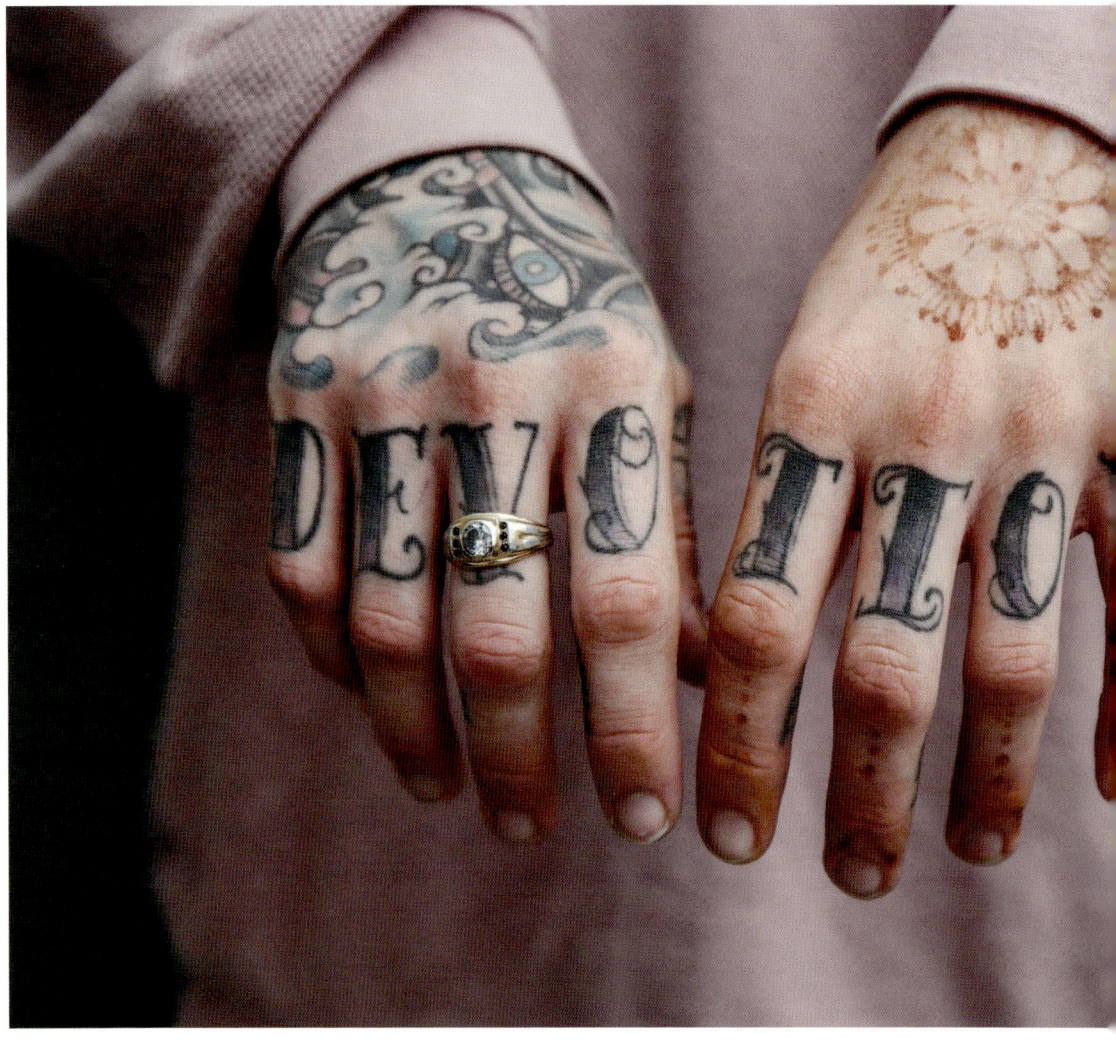

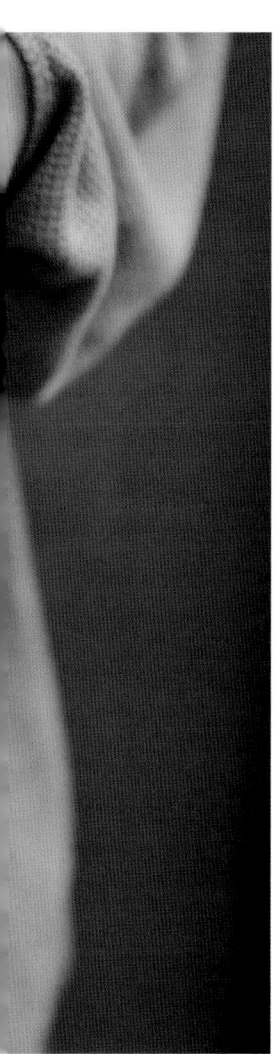

The Visual Draws

I was teaching the second day of a street photography workshop in Hollywood. I had planned to take the students to Downtown Los Angeles, but plans changed when I heard mention of a farmers' market being held just blocks away. This provided us with just as much potential for photographic opportunities as a visit to Downtown and allowed more valuable time for critiques in the afternoon.

On our second day, I wanted my students to begin photographing people and I gave them a variety of exercises, one of which was to focus on a subject's hands. I did not want the photographers to absently make photographs of passersby just to fulfill an assignment requirement. Instead, I wanted them to pay careful attention to who they were photographing and to emphasize some element that they found especially interesting.

As soon as the photographers dispersed, I began my own hunt for an interesting subject. While walking down the crowded street, I noticed a green door that was unusually positioned at the corner of a building. I was drawn to its color and shape. I immediately knew it would serve as a great backdrop for a portrait. I made a mental note for when the right subject arrived.

The streets were blocked off so I positioned myself in the middle of the intersection and observed hundreds of men, women, and children as they passed by. There were people of all ages, races, and ethnicities moving past and around me. I felt like a large stone in a river with the water continuously flowing around it. Rather than directing my attention to the faces or clothing of these people, I looked at their hands. I was not sure what to look for, but I was certain I would know it when I saw it. Eventually, I spotted a young man with tattoos on his arms and hands. He was carrying a white plastic bag with food that he had purchased from a vendor. I approached him and asked him about his tattoos. He was friendly and when I asked permission to photograph him, he quickly agreed. I directed him to the green door I had spotted earlier.

As usual, my camera controls had been set ahead of time for the overcast lighting conditions. The camera's ISO was set to 800 and my white balance was set for cloudy. The aperture was at f/5.6, resulting in a shutter speed well above my minimum of 1/200 second.

"The mistake
that many
photographers
make is relegating
photo-worthy
moments to only
special occasions
like vacations
and birthdays."

As I positioned the man at the door, I realized the color of his tattoos perfectly mirrored the color of the door, and his pink sweatshirt complimented those greens. I could not have asked for a better subject.

I knew that I wanted to emphasize the man's hands and tattoos, so I adjusted the aperture on my zoom lens to f/2.8 and asked him to extend his hands forward, making sure his fingers remained in the same plane of focus. My depth of field was shallow and I wanted the tattoos on his fingers, which spelled out the word "devotion," to be rendered tack-sharp. I made several frames, carefully refining the overall composition and making sure that I had critical focus (page 54).

I thanked the man and got his contact information so that I could e-mail him the picture later. I hoped that he would be as pleasantly surprised at seeing it as I had been in making the photograph.

Seizing Opportunities

The world is full of photographic opportunities; the challenge is whether or not the photographer is prepared to take advantage of them. The photograph of the young man with the devotion tattoo could have easily been lost to me. There was no lack of distractions to be had at that farmers' market. I was surrounded by hundreds of people. There were vendors selling any variety of arts and crafts, clothing, and food. The air was filled with the aroma of food and sounds of voices and music. Yet in the midst of all that, I was able to see the pale green tattoos on a man's hands that perfectly complemented a green door I had noticed mere minutes before. Was it just luck?

I might think so if it were not for the fact that I have countless stories just like this one. I've been in some location that was abuzz with activity and I was drawn to something in the scene upon which I built a photograph. Sometimes, those moments built up slowly. Other times they have happened within an instant. Yet I have many photographs that I believe were made possible because I was focused on seeing and not merely taking pictures.

I believe that I am able to open my eyes to the world's visual opportunities because I observe the world rather than simply look at it. We look at things all the time, but we do not really see them.

How many times have you driven yourself home from a long day and suddenly wondered how you got yourself there? You do not even remember navigating the highways and streets. You are amazed you got home safely. This is the kind of looking most of us practice in our day-to-day lives. It is not an active, conscious seeing, but rather an instinctual act that does not ask us to think about or evaluate what we are looking at.

Good photography demands that we stop looking and begin seeing. This begins with mastering the camera and reducing its potential as a distraction by setting the core settings. This is then followed by understanding how we are seeing a thing and how that can translate into a photograph.

I was running errands one day and parked my car on the roof level of a mall's parking lot. As I walked to the entryway, I saw the shadow of a light post on a short orange wall. I then noticed the color transition from the white of another wall, and then to the blue of the sky. I drew my camera and composed the scene, paying attention to the rails, the light fixture, and the small ledge.

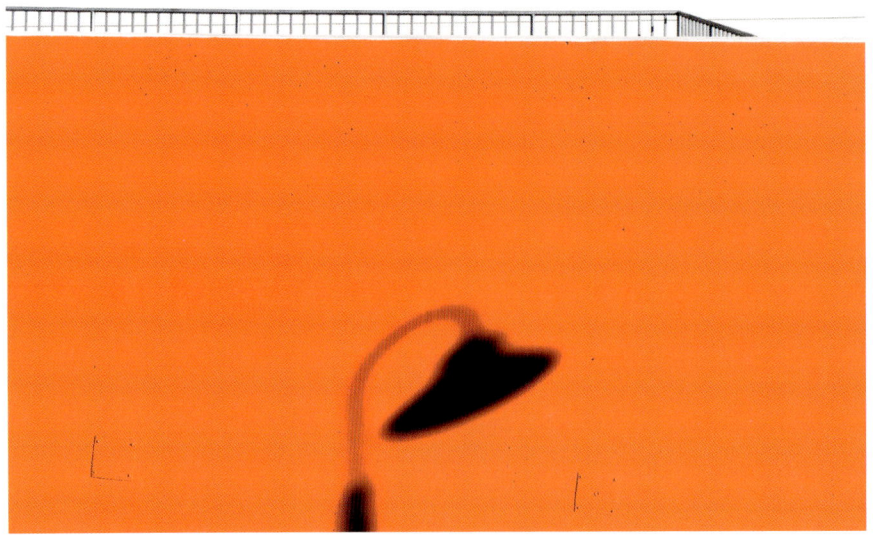

As I made the photographs, I felt amused that I had found such a beautiful scene in the unlikeliest of places. When I left home that day, I never would have thought I would find a beautiful scene at the top of a parking garage, but here I was doing just that. It served as yet another reminder that photographs are everywhere if I take the time to see rather than just look.

Stop Seeing Literally

The challenge for any photographer is to learn to be more than a glorified copy machine. You want to do more than document something's existence. There is no thought to that kind of photograph. You simply raise this box to your face and depress a button. It is nothing more than a snapshot.

To create visually interesting and engaging photographs, you must learn to stop seeing literally. By that, I mean looking at people, places, or things for how they function and move through our world. The chair is just a chair, meant for someone to sit on. The waiter is the person with whom you place an order and who brings you your food. The door is the portal through which you enter or exit a building. We see all these things for how they relate or do not relate to our lives. As a result, it is very easy to ignore virtually everything around us.

But the power of photography relies on making something extraordinary from the ordinary. Think of Edward Weston's classic photograph of a bell pepper. A bell pepper's function in our lives is clear enough—we eat it. We may sometimes appreciate the color, but even then, it is often about how the color will play in the look of a salad. But in Weston's photograph, the bell pepper possesses a beautiful sensual quality, whereby its lines and curves evoke the human form. The luminosity of the bell pepper's skin demands a complete reevaluation of what the viewer thinks he or she is seeing. We experience that vegetable not according to its function, but for how the photographer saw it and wanted the viewer to experience it.

To evoke experiences like this, you have to do more than rely on the camera to provide a sharp, in-focus photograph. You have to understand how you see and how you can use that to *make* rather than *take* photographs.

Pictures Are Everywhere

Photo opportunities exist everywhere and can happen at any time, even under the most mundane and ordinary circumstances. The mistake that many photographers make is relegating photo-worthy moments to only special occasions like vacations, weddings, and birthdays. Our lives are filled with more than those events. Ordinary moments can inspire wonderful photographs if we make the choice to observe life more carefully.

I walk my dog every day, usually following the same route, so I often see the same homes, streets, and landmarks day after day. There is nothing inherently special about any of the things I see, except for the occasional stray coyote. But one day, I walked past a house where I saw a Pontiac Skylark sitting in the driveway. I had seen the car before, but beyond admiring its classic stylings, I had never made a photograph of it. However, on that day, I saw a delivered newspaper protected in blue plastic sitting below the car's rear bumper. I saw a visual connection between the newspaper and the car and I made a photograph. I considered not only the car and the newspaper, but also the car's shadow and the elements at the edges of the frame. It is a simple photograph, but one that I find incredibly pleasing to look at, especially because I found it so close to home.

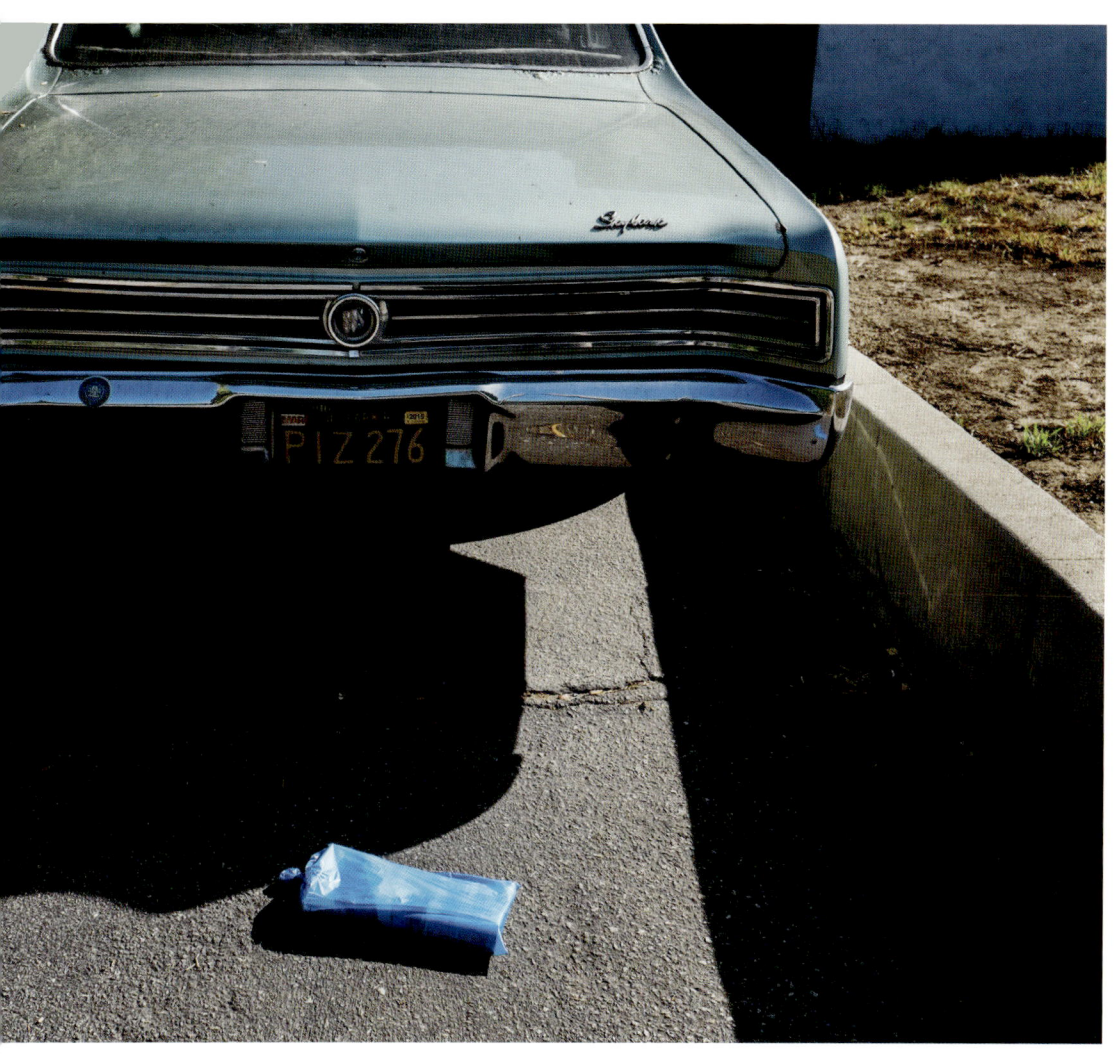

Moments like this serve as a constant reminder to me that I can find and make photographs whenever and wherever I am. This is why I am never without my camera. There are many days when my picture-taking occurs while I am running errands. Something will catch my attention and I will take a momentary break to create a photograph. This is often the only opportunity I have to dedicate time to my photography, but I nevertheless feel grateful for the chance to practice doing something I love.

Visual Draws

By studying the work of photographers and painters, I have come to understand the visual draws that affect and control how human beings look at a photograph or painting. These are the elements upon which I try to build my photographs when I create them, and which I use to analyze the effectiveness of those photographs when I look at them on my computer.

These visual draws are light and shadow, line and shape, color, sharpness, and gesture. Even though it is done subconsciously, each of these things influences the way someone experiences a photograph. By understanding the role of these elements in the visual experience, you, as the photographer, are able to make choices that allow you to control the viewer's experience of an image. This understanding also helps you to evaluate your images after they have been captured to determine why they succeed or fail.

Pull 10 of your better images and evaluate them based on the ideas expressed in this chapter. Go beyond merely documenting what you saw. What are the visual qualities of the subject or scene that make you like the image so much? If an image has a strong emotional resonance with you, try to take a step away from it and consider how light and shadow, color, line and shape, sharpness, and gesture make it an effective photograph.

Light and Shadow

It was early Saturday morning and I was out on the streets of Downtown Los Angeles. The storefronts had yet to open and there were few people around. Despite the inactivity, I liked wandering the streets, witnessing the city waking up to a new day. Shafts of sunlight cut down the street and sidewalks, illuminating the most mundane things and revealing them through a beautiful quality of light. It gave the city a magical glow.

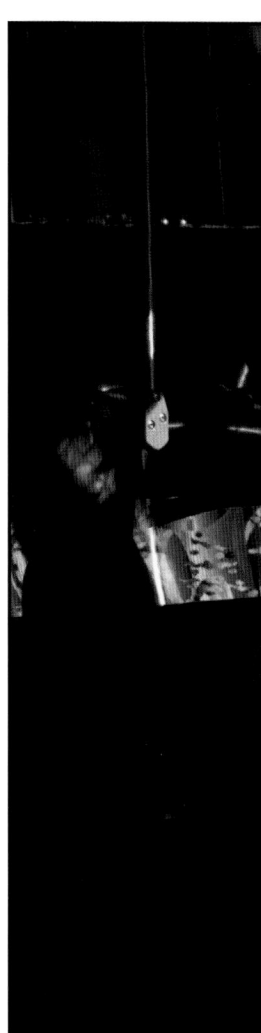

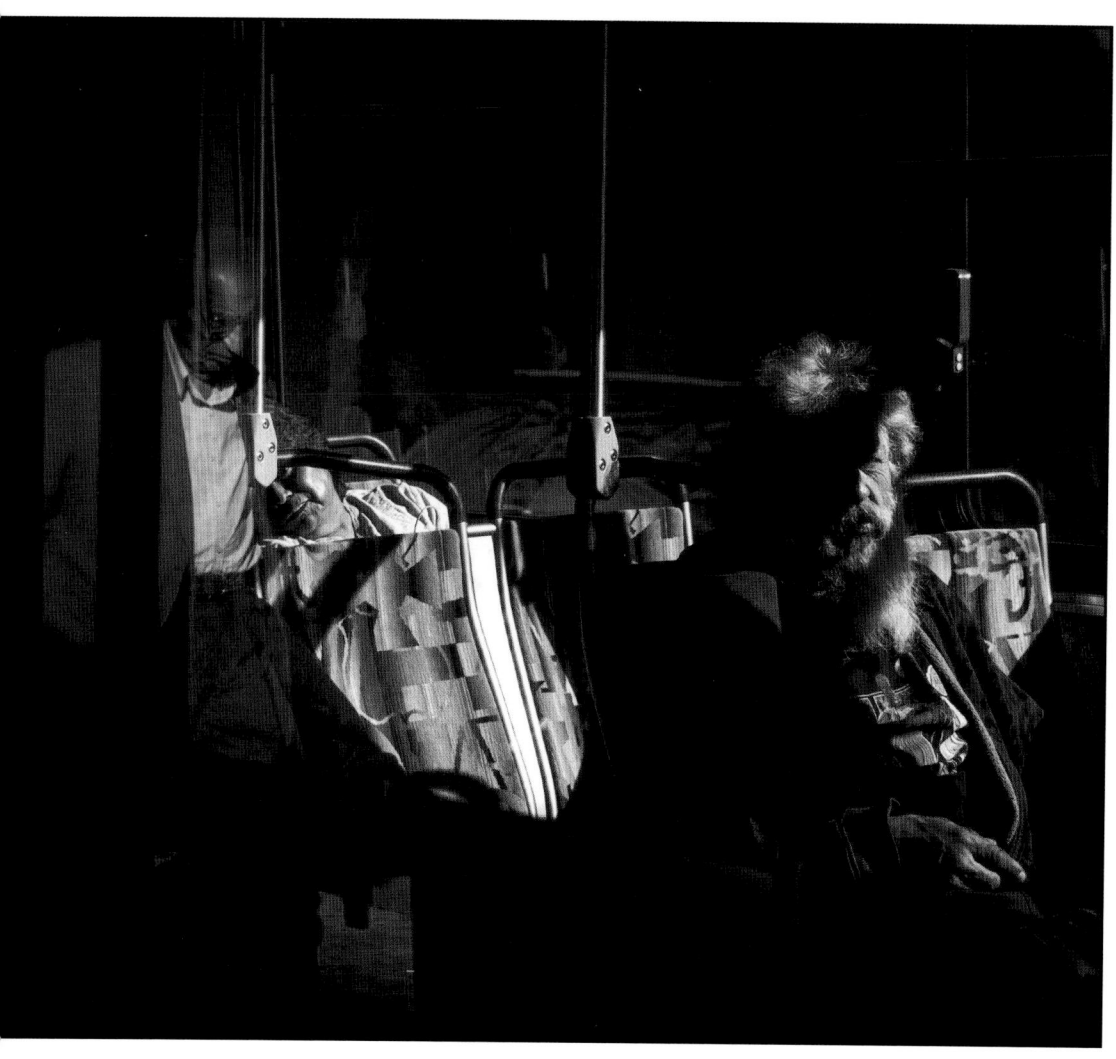

I adjusted the core settings of my camera. I decided to shoot in manual exposure mode and to bias my exposure for the highlights, which resulted in the shadows being rendered in deep black tones. I knew that I would lose details in those shadows, but I wanted to create images that would emphasize the brighter areas of the scene and accentuate the high contrast that I saw with my eyes.

I crossed the street and saw a commuter bus that had stopped at the corner. The sunlight shined through the interior of the bus, illuminating several of the seated passengers, including a man with an expansive white beard.

The play of light and shadow was dramatic.

I did not know how long the bus would remain in place, so I began to make photographs, moving closer to it to produce as clean a frame as possible. One of the passengers saw me and tried to duck out of my picture. I kept shooting. I managed to capture only four frames before the bus lurched forward to continue on its route.

Later when I reviewed the images on my computer, I saw a single frame in which the reflection of a man walking down the street appeared in the window of the bus. I remembered him walking past me as I shot, but I had not realized that I had managed to capture him in my frame. Nevertheless, his presence made the shot for me.

That scene and the resulting photograph came into being because I was observing the light. Had I been looking at the world literally, I would have just seen yet another of the many buses that move through the streets of Los Angeles. I had no interest in photographing buses. They held no personal fascination for me. They were usually distracting elements that I excluded from my compositions. But because I was paying attention to light and shadow, I saw the bus and its passengers in a completely different way. I recognized the potential for a wonderful photograph in which I documented a bus and the people inside it, but I did so with a creative eye for light, shadow, and composition. I took a normal, everyday moment in the life of the city and made art from it. And it all began because I had learned to see and understand the power of light and shadow.

Light as the Lure

One of the easiest and most important things to understand is that the human eye is frequently drawn to the brightest element in a scene. It is like a magnet that pulls the viewer's eye to that specific area in the composition. The viewer instinctually assumes that this is the most important area of the image and is where they should begin navigating the frame.

This is something you want to use to your advantage whenever possible. It not only helps you to consider where and when to photograph your subject, but also reveals situations where a brightly lit element in the background could prove distracting. If you are making a portrait, you want the warm direct sunlight to fall on your subject and any distractions to be relegated to the shadows. You do not want your subject to be sitting in the shadows with the light hitting a white car in the distant background. Whenever you are photographing anything, consider the quantity and quality of the light you have to work with.

You could be faced with different qualities of light that range from harsh, high-contrast noonday sun to soft, diffused light from a cloudy day. You could be working with soft, directional window light or weak, warm tungsten bulbs. Whichever you are working with, it is important to evaluate the quality of the light and how it impacts how your subject will be rendered in your photograph.

"One of the easiest and most important things to understand is that the human eye is frequently drawn to the brightest element in a scene."

If you have worked with your core settings, you will know that the quantity of light that you have to work with is directly related to your working ISO. You will then set your white balance to ensure the most accurate color. Once you have done these two things, most of the technical concerns have been resolved and it becomes more a matter of seeing the light and how it interacts with your subject and scene.

One of the best ways to assess the quality of the light is to ask yourself the question, "Where is the light coming from?" You can often do this by paying attention to the shadows. If there are long, well-defined shadows to the left of your subject, you can tell that the hard light is coming from the right. If the shadows remain close to the subject and you see strong shadows beneath a person's chin or the brim or their hat, you know that the light is coming from overhead. If the shadows are soft or barely discernible, you are working with diffused light, such as what you would find in open shade or on a cloudy day.

Harsh and direct lighting produces deep shadows that are sharply defined. This produces high-contrast images like the photograph that opens this chapter. If the scene is partly cloudy or overcast, the shadows are less pronounced, producing a much softer quality of illumination. Indoors, a large window provides a soft, directional light with shadows that gradually transition to gray or black. Halogen or fluorescent lights, which are often positioned directly overhead, provide any variety of contrast levels, but will produce diffuse shadows beneath a brow, nose, or chin.

By simply looking at the quality of the shadows, you can determine the quality of the light and decide how you want to use whatever level of contrast is available to you.

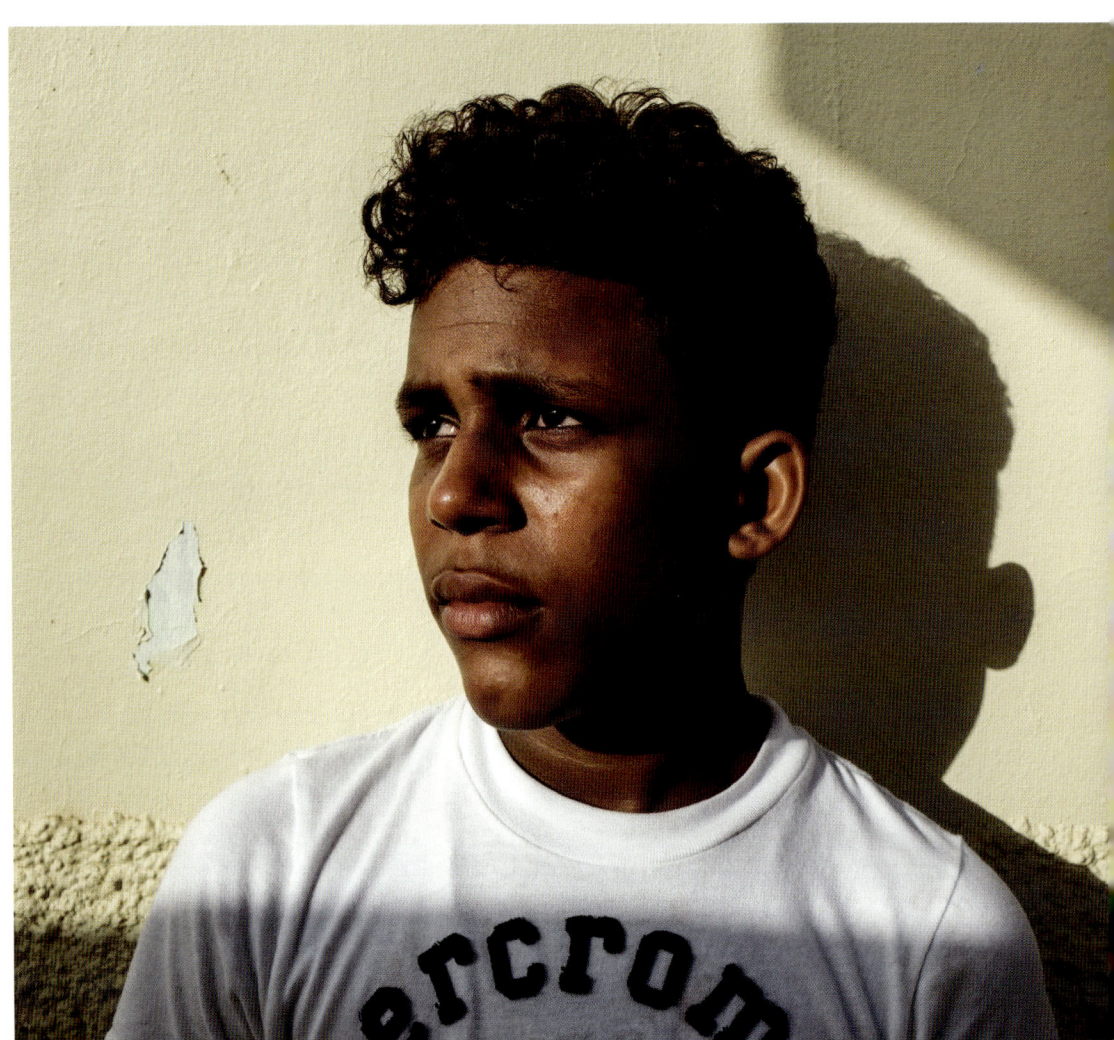

While tending to my father's grave in the Dominican Republic, I noted the play of light and shadow on a crypt. I appreciated the pattern the shadow created on the dull yellow wall and asked a family friend to pose for me. I purposely positioned him in the highlight area and used his shadow as another graphic element in the composition.

Even though direct sunlight is not ideal for portraiture, I have often used it to great effect, as I did with this image. Remembering that the viewer is drawn the brightest element in the scene, I positioned my subject so that he faced the light and allowed what was behind him to fall into shadow. I used the high contrast produced by the direct sunlight to control where the viewer would look first, and to give the image impact and gravitas.

On an overcast day, you can produce an image in which you do not emphasize a specific element with light, but instead allow everything in the scene to be considered. In this case, you can use other visual elements, such as line and shape or color contrast, to control the viewer's experience.

If you begin to assess the quality of the light by evaluating contrast, you immediately begin a more sophisticated method of seeing. Rather than seeing a chair as something to sit on, you look at the way the direct sunlight illuminates it and brings out its texture and color. You notice way the shadows of its body and legs extend from the base of its feet and stretch across the ground and wall. You see the strong graphic qualities of the chair and its shadow and consider them for the graphic potential in your photograph. The chair is no longer just a chair.

This is exactly what I experienced when meeting a friend for coffee. We were looking for a place to sit when I saw a trio of colorful chairs illuminated by a shaft of sunlight. I responded to how the color popped and how the legs of each chair were sandwiched between areas of shadow. Despite the fact that I was there to catch up with a friend, my eye was still sensitive to the visual qualities of the chairs that we found ourselves sitting in moments later.

Whenever I make photographs, I always consider the quality of the light first and foremost. This happens even before I have determined what my very first subject of the day will be. By paying attention to light and shadow, I observe the world by how it interacts with and reacts to the light that is illuminating it. This helps me to take that important step away from literalness.

Let the Light Lead You

When I was a young photographer, I would go out on a day's shoot loaded for bear. I had two camera bodies, an assortment of lenses, and dozens of rolls of film. They were all stuffed in my trusty Domke bag. Yet with all that equipment and gear, there were days when I came home with nothing to show for it. When asked how the day went, I would irritably respond that there was nothing of interest to shoot. I now know how wrong I was. It was not that there wasn't anything interesting to photograph; it was that I just was not seeing in an interesting way.

That began to change when I began to pay attention to the quality of the light. I did not set an agenda for the type of photography I wanted to produce on a given day. Instead, I convinced myself that I would observe the light and shadow and allow those things to set the day's agenda for me, from what side of the street I walked on to whether I turned left or right, and ultimately to what I would consider making a photograph of.

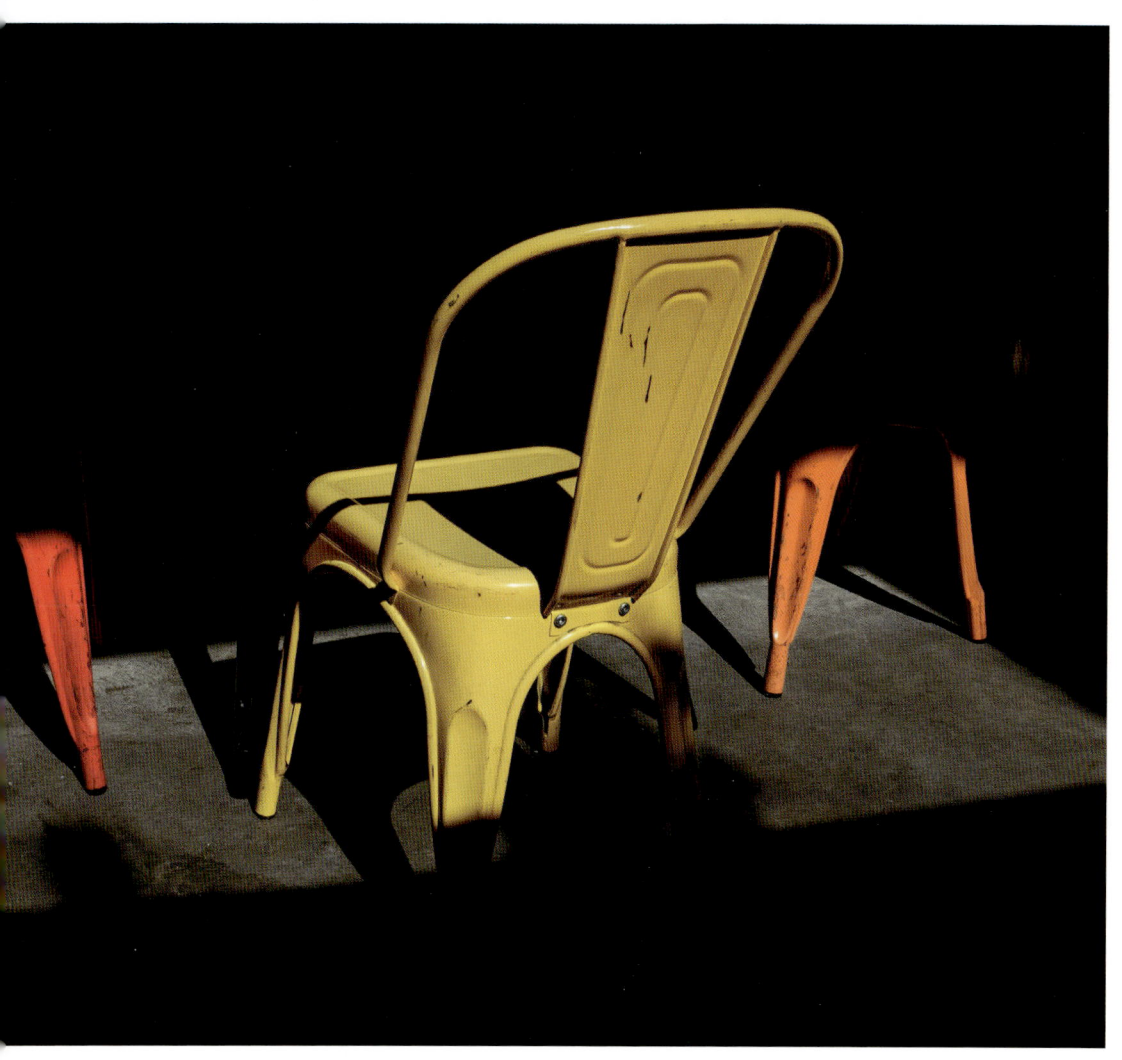

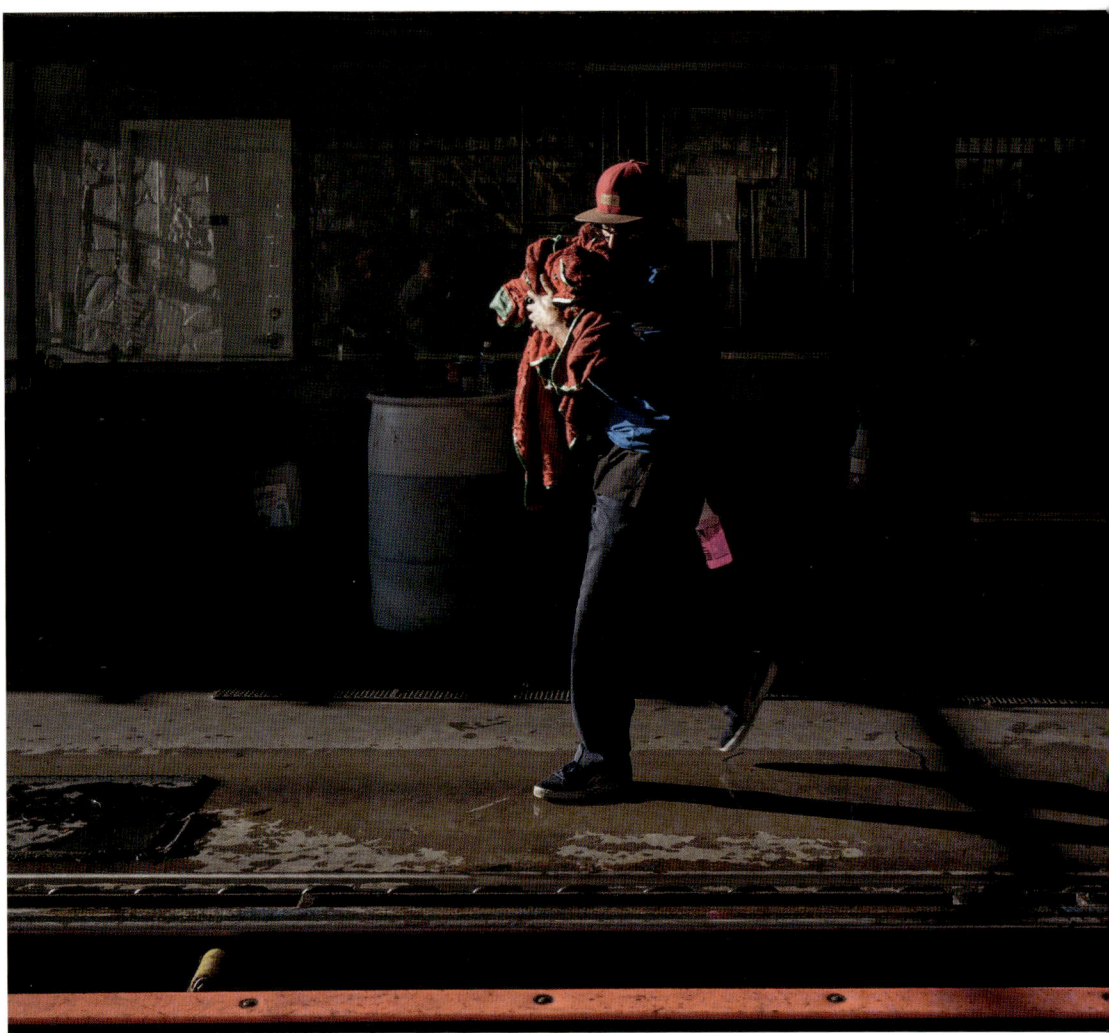

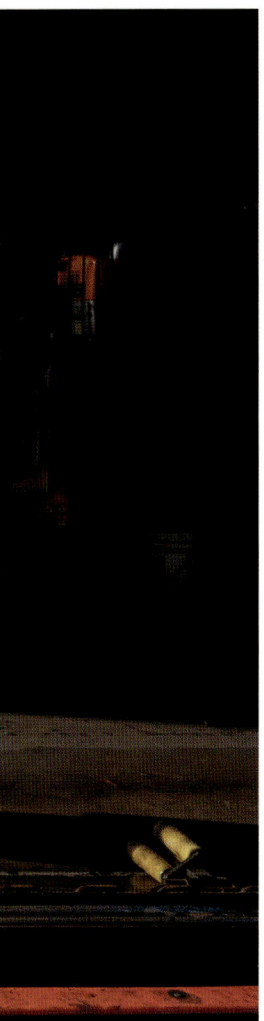

I was walking down the street one day when I saw the light illuminating cars exiting a car wash. The late afternoon light hit the cars and workers with a strong, hard quality that made the colors and shapes pop. It also produced long, deep shadows that stretched down into the depths of the car wash. I moved to the periphery of the structure where security gates separated me from the cars and workers.

I remained there for over 20 minutes as different cars came through and the men busily cleaned the vehicles' interiors and exteriors. I noted how the colors of the cars dramatically impacted the look of the images. Dark cars absorbed much of the light, bringing more emphasis to the workers, whereas white cars reflected the light and became a bigger visual draw in the compositions. Wanting to emphasize the workers more, I kept looking for darker cars to move through the line.

While watching these cars come through, I noticed that there was a young man frequently moving back and forth through the scene, his arms full of used towels. I assumed he gathered them to put through the washer and dryer. During a break in the procession of cars, he came through the scene and I captured him as he moved toward the light. The quality of the light made the reds, blues, and yellows in the frame pop with saturation, and produced a strong contrast between light and dark. The image succeeds in pulling the viewer's attention to the man, while still including details in the background that help tell the story of the moment.

Learn from the Light

By observing light and shadow, you learn how the world reveals itself to the human eye, and you can use that to your advantage when creating a composition. Even though you are often working with found light—light you have no direct control over—you can learn how to make conscious choices in terms of how you use what is there.

The wonderful thing is you can practice this at any time, whether you have a camera or not. You can observe light and shadow while waiting in line to buy theater tickets or pushing a shopping cart to your car, or even when stuck in a traffic jam. Use the time to observe what is happening with the light and the shadows. Learn from those quiet, disposable moments how light reveals and how shadows obscure details. Discover how the quality of light changes the saturation of colors or how textures and patterns are rendered.

Make the observation of light a regular practice that is not dependent on having a camera in your hand. By doing so, you prepare yourself for moments when you are intentionally seeing with the goal of making photographs.

On a bright, sunny day, make some photographs where the subject is more the quality of the light than it is a person or physical object. Look for a scene that is being illuminated by hard, direct sunlight and find a subject that takes advantage of those saturated colors and strong shadows. Photograph things in the shade or shadows as well. Try to produce an interesting photograph without the benefit of strong directional light.

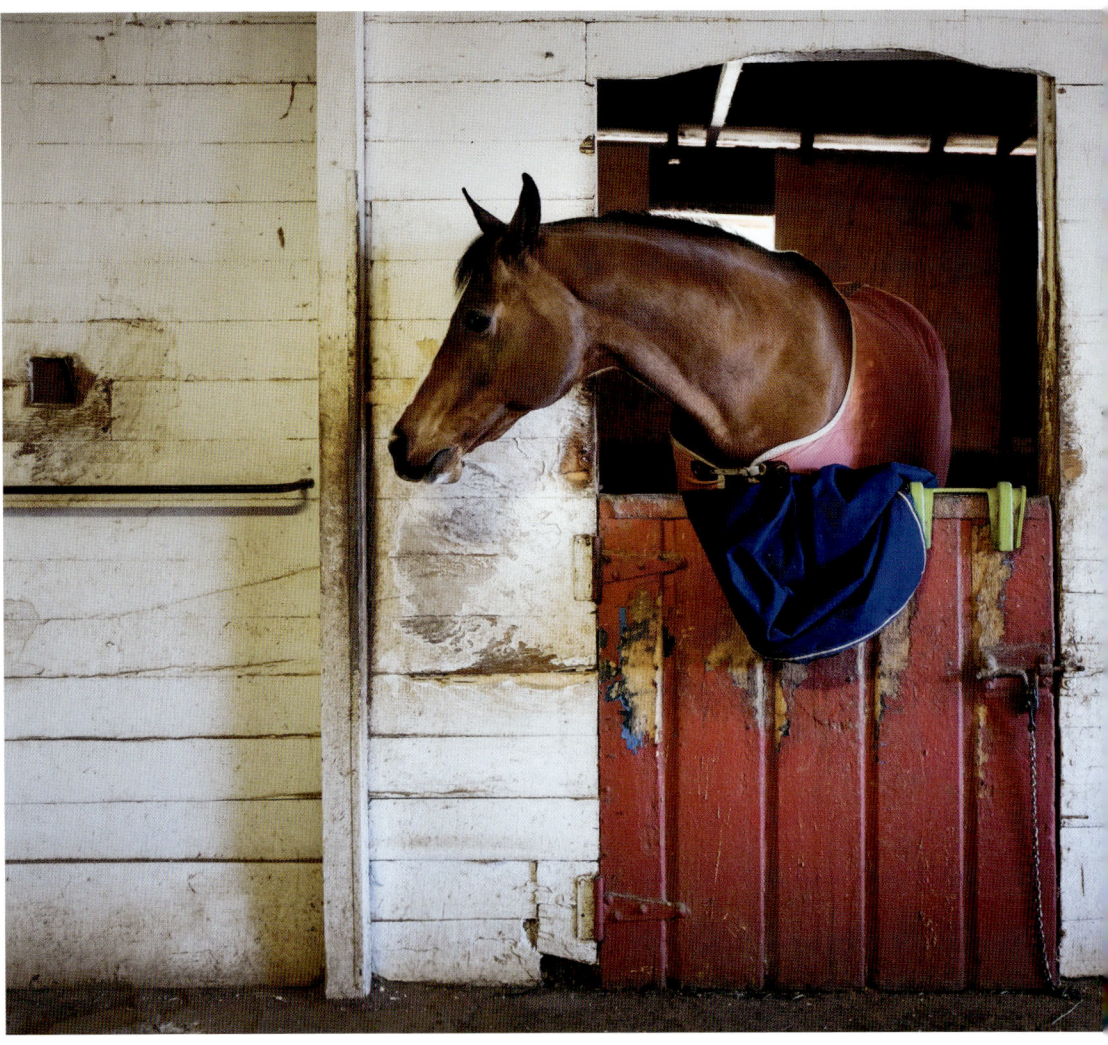

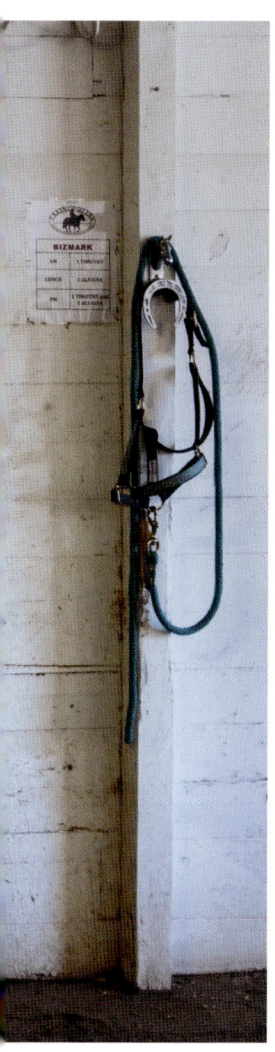

Line and Shape

I was asked to photograph for a local nonprofit that gives at-risk girls the opportunity to work with horses. Located only 20 minutes from Downtown Los Angeles, the horses are housed in the oldest continually used stables in the city. I was scheduled to meet with the director to discuss the images they needed for their various promotional efforts, but I arrived early, so her daughter took me on a short tour of the facilities and told me I was free to wander and make photographs until her mother returned.

I took the opportunity to observe the environment and I noted how dark the interior of the barn was. The light that came through the barn doors on either end quickly diminished to shadow. Photographing the depth of this barn would be a challenge. I needed to shoot at a fairly high ISO and a wide aperture in order to produce good photographs.

I noticed one of the horses housed in a stable about 25 feet from the east-facing entrance. I made several test frames to see what I could produce in this part of the barn. My camera was set for the day's outdoor lighting conditions, but that needed to change. I increased my ISO to 1000 and set the lens to its widest aperture of f/2. I would be shooting at a shutter speed of 1/100 of a second, which is one stop slower than I usually feel comfortable shooting at, but I stuck with those settings.

The beautiful horse stuck its head out through the opening of his stall and I loved the way the soft directional light illuminated his coat as well as the interior of the barn. Because of the relatively slow shutter speed, I knew I would need to capture the horse when he paused his movement, or his head would blur.

As I composed the shot I saw that the horse alone would not make for an interesting photograph. It needed the lines and shapes created by the various elements that made up the interior of the barn—the vertical and horizontal lines created by the slats of wood; the oval shape of the bridal hanging off of a peg; the square-like hole on the wall that mirrored the shape of the stall door. The horse's neck and head offered a curved, flowing shape that served as a counterpoint to the lines and shapes that existed throughout the frame.

I continued to make photographs, framing the scene while paying attention to the movement of the horse. I observed when his nose overlapped a wooden post to his right. I wanted clearance between his head and the post, so I refined my timing further to create that important separation.

I was pleased with what I saw, but I realized that I faced some technical challenges when I returned for the actual shoot day.

Seeing Graphically

One of the things that helped me to avoid seeing the world literally was to learn to see graphically. Instead of seeing things for their functions, I began to observe the shapes and lines that those objects possess. I examined the rectangular shape of doors and windows and bricks. I saw the round shapes of light sources and balls and buttons. I discovered the lines in sidewalk cracks, the ribs of an umbrella, or telephone wires. I saw these things and how they interacted with each other and my eyes opened up to subject matter I had never considered before.

Shapes and lines are everywhere—I had to look no further than my own office to see this. I began to see rectangles in the shape of my computer screen, phone, tablet, speakers, digital audio recorder, file drawer, business cards, and hard drives. I noticed circles when I looked at the Chinese lantern above my desk, the floor fan, the lid of a coffee mug, and a lens cap. I observed lines in the form of cables, folds in the curtains, the grain pattern of the hardwood floor, and the crown molding near the ceiling. When I actively looked for shapes and lines, their abundance was immediately revealed to me.

When I ventured out into the world, I made similar observations of things around me, whether it was in the shape and lines of manmade things, such as automobiles and structures, or natural things like leaves, shells, and rocks.

As an exercise, I challenged myself to look not only for standard shapes such as squares, circles, and rectangles, but also for triangles, octagons, ovals, and even shapes that I did not have a name for. It was much like a child's game, but a game that taught me to refine my eye and to take that all-important step away from seeing things literally.

When I photographed the things that I found, I learned the importance of cleanly defining a shape. It was important to not only find the shape, but also to consider the area immediately around it. Shape is defined as much by what exists around an object as the object itself. The shape of a door, for example, is cleanly defined by the existence of the wall around it. The square shapes of the keys on my keyboard are revealed because of the gray metal in which they are set. The lenses of my glasses are as much about the frame that houses them as they are the shape of the lenses themselves.

I paid attention to this as I made photographs that leaned more toward abstraction than documentation. By isolating the shapes that defined a thing, I emphasized the shapes and lines themselves.

In the photograph of my dog Zooey, I focused on the shape of the pads of her paws as she lay on our wooden deck. The shape of each pad is repeated on the bottom of her foot, resulting on a strong pattern. Each pad is separated by strands of fur that possess their own repetition of line and shape. The roundish shape of her foot pads are juxtaposed with the line and shape of the wood deck, creating contrast within the composition. The photograph is interesting because of its exploration of line and shape and not merely because it is my dog.

Take a moment to look at the space around you. What kinds of shapes do you see? Observe how frequently you see certain shapes and lines in your immediate environment. Think of how you might photograph some of those elements so that their shapes, rather than their functions, serve as the heart of your composition.

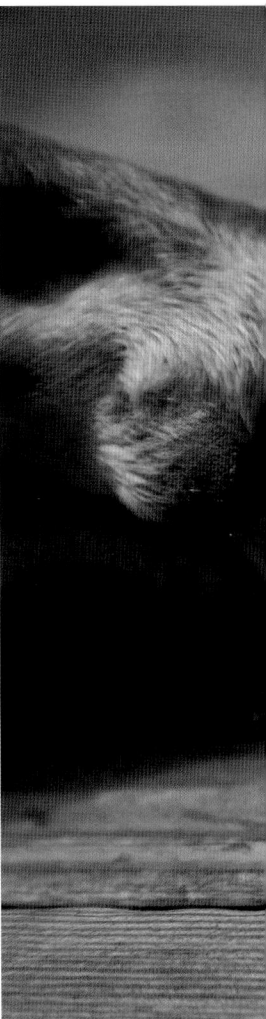

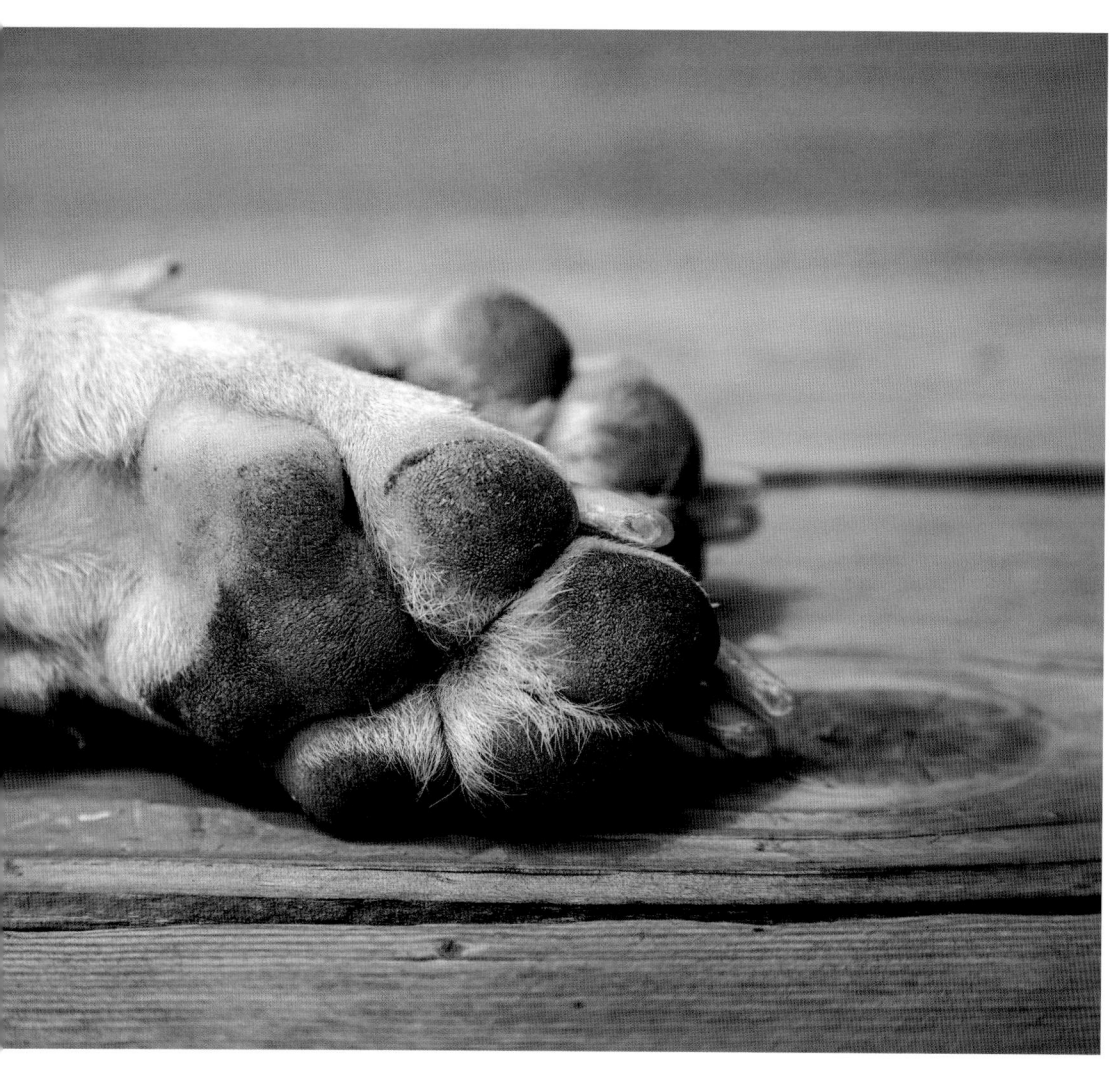

Seeing and Photographing Patterns

Where there are shapes and lines, there are patterns. Those repetitions are found in abundance in our natural and our manufactured world. They are not only pleasing to look at, but also help to develop your eye for line, shape, and form.

Pick up any leaf and you will see the beautiful patterns that Mother Nature has created. In this image of a leaf that I discovered during one of my daily walks, the leaf is defined not merely by its shape, but also by the repeating lines and textures found within it. More patterns are found in the water droplets that rest on the leaf, and even in the texture of the ground. Pattern and line exist in abundance in this natural object that others had walked past without any consideration or regard.

I increased my sensitivity to line and shape by making abstract images of virtually anything that I encountered. Instead of making a document of something, I focused on the graphic quality that drew my attention to it. These abstract photographs went beyond simple snapshots and emphasized the visual elements that piqued my interest in the first place.

In the image of a plant in my yard (page 88), I was drawn to the shape of the leaves and the pattern they created. The sun was behind the plant and highlighted the leaves in such a way that it also resulted in small shadows at the edges of each leaf. I framed the shot using an aperture that would keep the leaves on the stem sharp, while making the similarly shaped leaves and stem in the background appear soft and out of focus.

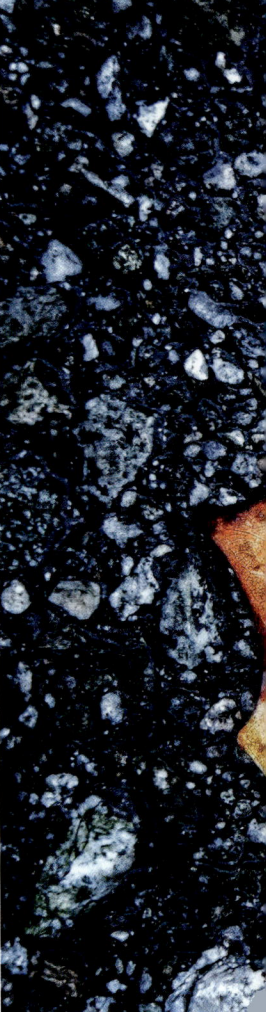

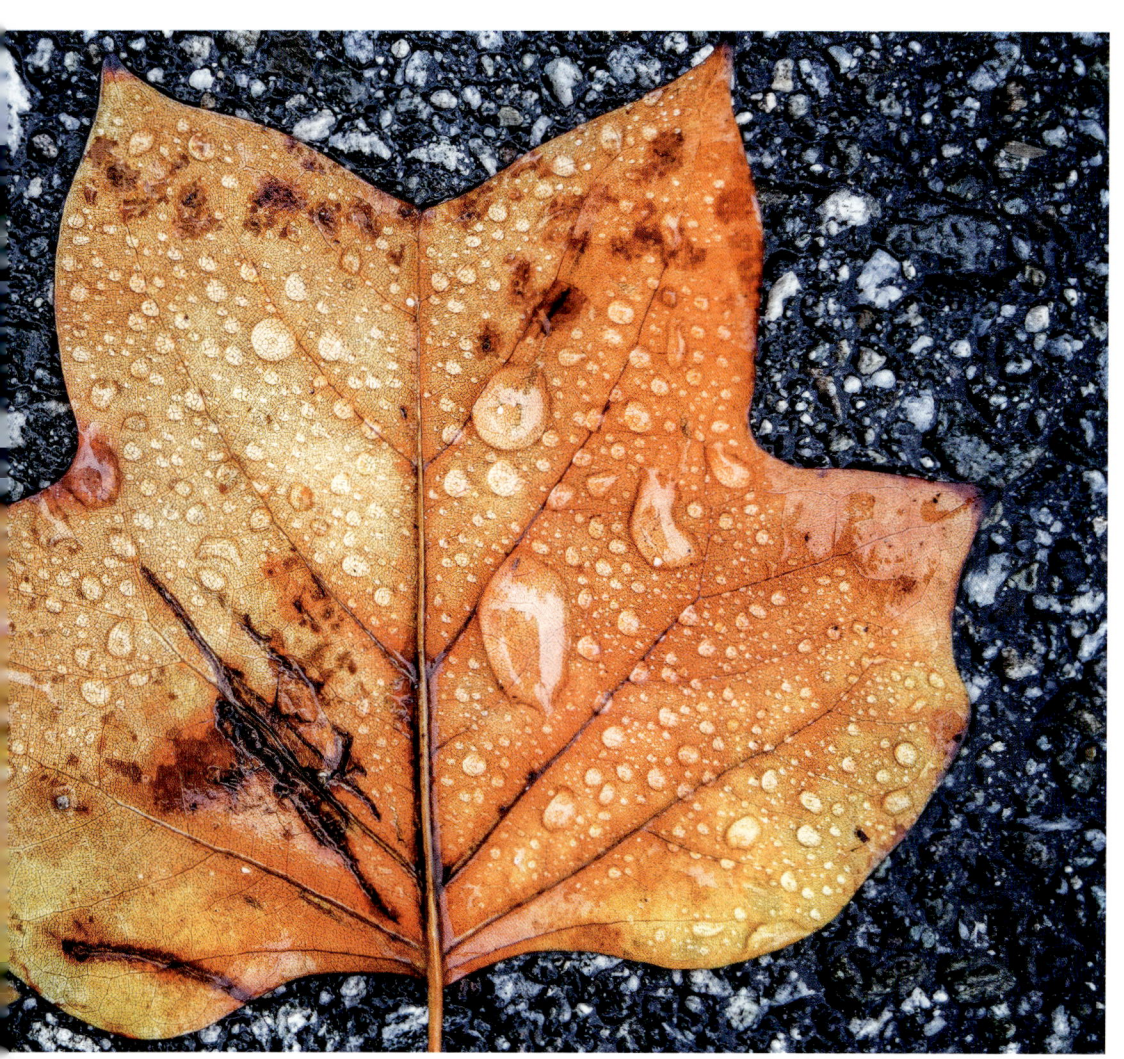

I had walked past this plant thousands of times and never considered it for a photograph before. But on this day, I observed how the sun illuminated the plant. I wanted to emphasize the shapes and lines created by the highlights and shadows, and the beautiful quality of light that illuminated the scene. All of that informed how I framed the composition to produce the final photograph.

I took this same approach when venturing out into the streets. I was on the hunt for lines, shapes, and patterns and I quickly discovered that they were everywhere. I began a process of discovering subject matter in the most unexpected and surprising places.

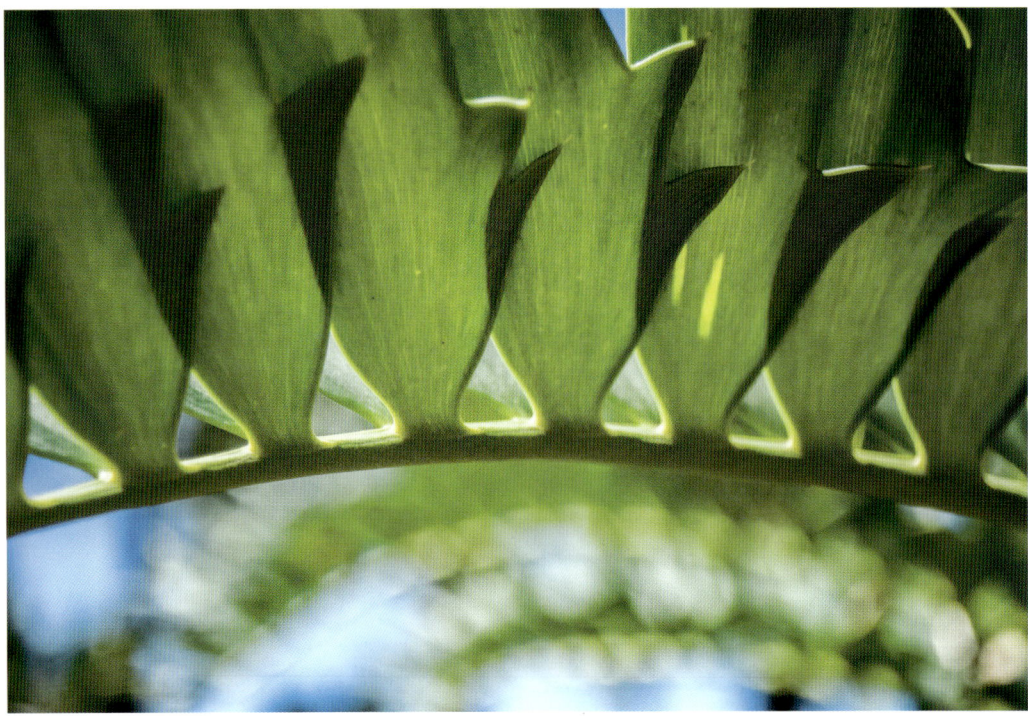

"One of the things that helped me to avoid seeing the world literally was to learn to see graphically."

I was crossing a bridge in Costa Rica situated over a river that is notorious for its abundance of crocodiles. I saw a few floating in the water and hoped the bridge was sturdier than it looked. When I looked down at the various crocodiles, there was one that drew my attention, not because of its size, but because of the way the curve of its body was defined by the muddy water around it. The ridges on its tail and back were made more pronounced by the shadows, making its skin appear horny and threatening.

I moved my camera out over the railing of the bridge and framed the composition to emphasize the shapes and lines that piqued my curiosity. The result was more than just a snapshot of the animal; it was a beautiful abstraction that revealed the animal in an unusual way. The photograph captured my personal experience of the subject in that moment.

Grocery Carts

For a period of time, I created photography assignments for myself. These were meant to get me out shooting on a regular basis and keep me on my toes visually. One day, I got it in my head that during the week I would only shoot grocery carts. I don't know why that idea popped into my head, but as soon as it did, I wanted to change my mind. It was a stupid idea. I did not want to spend what little time I had hunting down shopping carts to photograph. Could there be anything any more boring?

But I did not let myself off the hook. I felt that my resistance was exactly why I should do it. So I gritted my teeth and I began the exercise.

Suffice it to say, I surprised myself. Suddenly, I saw grocery carts everywhere. I saw them when I went to the market to do errands and when I was walking or driving down a street. It sometimes felt like an infestation out of a sci-fi horror movie.

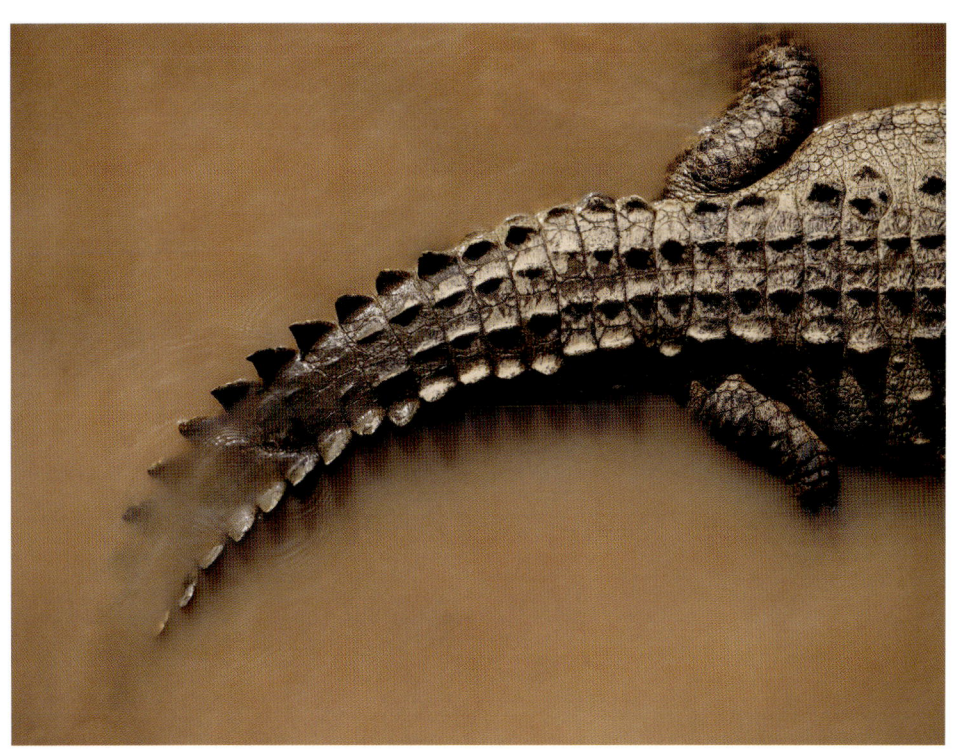

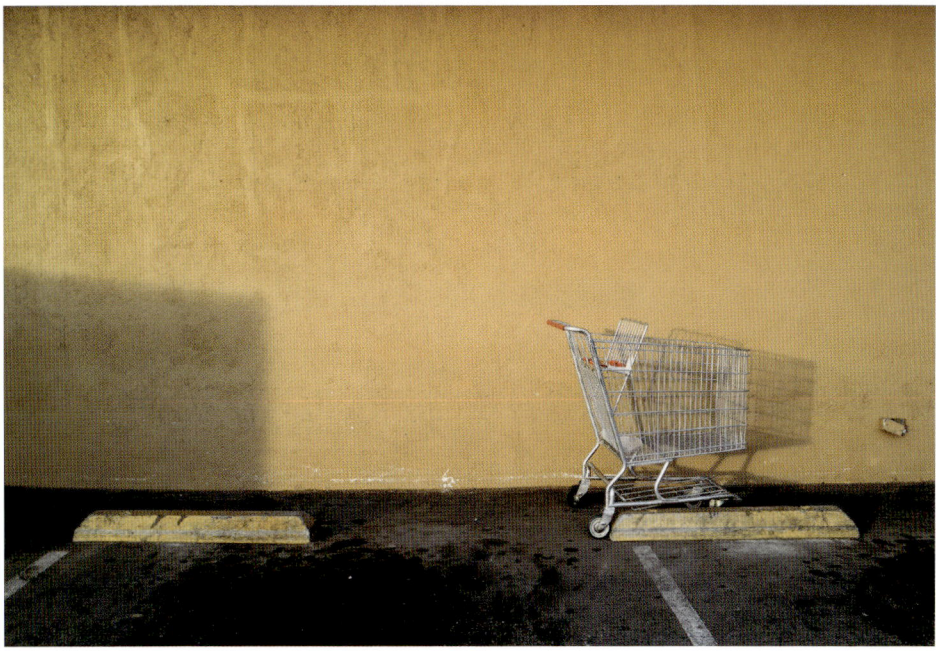

When I discovered one to photograph, the challenge was to make it interesting. The way I did that was by not looking at the shopping carts literally, but by observing the lines, shapes, and patterns they created. I looked at how shapes and patterns existed in the body of the carts themselves, and also how they interacted with the lines and shapes of the objects around them. Some of the photographs were tight detail shots of a cart and others looked like environmental portraits. With each image, I took that mental step back to observe the most ordinary thing in a completely new way.

That week-long exercise that I had been reluctant to begin filled me with excitement and eagerness by the end of the week. I felt that I saw the world with a different set of eyes. I did not produce the same photographs over and over again; rather, I challenged myself to see and create photographs in a different and unique way that informed everything I did afterward.

Spend a few days focusing on photographing a common object. It could be anything—leaves, doors, dogs, shoes, cars, etc. But instead of merely documenting the object you choose, create photographs that emphasize lines and shapes. Try for a variety of images and compositions. Shoot both close-up images of these items and images that draw upon other elements and the environment to help emphasize the lines, shapes, and patterns you see.

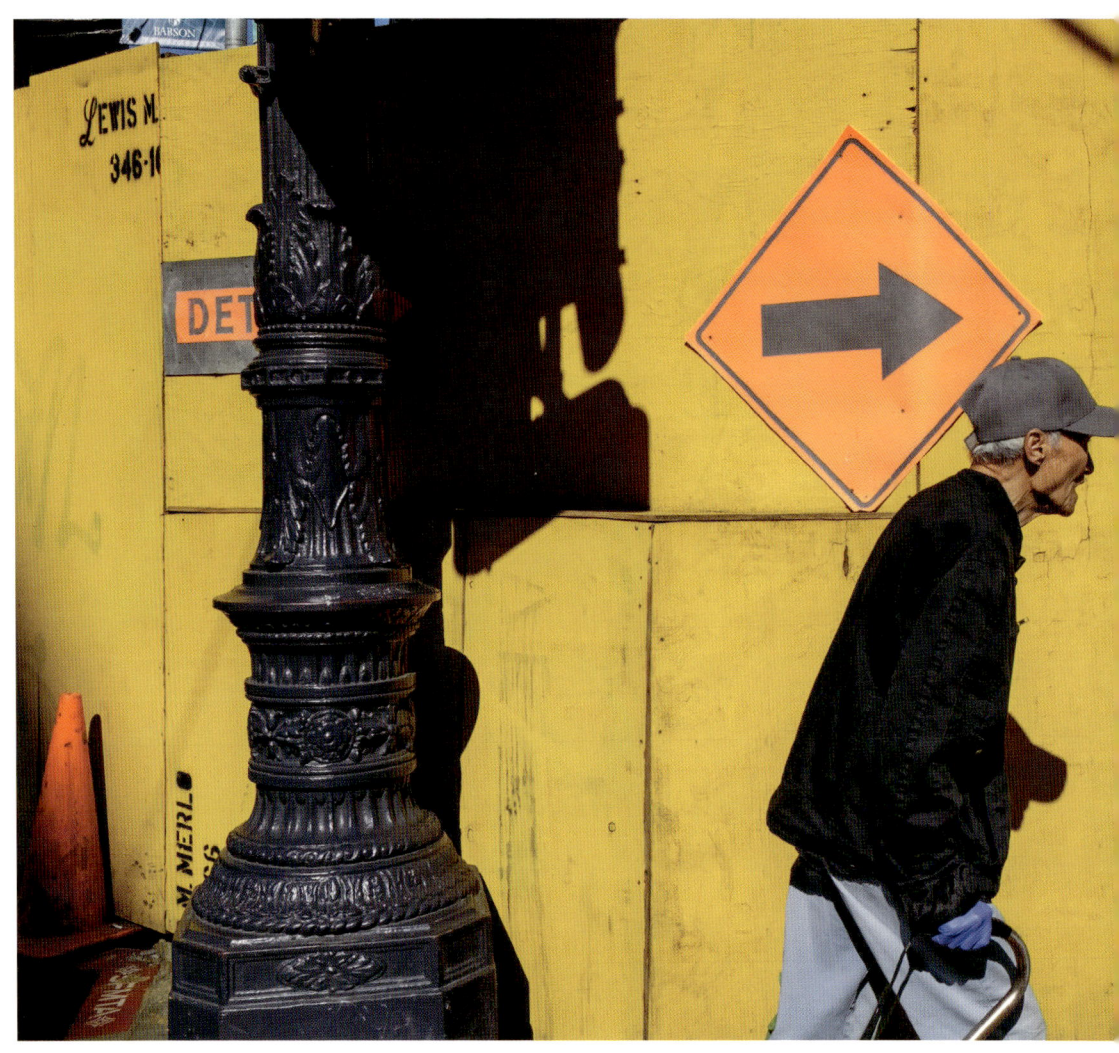

Color

I awoke in San Francisco and the last thing I wanted to do was get up and make photographs. I had a meeting in a few hours and I wanted to indulge myself and sleep in. I usually wake up at 5:30 a.m. each morning, and the idea of hugging the pillow for another hour or two was tempting. However, when I caught sight of the light coming through the hotel room window, I roused myself out of bed. As much as I would have loved a few more hours of sleep, I felt I had take advantage of a beautiful morning in San Francisco.

We were a few blocks from Union Square. I walked through the park and adjoining streets, observing how the light illuminated the architecture and the cable cars as they moved up and down Powell Street. Artists and craftspeople were setting up their stands in the square while dozens of other people made their way to work. The sky was clear, the air was crisp, and I took great pleasure in exploring.

However, I was not making great pictures. They were serviceable images, made more out of instinct than inspired by moments of discovery. After some time, I decided to head back to the hotel so that I would not miss my appointment.

As I walked, I saw light hitting a street corner, the location of a construction site. The light revealed an explosion of color made up of a temporary yellow wall, a red call box, and orange detour signs. I immediately realized that I might be late for my appointment.

I crossed the street and positioned myself at the very edge of the curb to evaluate the scene in front of me. I considered all the elements I had seen, including an orange cone and the ornate light post. But as I looked at the initial image I made, I knew the shot was missing something. I needed a human element to complete the composition.

I looked up and down the street, but there were few pedestrians this early in the morning. The people I did see were not walking past the spot where I wanted them for my composition. I saw a few people start to walk in my direction, but they eventually turned and moved on elsewhere.

I waited and waited, repeatedly looking at my watch as the minutes ticked by. When 15–20 minutes had passed, I realized I might be pushing my luck with time. I needed time to shower, get dressed, and drive across town. I kept calculating how quickly I could do those things and still arrive on schedule.

Just a few more minutes, I kept convincing myself. Just wait.

"Just as brightness and contrast and line and shape are visual draws for the human eye, so is color."

I had faced countless moments just like this in the past, and admittedly some of them had been a wash. The right character, the telling gesture, that special moment never arrived. But I did not allow such moments to dissuade me from staying where I was, because despite those failures, there had been moments when everything fell into place and magic happened. This scene was so close to perfection and I just had to trust that it would be worth the wait and the risk of being late.

I caught sight of an older man in the distance moving toward me. As he continued walking, I said a silent prayer, hoping he would walk past me. When I saw that he was, I raised the camera to my eye, framed the scene as I had previously determined, and depressed the shutter-release button just as he entered the right area of the scene.

I played back the image on the camera's LCD and after being satisfied that I had gotten the shot, rushed back to my hotel room to prepare for my appointment. As I rode the elevator, I looked at the image and saw that the universe had provided me with the perfect character to complete the photograph. Not only had he been walking in the right direction, but the beautiful color of the scene now included the powder blue glove he wore on his right hand. The color was a wonderful contrast to the warm tones that had surrounded the man.

Just as brightness and contrast and line and shape are visual draws for the human eye, so is color. Saturated colors like the reds and yellows in the photograph that begins this chapter draw you into the photograph and give the image its vibrancy and energy.

We are visually drawn to colors, and these same colors can influence us psychologically, evoking moods and feelings. Reds and oranges evoke excitement, sensuality, and anxiety, whereas blues are associated with melancholy, sadness, or isolation. Juxtapose certain colors against each other, and a scene can explode with visual tension and energy, even though the subjects are static.

These same colors can also be distractions if they are possessed by secondary elements in the scene. If the background includes a woman in a red dress, the eye is drawn to that part of the frame and may compete with your subject for the viewer's attention. It is important to consider how colors within the scene contribute to or detract from your subject. If colors in the background prove distracting, you will need to find a way to eliminate them, which could be as simple as shifting your camera position.

Color by Feel

There is certainly a science to color theory, of which I have a basic knowledge. But rather than becoming fluent in the logic of complex color theory, I have instead relied on my own gut reactions to colors as a graphic element in a photograph. There are times when I am walking down the street and I see a red door or the juxtaposition of a green wall against a blue sky and I am inspired to make a photograph. The trigger serves as the beginning of my process of evaluating the scene and breaking it down to its basic elements of light and shadow, shape and line, color, and gesture.

For the image on the following page, made in Chinatown, I was drawn to the various hues of red that dominated the scene. The ground and the Chinese lanterns were a saturated crimson, while the wall itself was a more muted version of the color. As I evaluated the scene, I noticed the yellow tails falling from the lanterns as well as the dark color of a lone bench.

I maneuvered myself to include each of these elements in the frame, but at this point, I primarily considered the lines and shapes that pervaded the space in front of me. In order for these various elements to play off of each other, I focused on the lines and shapes to build a balanced composition, where the result was not heavily weighted for the right or left, top or bottom.

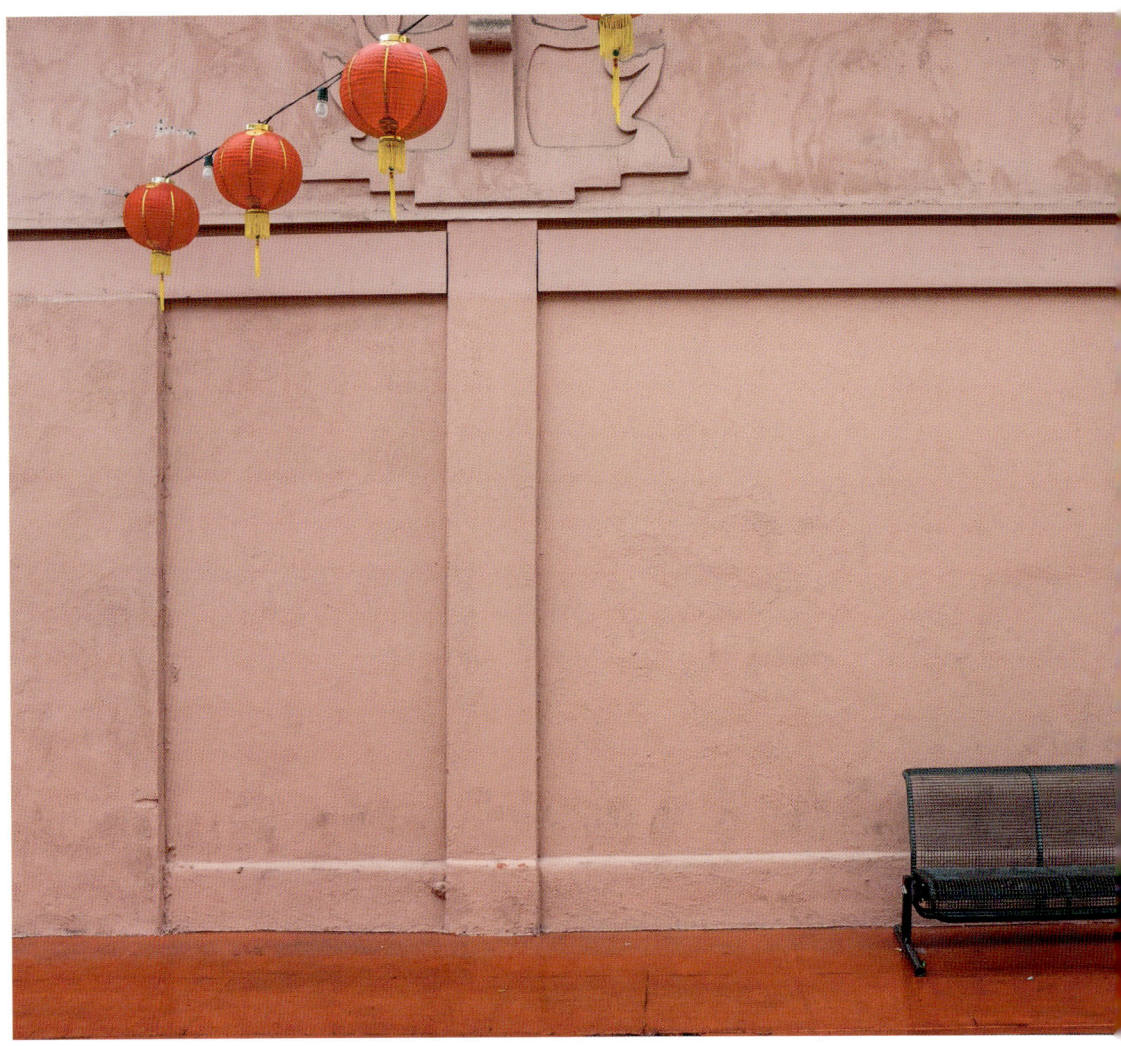

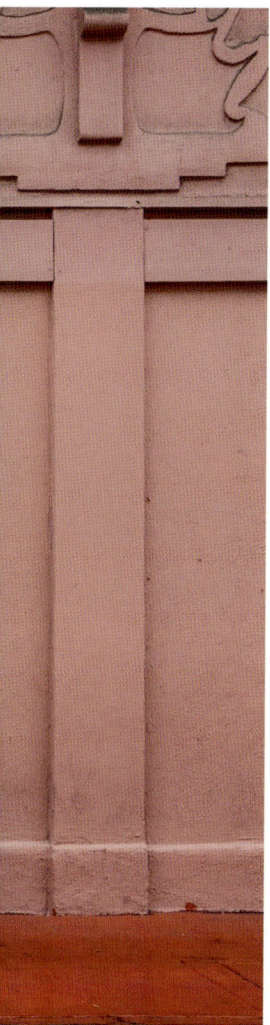

As a result, the final image used color, but it was not a photograph solely about color. It was successful because of the use of light, shape, and line that helped me to build the composition.

Color as a Starting Point

I see color as a starting point and not an end in itself. Trying to create an image that is solely about color is like trying to compose music with a single note. A successful and interesting photograph has to be more than just a punchy hue. If it isn't, it may inspire a cursory glance, but it is unlikely to hold the viewer's attention for very long.

Just as I am often drawn into a scene because of light and shadow and the resulting contrast, I can find myself drawn into a scene because of color. However, I make a mistake if my seeing stops there. Instead, I use color as the beginning of an exploration where I build a composition that is complex, pleasing, and occasionally challenging.

I was walking in Downtown Los Angeles when I saw a powder blue wall with two whitish rectangles of paint (page 103). I also noticed the red curb. Luckily, the street had been changed so that I could safely stand several feet away from the curb and still include the wall, a bike rack, and a light post in the composition.

I made a series of images evaluating the relationship of each of these objects within the frame. I made adjustments to my standing position to ensure I had enough space at the top and left sides of the frame to cleanly define the edges of the white patches.

I knew I wanted more than a still life, so I photographed several people walking through the scene, but it was evident to me that I risked repeating myself. How many times had I found an interesting background and hoped for the right interesting character to walk by? Yes, I had succeeded many times before, but I wanted to challenge myself to do something different. Though I was tempted to stop shooting and move on, I urged myself to stay put and linger.

It was then that a flock of pigeons flew through the scene and I captured a single bird just as it was about to exit the frame. In that moment, I had that something different I had hoped for, a moment that I could not have anticipated when I stopped to consider the scene. What began as a response to color became a more much complex and interesting composition that was completed by the magic of the unexpected.

Reconsidering a Relationship to Color

Responding to color in this way is another way to avoid seeing the world literally. It is a way to examine the various elements in your line of sight as abstractions, and then use those elements as compositional building blocks.

We can and do have a visceral reaction to color, but we more commonly associate such reactions to smell or taste. This reaction is something to use because the goal is to recreate the moment of discovery for the viewer when they see the photograph. In a photograph you can evoke the same thrill of discovery you felt in another human being.

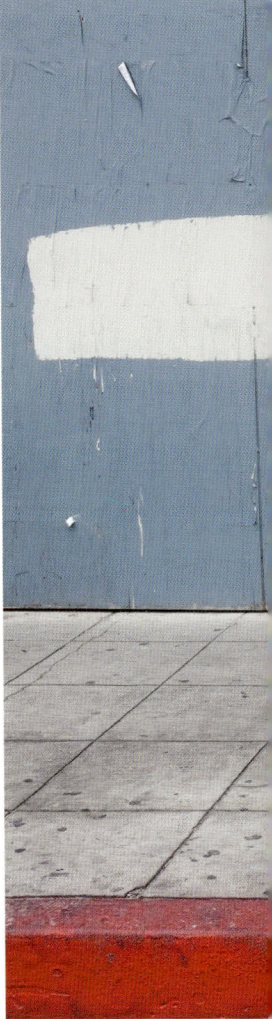

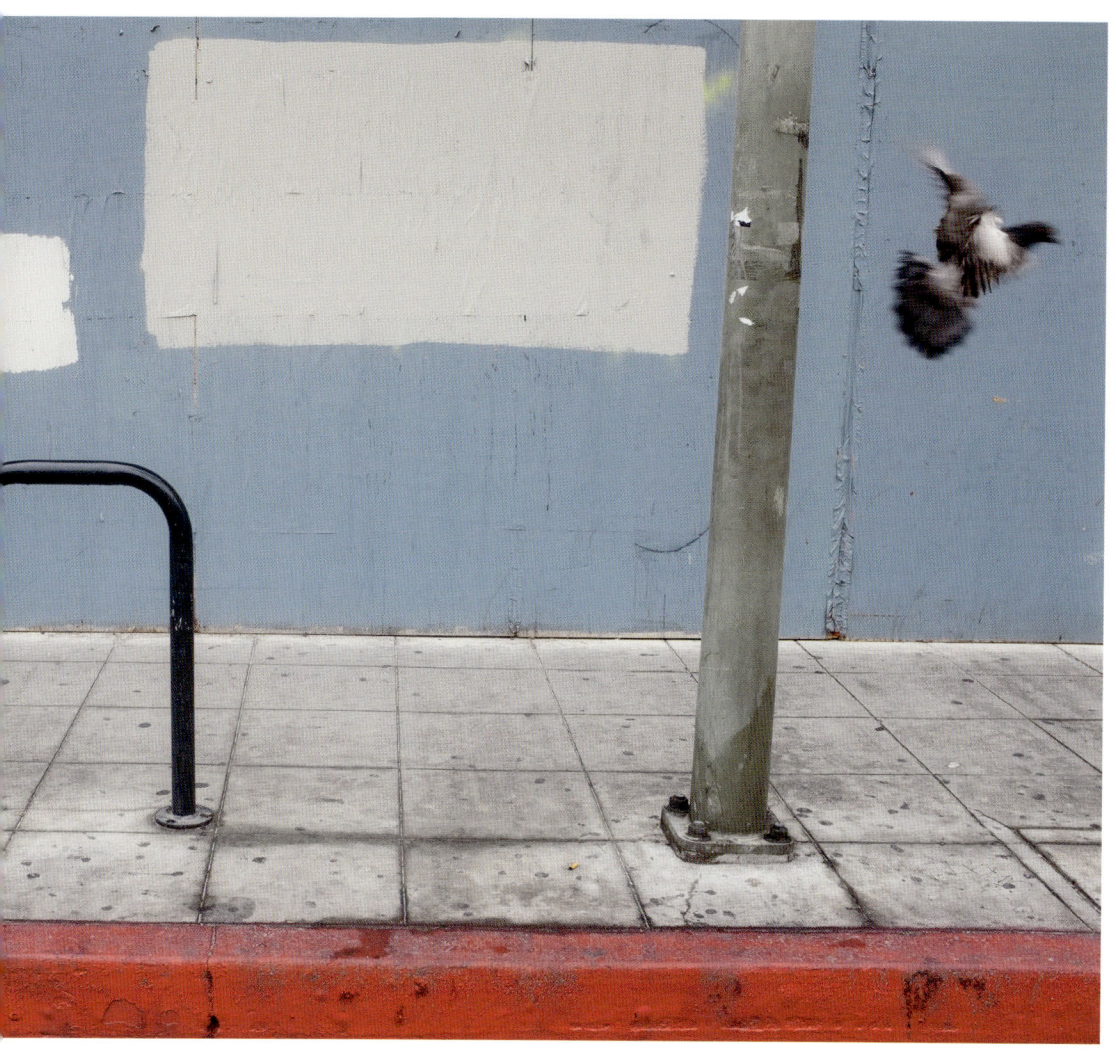

That is what I hoped to do with this image of a woman about to cross the street holding a red-and-white umbrella. I responded to the scene because of the contrasting colors of the umbrella and how they played off the yellow lines of the crosswalk. But that reaction to color also led me to consider the importance of the repeating shapes and patterns, which included the triangles of the umbrella and the lines in the crosswalk and street. It also led me to think about the importance of light, including the umbrella's shadow.

Yes, the images in this chapter have color, and to some degree are about color, but they are also about the feeling they helped evoke in me when I discovered each scene. The challenge for me was to use my skills as a photographer to create a composition that allowed the viewer, who was not with me in that moment, to experience the scene vicariously through my eyes.

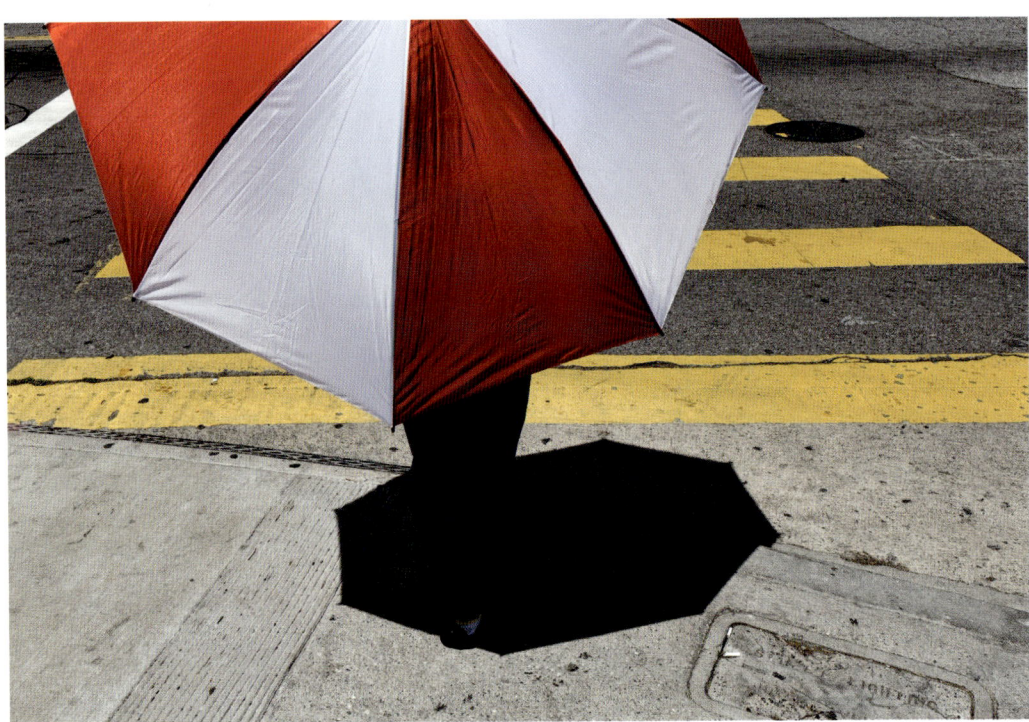

Explore a scene that you are drawn to because of color. Use what you have learned about light and shadow and shape and line to create a composition that builds on your discovery of color. If possible, use the juxtaposition of two or more colors to create visual contrast.

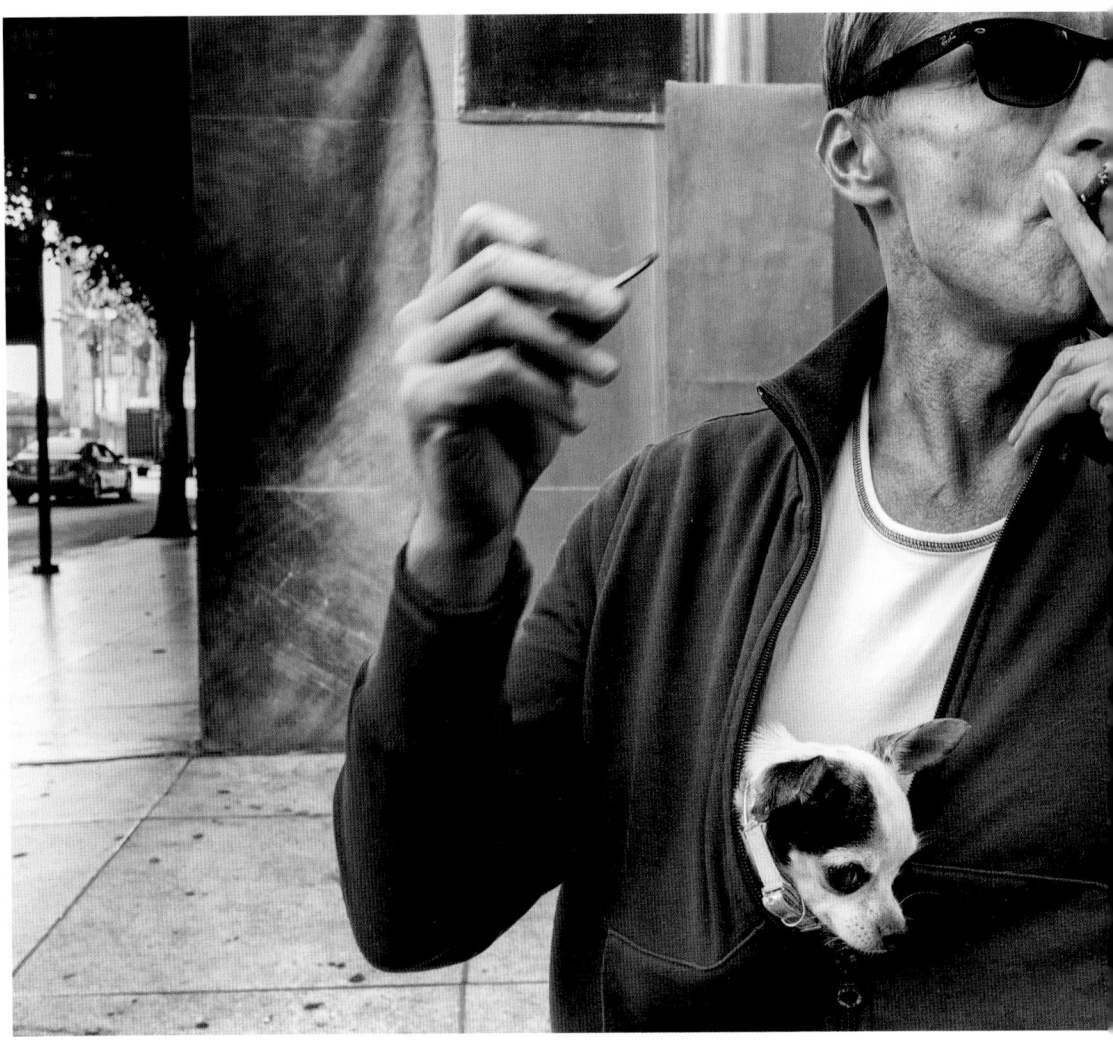

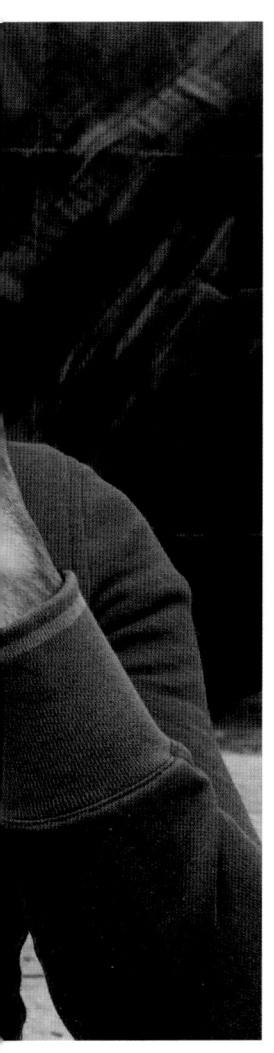

Gesture

When I was younger, I had boundless energy. I could walk for hours with a bag loaded with cameras, lenses, and film. I was a perpetual motion machine with a camera. How time has changed all that.

Nowadays, I need periodic breaks when I am out shooting. On this particular day, I was headed for a local Starbucks that is frequented by many other street photographers. As I waited at a crosswalk, a man walked up to me. Peaking out of his partially zipped jacket was the head of a small dog. I knew I had to make a picture.

I complimented the man on his dog and asked him if I could make a picture of it. He agreed, and I positioned myself in front of him. I knew I wanted to do more than just take a picture of his dog. My intent was to include the man in the composition because it was the intimate connection between him and his dog that interested me.

As I was figuring out my composition, he asked me if I minded him lighting up a cigarette.

"Please do," I said, amazed at my luck, because it was the moment that he lit his cigarette, took a drag, and whipped the match through the air that provided the gesture that made the photograph. What would have been just another cute shot of a man with his dog became something more as a result of the gesture of the man's hands, the tilt of his head, and the expression of the dog. It was the flourish that completely transformed the photograph into something special.

What is Gesture?

When you think of gesture, the first thing you likely imagine is a person moving their hands as they try to explain or emphasize something. Human beings use their hands all the time to express emotions such as joy, anger, and sadness. There are moments when gesture expresses a feeling better than words can. This is one of the reasons gestures can be so important in a photograph, a medium that does not have the benefit of sound.

However, gesture is more than just a person gesticulating. It can also be the slight tilt of a head, the hunching of shoulders, or a facial expression. Gesture is often that little something that elevates the ordinary to the extraordinary. And the amazing thing about gesture is that it is often the smallest of details that completely transforms a shot.

Though a gesture is often associated with human physicality, it can also be a ragged piece of yellow cloth clinging to a chain-link fence or the peeling paint of a wall that reveals an old poster underneath. It is a detail that, whether human or not, makes an image more than just the sum of its parts.

In this photograph I made while listening to a presentation at the Miami Street Photography Festival, the gesture was the sunglasses sitting atop the man's head. Though his silhouetted bald head makes for an interesting visual draw, it is the sunglasses and the color they produced that makes the shot especially interesting. It is a small thing, but a small thing that carries weight, which is something to always look for in a gesture.

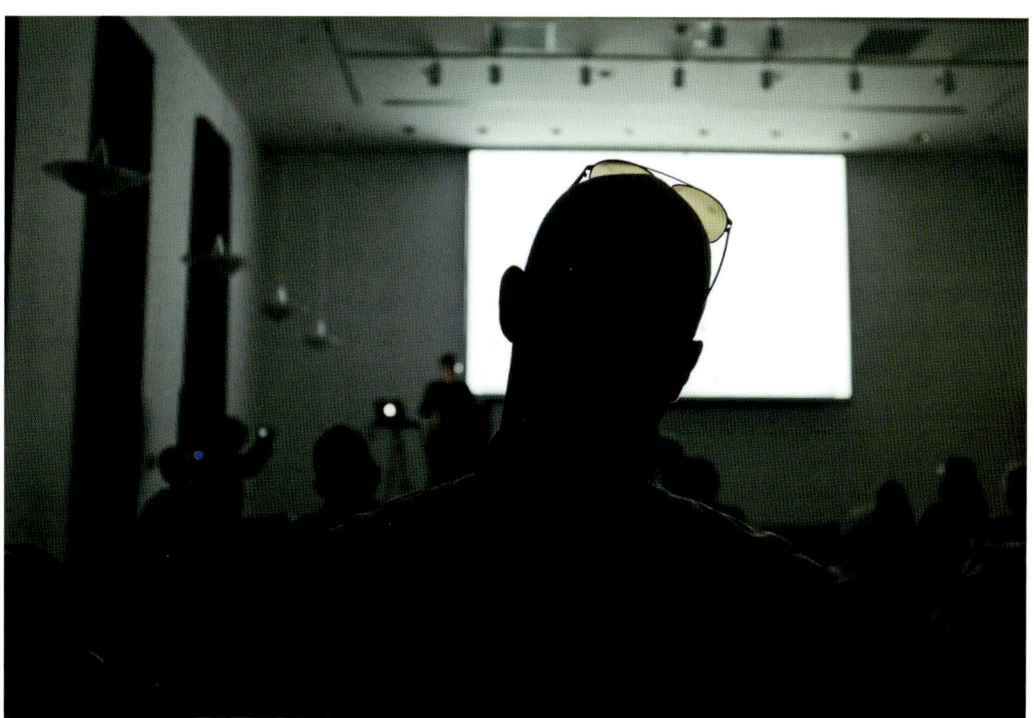

The search for gesture is often the last thing I consider for a shot. The evaluation of light and shadow, line and shape, and color serve as the building blocks for each composition. It is the consideration of each of those elements that allows me to decide what to include or exclude from the frame, thus refining the composition. Once these decisions are made, the gesture is the one element that I cannot completely predict, but which precise seeing and patience often reveals.

This is why having a systematic way of seeing becomes so invaluable. If you don't, you are often too preoccupied with the camera and its settings, or relying far too much on fast reflexes, to respond to an unfurling moment. By processing the scene visually in the way that I have described, you can focus your full attention on that one telling flourish that completely elevates an image.

Anticipating Gesture

For this image of skateboarders in France, I saw the potential of the scene to make a remarkable shot. I knew I wanted to do more than capture a single skater performing a trick. I wanted to capture the fluidity and the energy of the entire scene and the multiple skaters.

As I evaluated the action, I determined where the skaters who were catching air launched and landed. To emphasize their flight, I positioned myself low to the ground. From there, I considered the lines and shapes of the scene, including the block of concrete, the pole, and the other skaters that moved through the area. The abundance of light ensured that I could achieve both a fast shutter speed to freeze the action and a small aperture to increase the depth of field. The expanse of blue sky would play an important part in the shot because of the low angle from which I was shooting. I also noted that the clothing of the skaters might play an important role in the photograph.

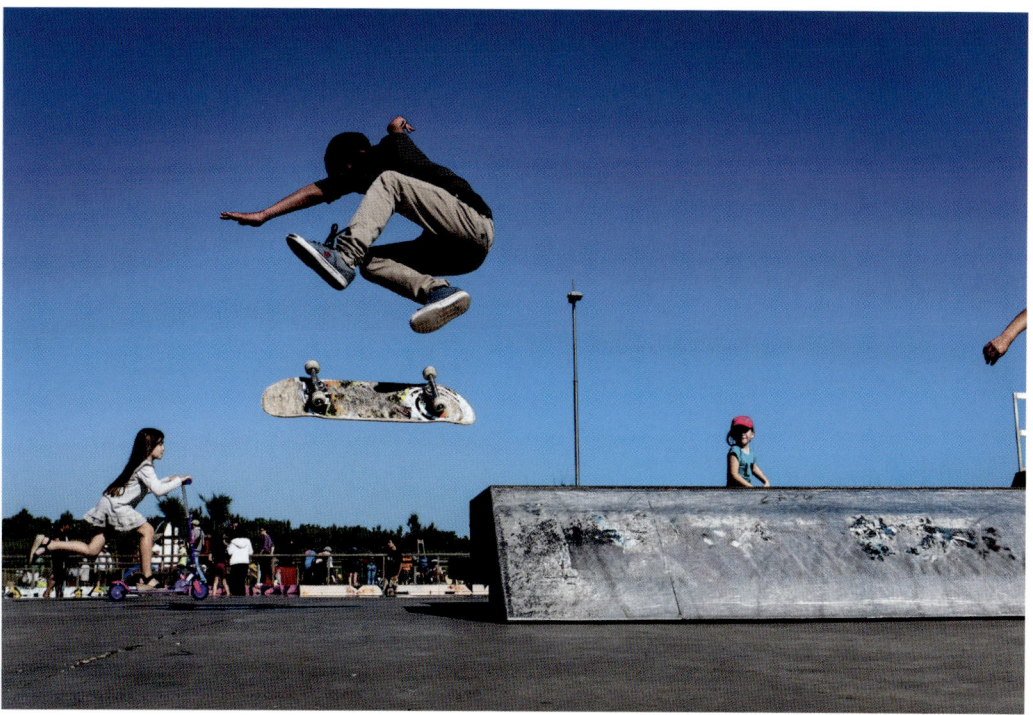

Once I figured out my overall composition, it became a numbers game. By that, I mean creating a series of images of a skater juxtaposed against the expansive blue sky that also considered the other skaters in the background. I paid attention to both when the individual skater launched into the air and where the other kids were positioned in the background and at the edges of the frame.

This final image provided me more than I could have hoped for. I captured a wonderful gesture produced by the skater in the background, and the body language of the girl on the left provided a fantastic counterpoint to him. The angles produced by the skater are mirrored beautifully in the girl's body. But that is not the only gesture in the photograph. There is also the gesture of the red hat against the blue sky to the right of the light pole. And finally, there is the arm and hand at the far-right edge of the frame. It is a little detail that other photographers would avoid, but that for me adds an important and balancing gesture that helps complete the image.

An image like this would not have been possible had I been focused only on capturing the action of a single skater. That might have been an interesting shot, but it would not have been much different from the tens of thousands of images made of skateboarders every day. This shot takes it to another level as a result of slowly building the composition and then waiting for the final, telling flourishes. This image relies on the power of gesture.

Humanity in a Gesture

I am increasingly aware of the importance of capturing something genuine in a photograph. As much as I love to create aesthetically pleasing photographs that are well lit and composed, I am always trying to challenge myself to produce photographs that reveal what it means to be human.

Having critiqued numerous photographs in competitions and portfolios, I am aware of the fact that whether images are sloppily or well composed, they can sometimes leave me feeling a bit hollow. It is not so much how the image was captured or with what camera, but what the photographer was responding to.

When I photograph people interacting with each other, an animal, or even an inanimate object, I look for something that reveals some aspect of that person's experience in that particular moment. This is a lot harder to do than one might think.

I find that when I have considered all the other visual elements of light and shadow, line and shape, and color, I can keep my full attention on identifying a gesture that not only provides visual flourish, but also gives the image a sense of humanity.

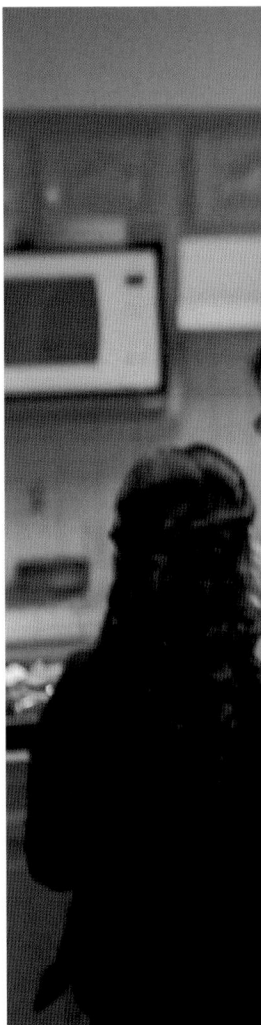

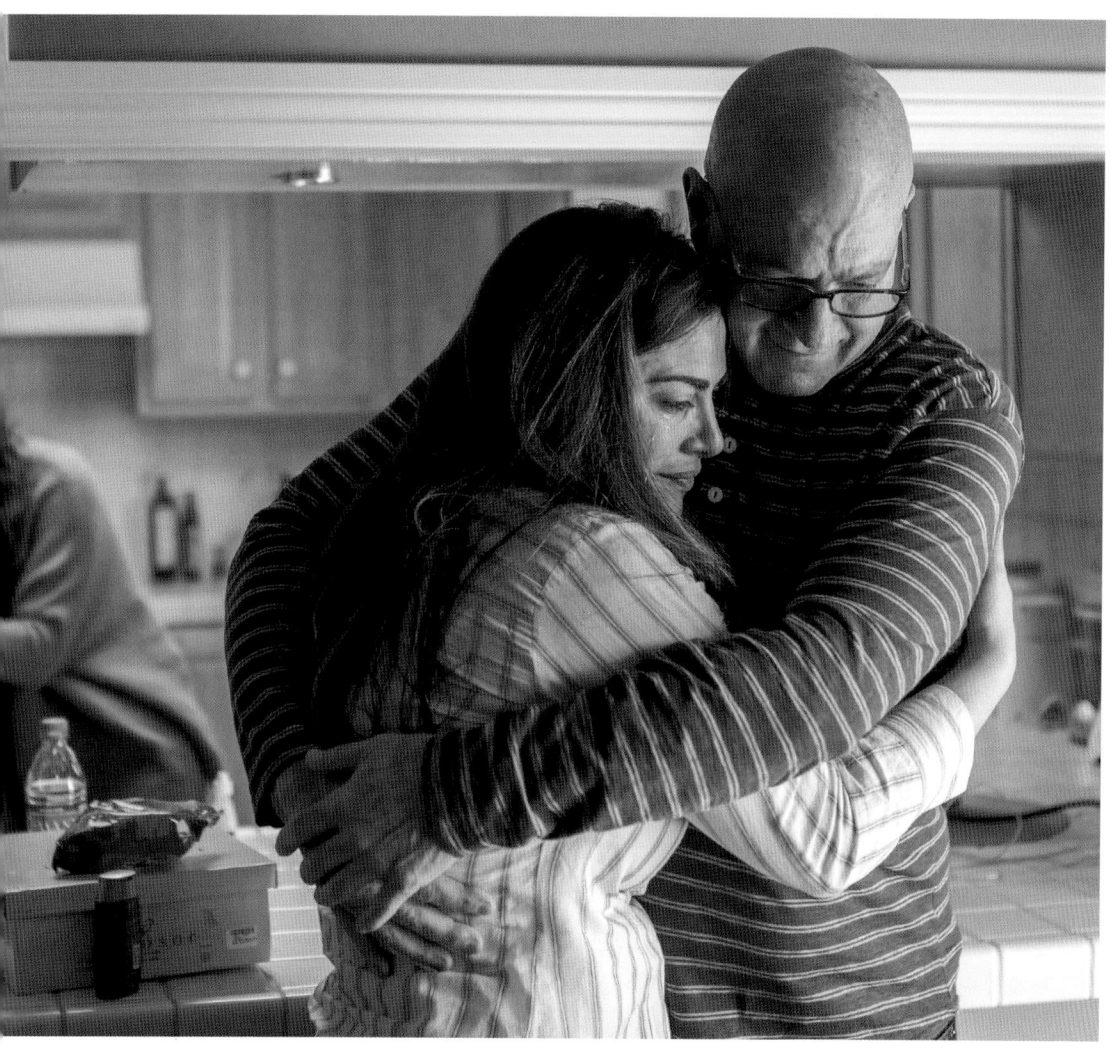

I see humanity in the photograph of a father and daughter embracing on the day of his wedding (previous page). The way they hold each other expresses the love and affection that they felt for each other in that moment. As a counterpoint, there is another gesture that exists in the background with the makeup artist applying makeup on the bride. In addition to helping tell the story of the moment, the contrasting gestures, in their own way, demonstrate the relationship between people.

Special events like weddings, birthdays, and reunions can provide rich opportunity for such gesture, but these gestures actually happen all the time. Think of a mother brushing her child's hair, a dog licking its owner's face, a woman trying to avoid stepping into a puddle, or a man blowing on a hot cup of tea. Each of these ordinary, everyday moments are gestures that, through the eyes of the observant photographer, can be pure gold.

Find a scene that involves
people doing something
together. Observe how
they act and interact
with each other. Look
for hand gestures, facial
expressions, and gestures
of affection. Look for
and refine your overall
composition and focus
your attention on the
gesture, that final critical
detail you feel makes
the difference in the
photograph.

Building a Visual Workflow

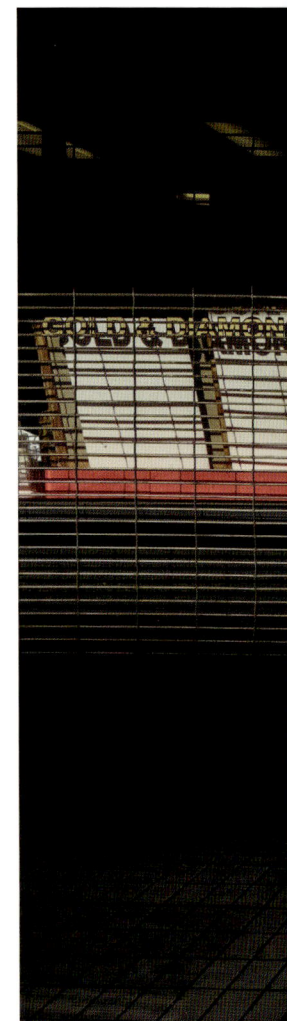

It had been a long day and I was tired. I had conducted an interview for my podcast, written a magazine article, and tended to other business. I then traveled downtown to conduct a one-on-one workshop. I still had several things left on my to-do list and I was seriously considering adding a short nap to that already lengthy list.

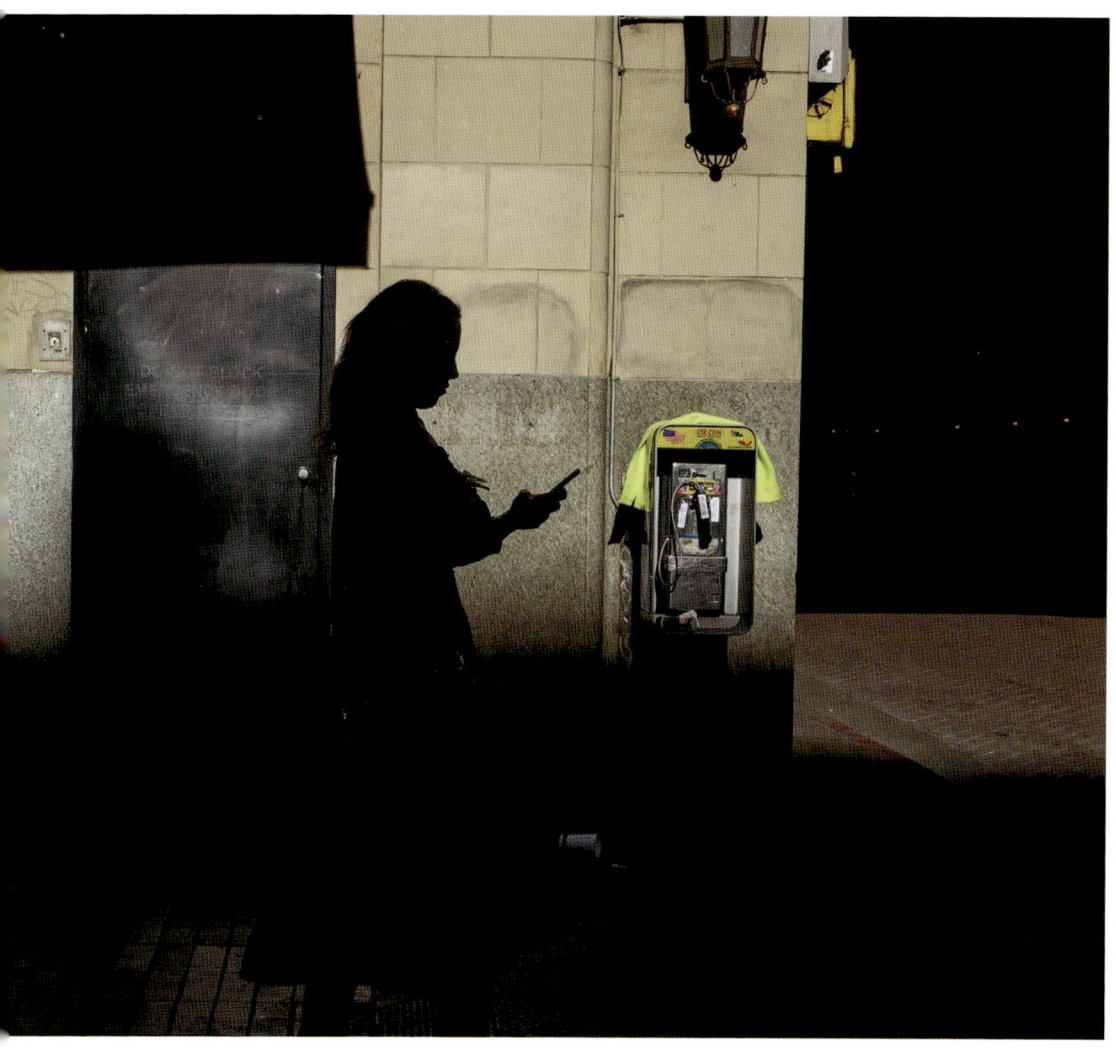

I made photographs, but I was not at my best. I was struggling. My mind wrestled with concerns of the past week. Admittedly, I had put too much pressure on myself to get so much done within a very limited period of time. As much as I wanted to push those feelings aside, they returned with the relentlessness of a needy stray dog. I could not shake it.

It was hard to make images on a day like this. It resulted in me *taking* rather than *making* photographs. I found nothing but empty solace in hearing the click of the shutter, rather than enjoying the careful process of seeing. I grew frustrated and angry at my inability to get into a seamless space of creativity.

I took a break at a café for a cup of coffee. Instead of fighting my demons, I put the act of making pictures aside. I drank my coffee and watched life happen around me without the pressure of making a photograph. Instead, I directed my attention to enjoying the taste of my latte.

I sat there and managed to slow my mind down. By focusing my attention on something as simple as drinking a cup of coffee, the noise in my head diminished, as did the pressure to produce something great with my camera. When I was done, I stepped back out onto the street feeling refreshed and open to opportunity.

At that moment I saw the light cutting across the building facade and a nearby alley. I was lured in by the contrast of light and dark that it created, especially the sharp line between light and shadow. The shadows created lines and shapes that mirrored the lines and shapes of the building, the security gate, the sidewalk, and a lone pay phone. The red and yellow elements in the scene took on a vibrancy as a result of the hard sunlight. It was the perfect stage for a photograph.

I revaluated the scene through the camera's viewfinder, considering the placement of the pay phone, the alley, the light fixture, the sidewalk, and the security gate. As people walked past, I determined where I needed a human figure to be to complete the photograph. Despite the strength of all the visual elements, I knew the image would not be complete without someone in the frame.

I noticed that those who walked close to the wall were illuminated by the sunlight, while those who walked closer to me were rendered as silhouettes. If they were close to the wall and walking from my left to the right, their faces were illuminated. If they walked from the other direction, the light only illuminated their backs. If they were rendered in silhouette, I could make it work regardless of the direction they walked.

Now it was just a matter of waiting. I made a series of images of people walking through the scene, determining exactly where I wanted them to be in order to create a balanced composition. There was an area of negative space between the phone and the black door in the wall that was ideal. However, most of the characters that moved through the scene were less than perfect, or I just failed to time the release of the shutter.

Unlike earlier, I became completely focused. I was no longer distracted by my own thoughts. Instead, I was immersed in the ebb and flow of the street. There was a rhythm there and I slowly synced myself with it. There was no rush or feeling of impatience; I was just in the moment.

When I caught sight of the woman walking from the left looking at her smartphone, I knew that I might have what I needed. I used the timing of the previous shots to anticipate where she needed to be in order to complete the frame. Just as she was about to step into that area of negative space, I released the shutter and created the image. The flourish that I had hoped for revealed itself and provided me with a wonderful gesture and an ironic contrast between the modern smartphone and the old pay phone. It was the perfect addition to a perfect moment.

"The technique that once required intense concentration and practice becomes instinctual and fluid, a natural extension of you."

Relying on Methodology

Having a practiced and repeatable way of seeing is an invaluable tool for a photographer. During those moments when the mind is full of distractions, anxieties, and self-doubt, you can fall back on an approach that has proven itself in its reliability and consistency. Because negative feelings do not always go away as much as you might hope they would, knowing how to work despite them becomes more important than the equipment you are using.

When I am in such moments, I stop and gather myself. Sometimes I sit down and take a break or practice a breathing exercise. When I return to shooting, I break up the scene and subject into the basic elements that I have been sharing with you: light and shadow, line and shape, color, and gesture. It is this series of actions that supplants the distractions and provides me with the means to not only make photographs, but to discover things that I might not otherwise see.

It is like relying on muscle memory when swinging a baseball bat or tennis racket. The technique that once required intense concentration and practice becomes instinctual and fluid, a natural extension of you. You do not have to concentrate on the action, but instead allow yourself to be completely in the moment. The depressing of the shutter-release button becomes the culmination of all of these things, resulting in the photograph.

I was sitting on a bench outside of a ramen restaurant waiting for my friend and I to be seated. Though tired, I did not allow my fatigue to stop me from actively seeing. I noticed the quality of the light illuminating the curb and street, and the shadows produced by people walking past me. I decided to create a challenge for myself to photograph the people walking by with the goal of including as many feet as possible.

This was difficult because each person had to be cleanly defined within the frame, and I needed a person to serve as an anchor to the entire composition. I made numerous shots, most of which failed miserably. Either a solitary figure walked past, which I found boring, or people were positioned too close together.

I did not feel any pressure since this was more of a visual game for me and I had nothing better to do as we waited. As I saw a small group of people walking toward me, I took notice of one person's white sandals. She was walking closer to me than to the curb, making her the ideal candidate for my visual anchor. As she walked past, I gauged her stride to ensure that her legs would be splayed at the moment of exposure. I also scanned the edges of my frame to ensure that I included the three other people walking along with her.

I felt good that I had taken a moment when I could have distracted myself with my smartphone and used it to practice my way of seeing.

Where to Begin

When you observe a subject or scene that inspires you to make a photograph, that is the very time to begin thinking about how you see. You may be tempted to raise the camera to your eye and shoot, but if you are not aware of how you are seeing in such moments, you are just taking pictures. Whether or not they are good photographs is secondary. You are relying on chance and luck.

The impulse we all have is to simply take the photograph—take it before we miss it. It is this impulse to press the button before the moment disappears that drives the moment, even if we have not completely evaluated it. It is not

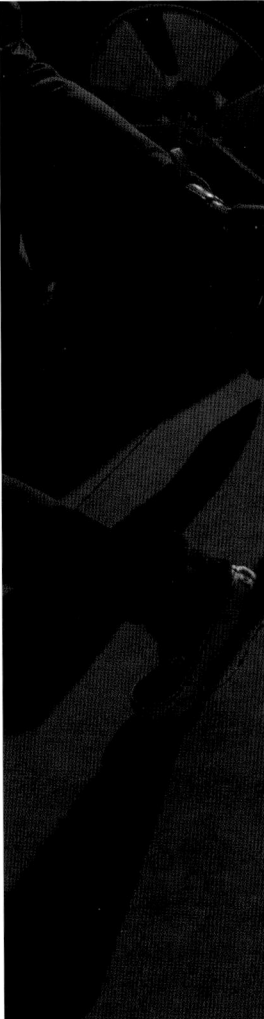

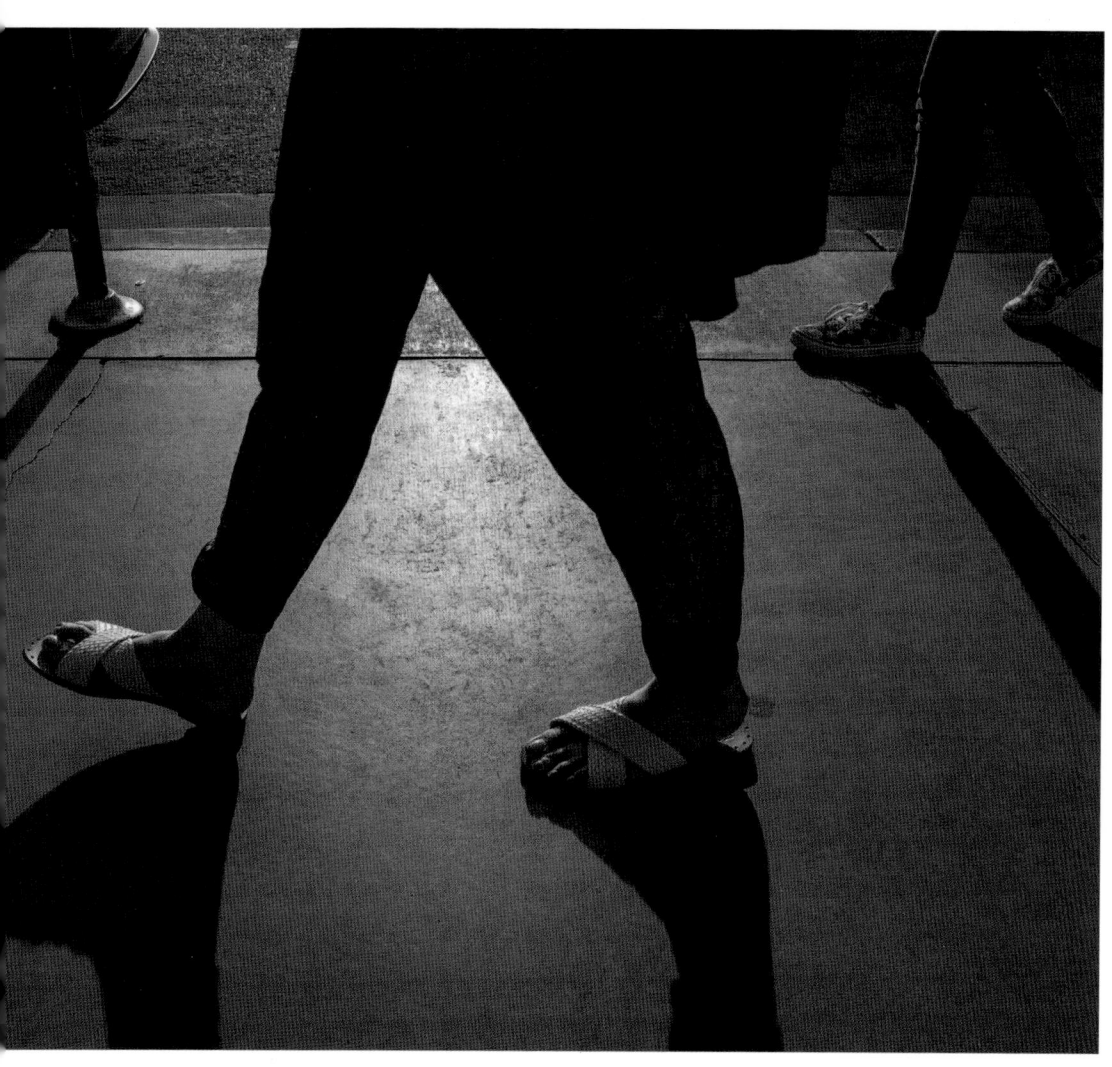

about seeing, but rather hoping that this technology on which we spent hundreds, if not thousands, of dollars will figure out everything for us. It usually does not, leaving some of us believing that the next and greatest camera will do for us what the current technology cannot.

So it all begins with what you are seeing, the thing that drew your attention. But instead of absently taking the picture, you begin the process of analyzing the scene for light and shadow, line and shape, color, and gesture. You answer the questions that those things pose to you and begin the process of making rather than taking a photograph.

Though I spelled out this approach of seeing in a particular order, it does not mean that you have to approach a scene in exactly the same way. There will be times when you are drawn to a scene because of color or line or gesture. That is good. Whatever it takes to jump-start the process is fine. It is evaluating the other visual draws that helps you to make the choices necessary for producing a good photograph.

When I spotted this young woman in South Africa, I immediately knew I wanted to make her photograph. I was struck by her beauty, braided hair, and luminous black skin. I knew that I would not forgive myself if I did not ask to make her portrait.

But even before approaching her, I considered how I would use the visual draws to build a photograph around her. I noticed that just a few feet away from her was a gray wall that was located in open shade. The light there was soft and diffused and would help me to avoid the harsh noonday light. The gray textured wall was uniform and simple and would perfectly compliment her skin, hair, and white blouse.

I approached her and her mother and explained who I was and what I wanted to do. Her mother graciously gave me permission to make a photograph and I moved the young woman to the space in front of the wall.

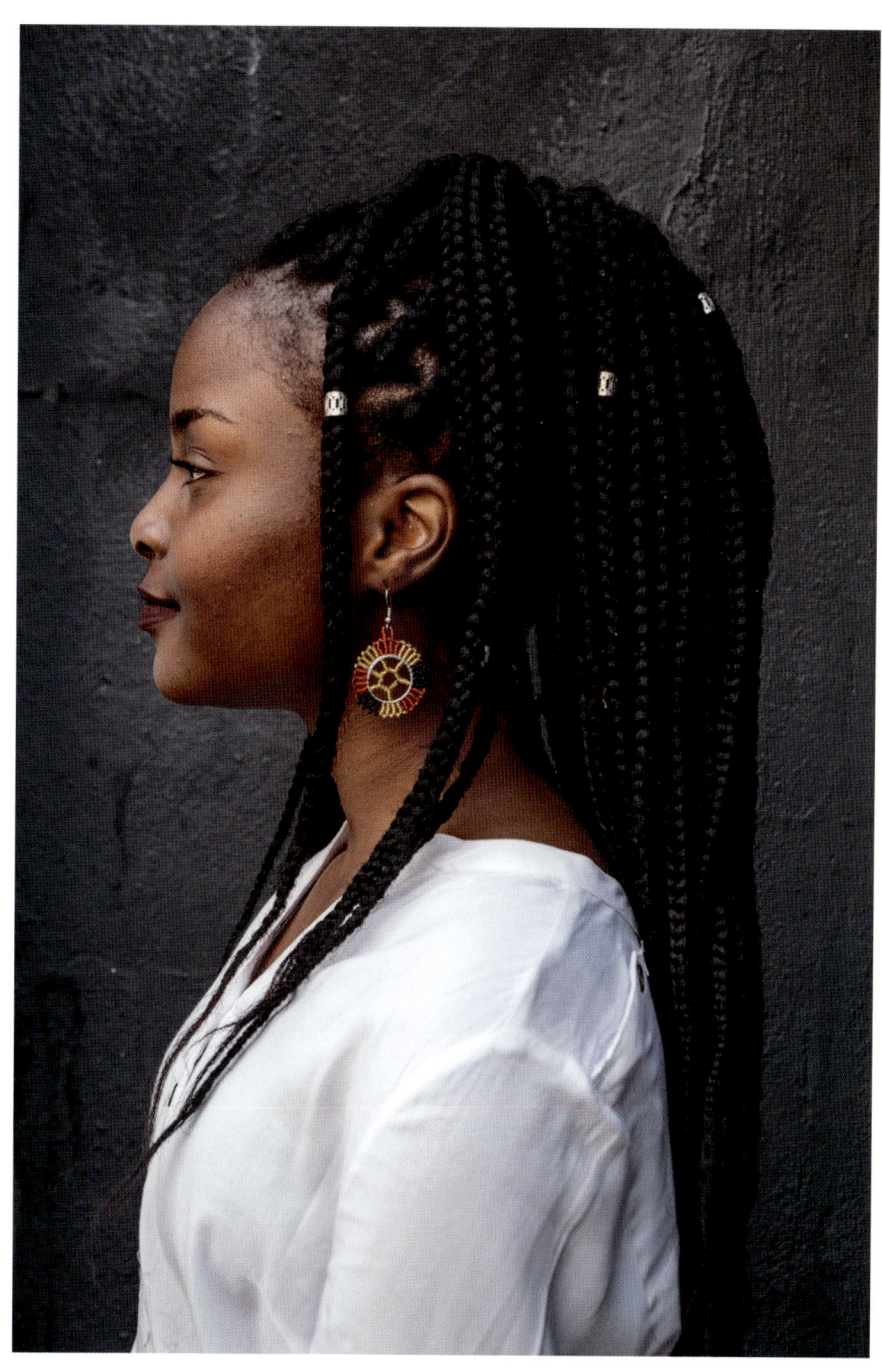

I wanted to create a photograph of her in profile to capture not only the wonder of her braided her, but also the outline of her nose, lips, chin, and neck against the gray wall. I had been wanting to create a strong profile portrait for a while and I knew that this was my opportunity.

As I looked through the viewfinder, I noticed a few of her braids were in front of her ear. I asked her to push them back and when she did, it revealed a round earring with gold, red, and black colors. The earring provided a wonderful gesture of shape and color to a shot that otherwise consisted of black, brown, gray, and white.

Though I made some portraits of her facing the camera, I knew it was the profile portrait that I was most happy with. And of all the photographs that I made in Johannesburg, South Africa, this is easily my favorite. If I had made no other photograph during my travels, I would have been happy with this one.

The Importance of Slowing Down

Whether I am shooting street photography, a portrait, or sports action, my consideration of the visual draws is always at play. I am always processing and reading the scene, which leads me to make compositional choices.

This is an approach that has become natural to me. I do not have to concentrate or think about it in the way that I used to when I first started practicing it. I consider all of the visual draws upon discovering a subject and scene, which leads me to immediately make adjustments for camera settings, lens choice, or where I choose to stand, crouch, or lie down in order to make the photograph.

An important part of my learning to do this was to appreciate the importance of slowing down, of not putting so much pressure on myself to take the photograph. I had to give myself permission to take the time required to evaluate the scene, parse it out, and make my creative choices. Sometimes that time can be measured in seconds or minutes, but it is not the duration that matters, rather it is the attentiveness that I dedicate to seeing the scene.

Far too many photographers are in a rush. They find something to photograph, take a couple of frames, and are off to find the next thing to capture. It is of no surprise that they are often less than satisfied with the resulting photographs. It is like fishing with a shotgun. Yes, you will likely score some fish, but you will have completely missed the point. Because as with photography, the pleasure in fishing is the quality of the time spent doing the activity.

You have to give yourself permission to take your time. Not doing so results in rushing, which inevitably leads to bad choices and bad photographs. Though your work and family life may be filled with the pressure of having everything done by yesterday, you have to let such thinking go by the wayside when it comes to your photography.

Whenever I find a subject or a scene, I evaluate and reevaluate it. I photograph one way and then I make another choice, which may involve me changing camera position. I may navigate to the side of or behind the subject to find a better angle or perspective. I do not assume that my initial choice is my best choice. My best photographs are frequently a result of numerous considerations, which I am able to make only because I give myself the luxury of time.

This is one of the reasons I usually photograph alone. Along with not desiring the distraction of socializing with another photographer, I do not want to feel obligated to keep up with the group. During the few photo walks I have attended, I sometimes want to yell at everyone to just pick a spot and start making pictures.

The few photographers who I do go out with understand the importance of lingering, taking one's time, and practicing patience. We will often lose each other only to find each other once again. Each of us has given ourselves permission to work in the way that works best for us. We do not allow others to deter us from doing things in our own personal way. Even though we are photographing in the same community and area, we are guaranteed to produce distinctive images that are unique to our way of seeing. We are often surprised at how the others saw a scene that we had walked past or even photographed ourselves.

This is not to say that socializing with other photographers is a bad thing. It is a great opportunity to socialize, compare experiences and techniques, and draw inspiration. However, if you are not careful, you can spend more time socializing than practicing a deliberate way of seeing. Making a choice to slow down and give yourself time may seem selfish, but I believe that it is necessary to improve one's skills as a photographer and as an artist.

Applying What You Know

Though I do not often photograph sports, I could not pass up an opportunity to photograph Supercross. The event was held at Angel Stadium of Anaheim, but instead of a pristine baseball field, I found tons of dirt laid out in a complex web of turns, straightaways, and jumps. The roar of the motorcycles was loud and palpable. I felt the vibrations of all that horsepower through my feet to the top of my head. The sounds and sight of these young men launching themselves and their machines into the air was awe-inspiring.

Photographically this was going to be a challenge. I needed a fast shutter speed to freeze the action and I settled on 1/1000 second. I set my camera to shutter-priority mode, a mode I rarely use, to ensure the fast shutter speed. A meter reading of the scene at ISO 6400 gave me an aperture of f/5.6, which provided valuable depth of field.

After setting my camera to continuous focus, I photographed individual riders as they moved through the course. I picked a specific spot where they would launch themselves into the air, and I gained confidence in my timing as each of them rode past.

I realized that just having a single rider in the composition was not particularly interesting. I had seen that kind of shot before, even though I was not a regular patron of the sport. Nevertheless, I knew that there was a more interesting image to be had.

I decided to compose a photograph with multiple riders in the frame, hoping I could capture two or three riders who were airborne simultaneously. I moved my location to get a better vantage point while considering what would be included in the background. There was a lot of branding throughout the stadium, but I chose a location where I could keep that to a minimum and instead focus on the thousands of fans in attendance.

It then became a matter of tracking the riders as they moved through the course, paying attention to when a tight group made the turn and were on their way to the series of dirt hills off of which they launched themselves.

I made dozens and dozens of images as the riders appeared and disappeared from my line of sight, until I captured a single moment that provided me with what I had hoped for. The image caught three athletes in flight, positioned as if illustrating the three stages of a jump.

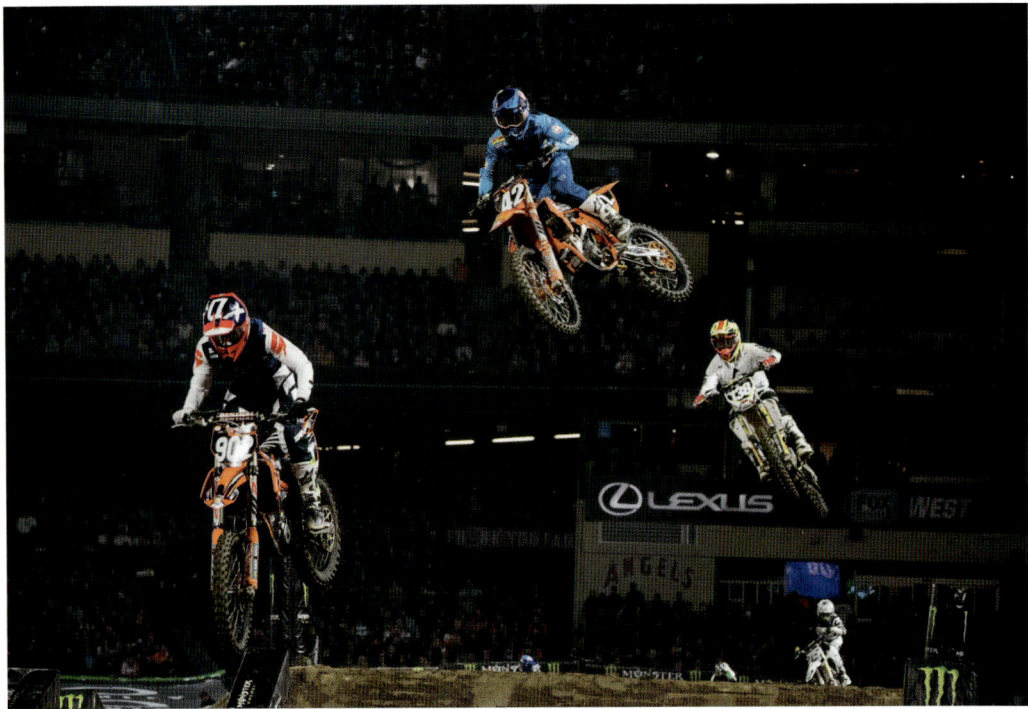

Though I had never before photographed Supercross, I relied on all my experience

and skills as a photographer. I first resolved all of the technical issues with respect to

exposure, white balance, and focus. Then I considered the kind of shot I wanted to

make and evaluated the scene. Some elements were static, such as the stadium, the dirt

track, and the advertisements. The athletes were fluid and ever-changing, but because

of the nature of the sport, that was a level of predictability that I used to my advantage.

Despite my inexperience and nerves, I fell back on the familiar visual workflow of

breaking down a scene and making the individual choices necessary to pull off the

photograph.

Spend 15 minutes
exploring your nearby
surroundings using the
principles of your new
visual workflow. Once
you find a scene, create
a variety of photographs
of the subject or scene
until you feel you
have exhausted all
possibilities. Do not
rush yourself. Enjoy
taking your time
exploring your subject.

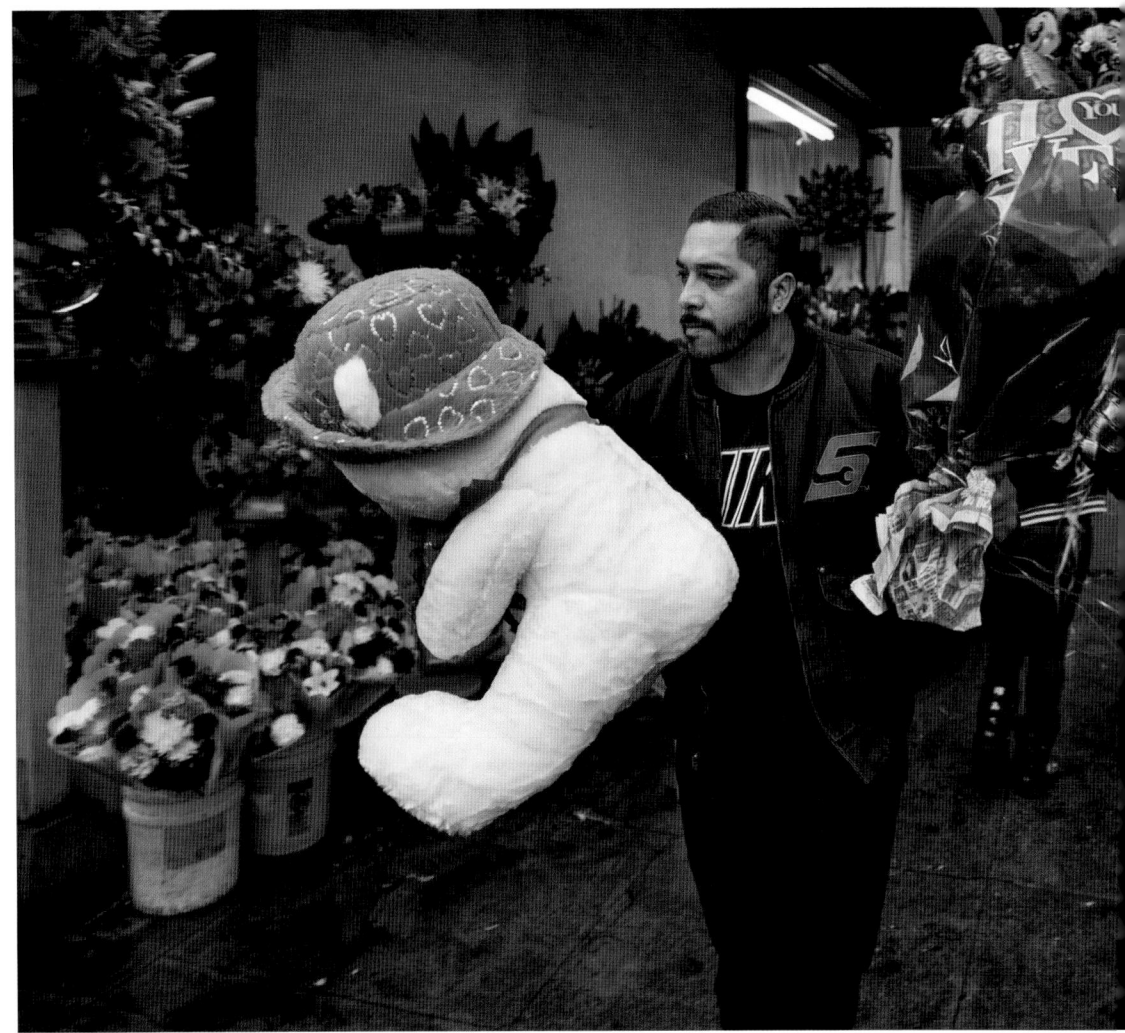

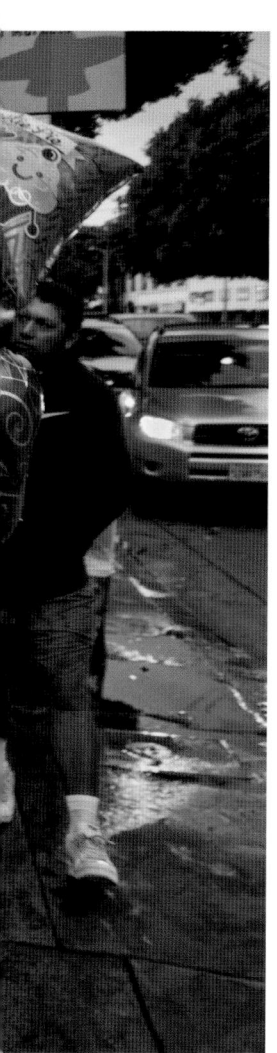

Making vs. Taking

It was Valentine's Day morning and I was in the Los Angeles flower district. The sun had yet to rise, but the street was active with flower vendors opening up shop, preparing for the thousands of people who would arrive to purchase bouquets and flower arrangements for that special someone in their lives.

It was a cold morning and the streets were wet from the previous evening's rain. Fluorescent light spilled out of many of the stores' large entryways, reflecting off the puddles on the sidewalk. Men with large trolleys rushed past as they moved dozens of bouquets and arrangements up and down the street. A middle-aged couple busily loaded a minivan with flowers that were to be resold elsewhere.

The streetlights were still on, but they produced little usable light. I assessed that I would need to find scenes where people were illuminated by the lights from the storefronts. Having not shot in this location before, I wondered whether my presence would be an issue with the storeowners, but I was completely ignored. As long as I did not interrupt their ability to earn money, I was not a nuisance.

Despite the flurry of activity in my first hour there, I struggled to find my footing. As I made photographs, I lacked confidence that I was seeing as carefully as I wanted to. The challenge of the poor light and the busy backgrounds made it difficult to find an effective composition. I was reacting more to gesture than anything else, but I struggled to consider and manage compositions around the other visual draws.

When the sun finally made an appearance, I found that I could work on the streets themselves, which were increasing with activity. It was during this time that I reconsidered what I was trying to do. I was using my understanding of the visual draws to lead me to a subject to photograph, but I was looking for the wrong things. My attention needed be on the nature of the day. The story revolved around Valentine's Day, so I needed to think of the story first and then use the visual draws to build as strong of a photograph as I could.

With that perspective, I recognized that it was the customers who should be the focus of my attention. As I observed the traffic on the street, I looked for a good location to position myself. I evaluated the quality of the light and the lines and shapes created by the various elements in and on the street to determine a good spot. More importantly, I made sure that the elements in the background helped to tell the story of the day, and thus included the flowers of the storefront and the wet streets.

As I stood there, subjects flowed around me. I scanned up and down the street, evaluating people who moved in my direction and who might make good fodder for a photograph.

I spotted a man with a large white teddy bear and a bouquet of balloons walking toward me. I adjusted my position slightly and took the photograph just as he began to turn the corner. He was completely oblivious to me as I made the photograph, and he continued uninterrupted.

What's the Difference?

I was surprised when people pointed out that I expressed my process for photography as making rather than taking pictures. There is no real intent behind this, but rather it is an accurate expression of what I do when making photographs.

For me, taking photographs suggests the physical act of depressing the shutter-release button and taking the picture. There is not much thought involved beyond reacting to something and trying to document it with a camera.

Making a photograph requires a more careful examination of a subject and scene, where consideration is made for everything that finds a home in the final composition. That consideration does not necessarily have to involve long minutes parsing through a scene. It can happen in seconds, but it still involves awareness of what one is choosing to include and exclude from the frame.

When pressed, I explain the difference this way: If you are producing lots of photographs and are endlessly surprised by things you did not see when you released the shutter, and that you feel ruined your photographs, you are likely just taking photographs. Seeing and discovering things only when the image is up on your computer screen means that the picture-taking was just a reactive process. Making photographs and practicing a careful way of seeing does not mean that you will never discover surprises when you thoughtfully compose a photograph, but in my experience, those surprises are often the kinds that benefit the photograph rather than diminish it.

"If you want to increase your chances of succeeding as a photographer, you have to dedicate yourself to a process that is thoughtful and patient."

Be Thoughtful

Most of the photographs that many photographers make, even the great ones, fall short. It may be because the light is not right, or the gesture is wrong, or the moment is just not there. But they keep shooting, and when the moment reveals itself, the photographer, using all their skills and experience, makes the shot that matters. The "failed" images that led to that moment were necessary to eventually achieve that perfect shot, and thus were an important part of the process. It would only have truly resulted in failure if the photographer had stopped shooting before the moment finally presented itself.

If you want to increase your chances of succeeding as a photographer, you have to dedicate yourself to a process that is thoughtful and patient. By developing a repeated method of seeing, you naturally flow into a practice of patience. You have to take those brief moments of time to assess the visual draws, but all in consideration of the story you are trying to tell. Simply wanting to "catch something" is not enough to sustain and nurture a developed way of seeing.

Answering the Question of Why

Why are you making the picture? This is an important question to answer whenever you are making a photograph because the answer will naturally inform how you choose to photograph the subject or scene. Whether it is a child's first steps or a splash of color against a white wall, knowing why a subject, scene, or moment is important to you informs the subsequent choices you make as a photographer.

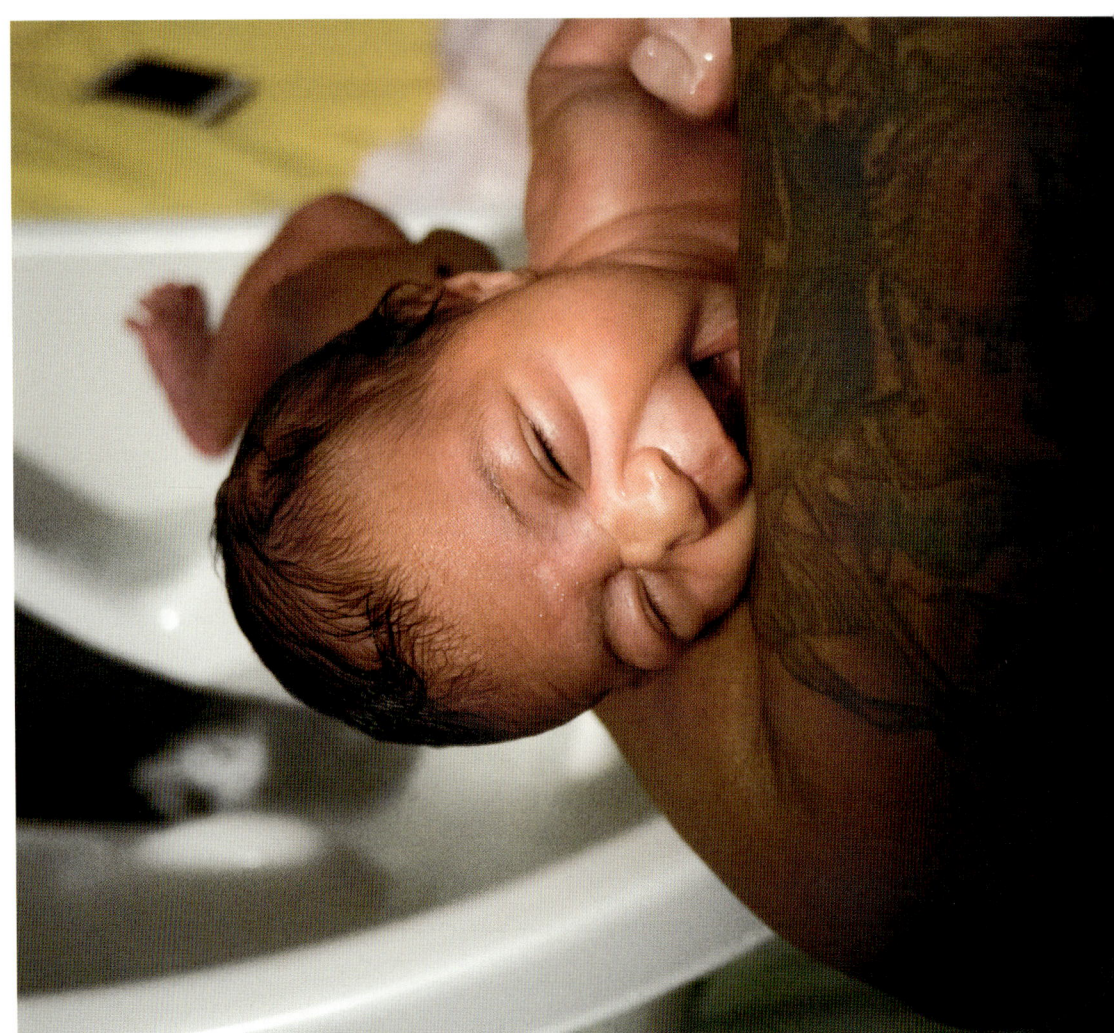

When I photographed my newborn niece for the first time, I wanted to capture the love that my family had for her and her vulnerability. I had just such an opportunity when I photographed my stepmother bathing her. This activity provided those qualities of affection and tenderness I was hoping to capture. It was a moment of humanity that I am continually in pursuit of, especially as I get older.

When I first began to photograph, I instinctually responded to a scene and made the photograph, not really thinking about how I was creating the photograph. I just hoped that it was well-exposed and in focus. That was the extent of my creative thinking and I was happy just to have produced an acceptable snapshot. But as time passed and I demanded more of my photography, I questioned how I could adeptly capture the feelings of wonder and discovery that I felt when I witnessed a scene. This is where thoughtful seeing came into play and why it is so important to me to be conscious of those beats that occur between discovering a scene and depressing the shutter-release button.

Asking yourself why you are making a photograph allows you to evaluate what is important in the scene and what is not. You then begin to think about how the visual draws either benefit the subject or detract from it. You make choices that strengthen your photographs rather than weaken them.

Asking yourself the question of "why?" provides you with those brief moments of time that are necessary for being thoughtful with your process of seeing.

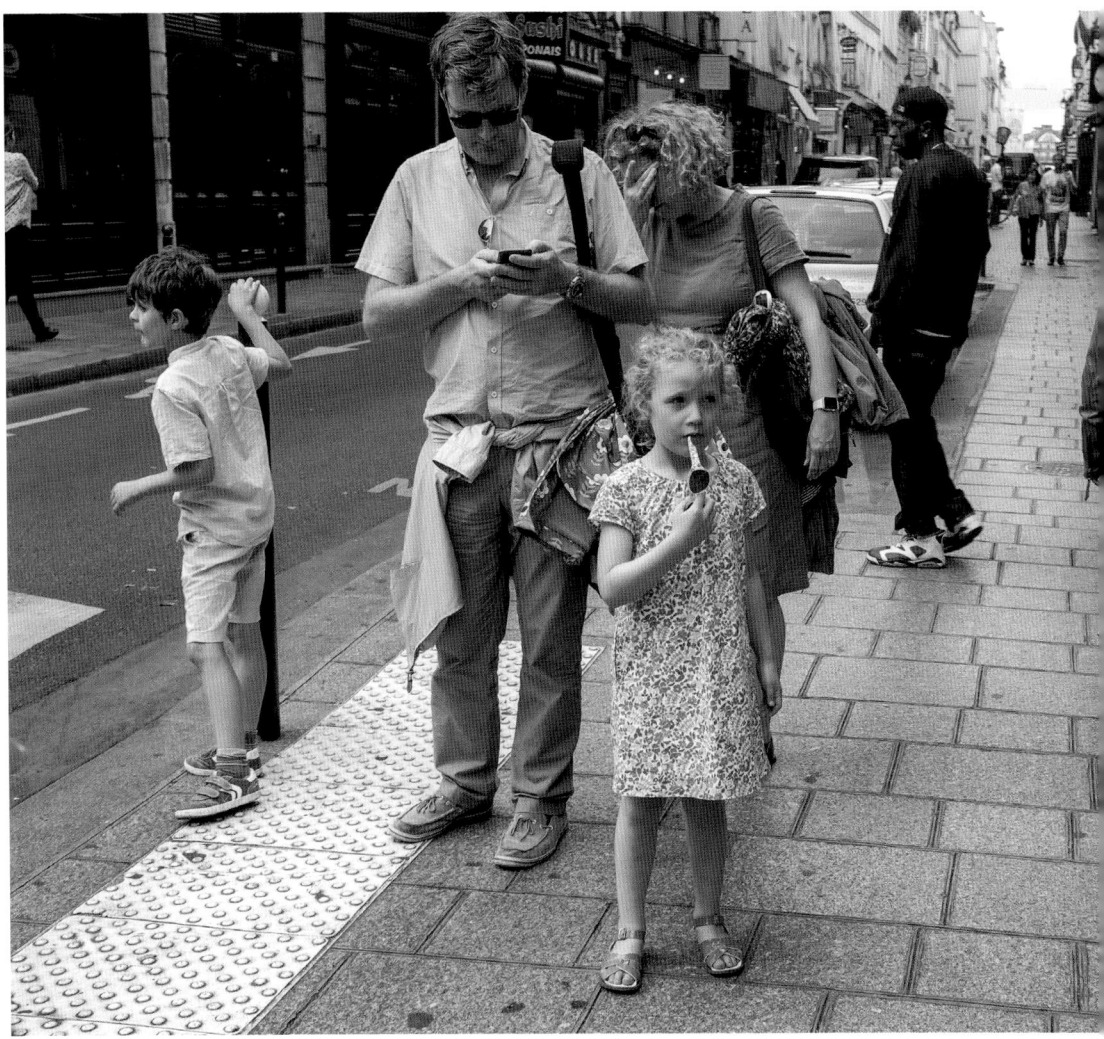

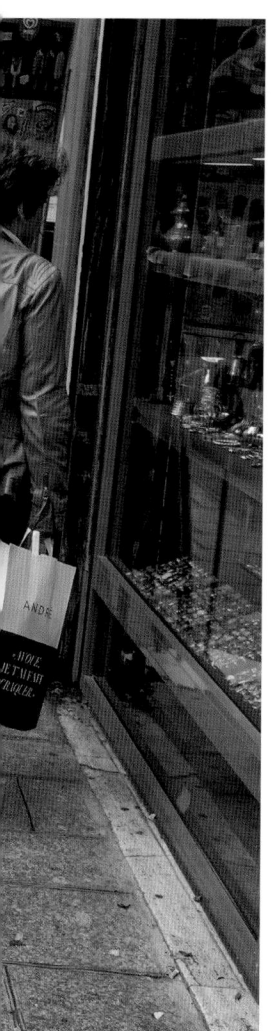

The answer to this question can vary. It certainly does for me. There are times when the answer to why I am making a photograph has everything to do with aesthetics; it is simply about making a satisfying and pleasing photograph. There are other moments when it is the mood or emotion that inspires me. The mechanics of making the photograph may be the same, but what drives me is often subject to change.

Moments

When I turned this corner on a Paris street, I knew what it was about the moment that I wanted to capture. Each member of this family, as well as the other figures on the street, were in a different world, their own personal bubbles. Even though the family of four was obviously together, they were each experiencing this moment in a very different way.

The father was busily looking at his phone, likely looking for directions. The mom seemed fatigued. The boy was distracted by something across the street, while the young girl was similarly distracted by something else, absently chewing on the arm of her sunglasses.

It was that feeling of disconnectedness that fascinated me. Yet in that fraction of time, I also considered the movement of the two figures to the right of the family. They were an important part of the shot, and I shifted my position to create as clean of a separation between all the bodies as I could.

The time between me discovering the scene and actually making the photographs was a matter of seconds, but that did not keep me from considering many things on my way to making the photograph. Because my camera settings had already been set for the lighting conditions of the day and because I have a consistent workflow with regard to the visual draws, I was free to focus completely on composition and the story of the moment.

Remember to Slow Down

Though I repeat this endlessly during my workshops and in this book, I cannot emphasize it enough. You have to slow down. You have to slow down not only in making the photographs, but also with the thinking that goes on in your head when trying to make photographs.

Our minds are constantly racing with thoughts, feelings, and distractions, all of which interrupt the creative process of seeing. This is the biggest disruption that we fight against when making thoughtful photographs. But by slowing down your visual workflow, even for a few moments, you afford yourself the luxury of thinking about why you are making the photographs and how you do so.

It can be difficult at first, but this is why I believe it is important for you to take note of how you are feeling when you are making photographs. Identifying when you are calm and relaxed versus anxious and nervous helps to determine how those feelings inform and affect your photography.

When you recognize that negative thoughts or distractions impair your ability to be consistent, you see the value of slowing down and taking your time. Though it may slow your process at first, over time it will become so natural that you are able to make important decisions within a fraction of a second.

Choose a subject of your choice and spend 5–10 minutes photographing it. Ask yourself why you are drawn to this subject or scene, and then use the principle of the visual draws and your knowledge of composition to create a series of photographs. Think about what feelings are evoked when you look at this subject, and create an image that emphasizes the qualities of the subject or scene that elicit those feelings.

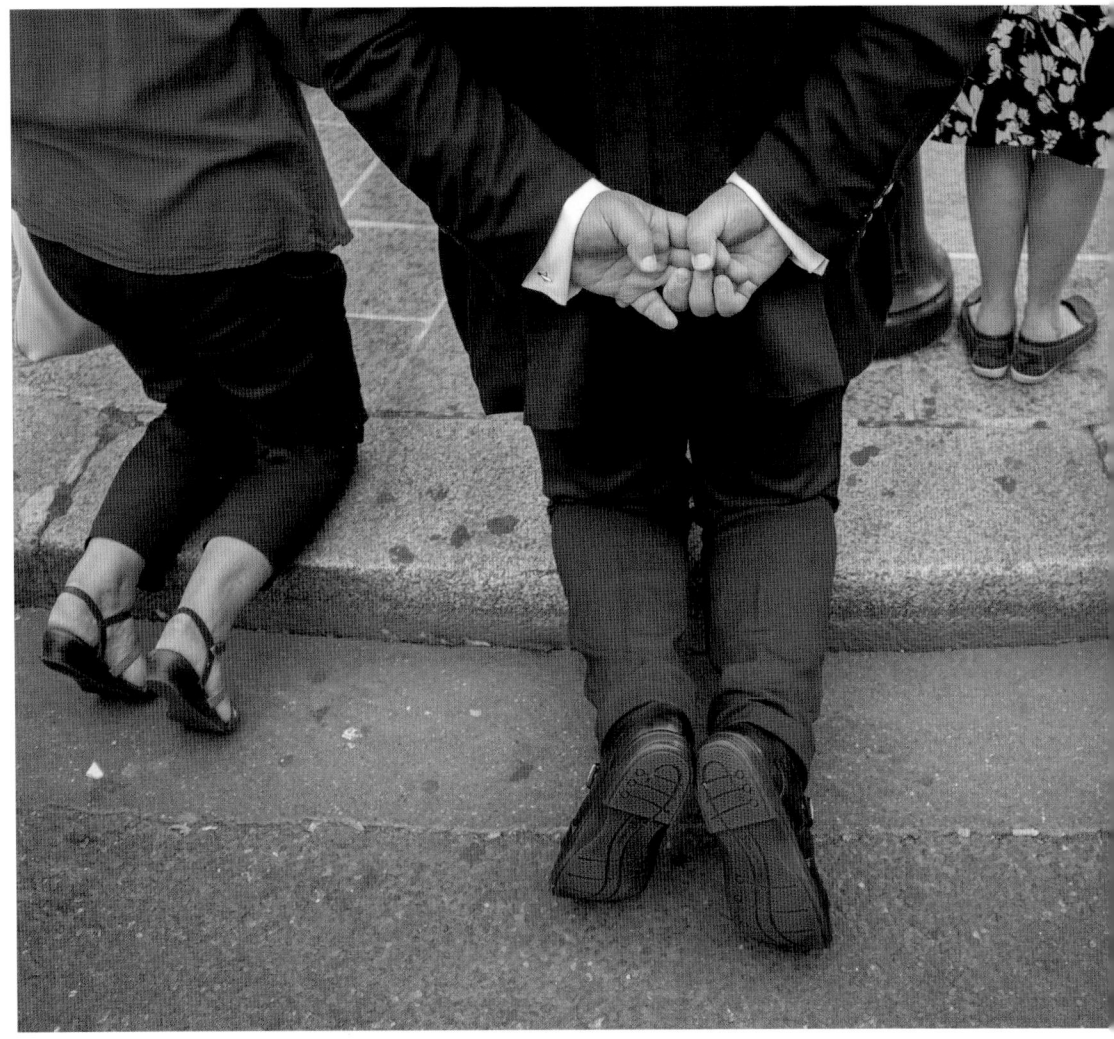

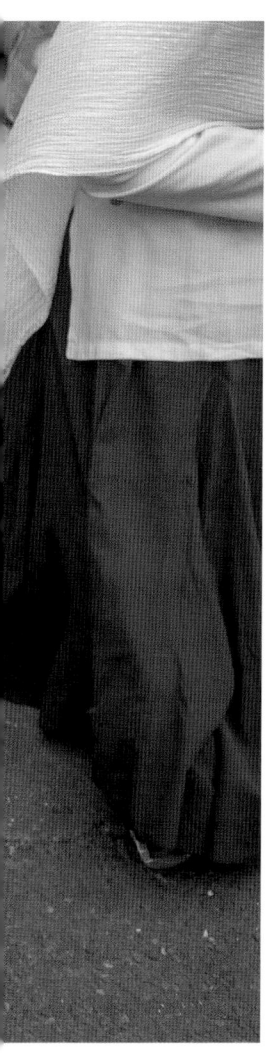

Inclusion
and Exclusion

It was overcast on the morning that
marked our second week in Paris.
We chose to make this a lazy day that
involved sleeping in late and not adhering
to any particular schedule. There were
no must-see destinations and as a result,
we were not busily checking the clock or
submitting a request for an Uber.

By the time we left the hotel, we were ready for lunch and we walked to a restaurant in the Latin Quarter. As we sat down, I noticed the street had been blocked off and there was a police presence. It did not seem to involve anything bad because the officers appeared relaxed as they talked among themselves.

I then saw a procession of people moving toward us led by priests and altar boys. My wife took one look at me and said she would place my lunch order for me. She knew exactly where I was going.

The procession stopped in front of the Fontaine Saint-Michel where people created an open space in which the priests and other officiates began a service. One of the boys carried a banner of the Virgin Mary and I quickly determined that this was a celebration of the ascension of the mother of Jesus.

I weaved my way through the crowd making photographs, trying to be as unobtrusive as possible. While there were many people making images on the periphery, I wanted my images to be more intimate and this required me to be within the crowd rather than outside of it. I was using my Fujifilm x100s, which provides a single focal length, the equivalent of a 35mm lens, and I was able to move in close without becoming a distraction.

At first I focused on the ceremony itself, but then I switched my focus to the parishioners. As they sang and prayed, I moved through the public demonstration of faith and devotion. I wondered whether I could capture that sentiment in a photograph. I had captured images that included the religious iconography, which helped differentiate this scene from just a random crowd of people. But could I do something that did not rely on the banners, the cross, or the priests' or nuns' garments to capture what was special about this moment?

I moved outside of the gathering and tried to determine a new position from which to photograph when people got down on their knees in supplication. I was drawn to an older man in a black suit who knelt at a curb, his hands clasped behind his back. I liked the contrast of the white cuffs of his shirt against his black suit, as well as the gesture of his interlocked fingers. I moved and made several images that isolated those elements in the frame.

I knew that the image did not tell the story of the moment, so I pulled back and began observing the other people in the man's immediate vicinity. There were two women who were also kneeling on either side of him, while another woman remained standing in front of them. I realized that if I included all four subjects in the frame, I would more accurately capture the solemnity of the moment. I took a few steps back and framed the composition so that each figure was cleanly defined within the frame. The clenched hands were still the anchor of the photograph, but now they included much more context. This became the image that I had been hoping for.

The Frame is Yours

To produce great photographs and to do so consistently requires you to make a series of choices, including your choice of focal length, where to stand, whether to orient your camera vertically or horizontally, and what your point of focus will be. All of these are decisions made by you when making a photograph. But to me the most important consideration that you make as a photographer is what you choose to include and exclude from the frame.

When you look at the world with your naked eye, everything is equal. Your eyes will flit around a scene and you will focus your attention on one thing and then another. If you see something of interest, you may appreciate it, and if you are with someone, you will nudge them and point it out to them. But you are not only seeing that thing. You are also hearing and smelling and touching the things around you. You experience the moment. That is not the case with a photograph, which limits you to a single sense.

In the context of a photograph, the whole world is encapsulated into that single frame. The world begins and ends there. The experience that is derived from that photograph succeeds or fails on the various visual elements that find a home in that frame. And so, as the photographer, it is your responsibility to be aware of those things when you compose your photograph.

As I often tell my workshop students, you own the frame. Everything that finds a home in your photograph is your responsibility, so own it. Own the frame. Failing to do so just increases the chance that your photograph will be weakened or fail completely.

Like me, you have made a photograph that you thought would be great only to discover later that there were elements in the background or at the edges of the scene that ruined the shot. It was the tree immediately behind the subject that looks like it's growing out of the subject's head. It was a bright-white van that suddenly appeared at the edge of the frame. It was that attention-seeking relative who was in the background, mugging for the camera. Whatever form it took, it was enough to ruin the image. We can only look at that image in disappointment for what it could have been.

So you have to own the frame and be conscious of it until you make the photograph.

When I photographed this play of shadows on a blue wall, I had a lot of choices I needed to make. Do I shoot it horizontal or vertical? Either choice resulted in different elements being included and excluded from the frame. When I tried horizontal, I also thought about whether to include someone walking into the scene. Do I use their whole body or

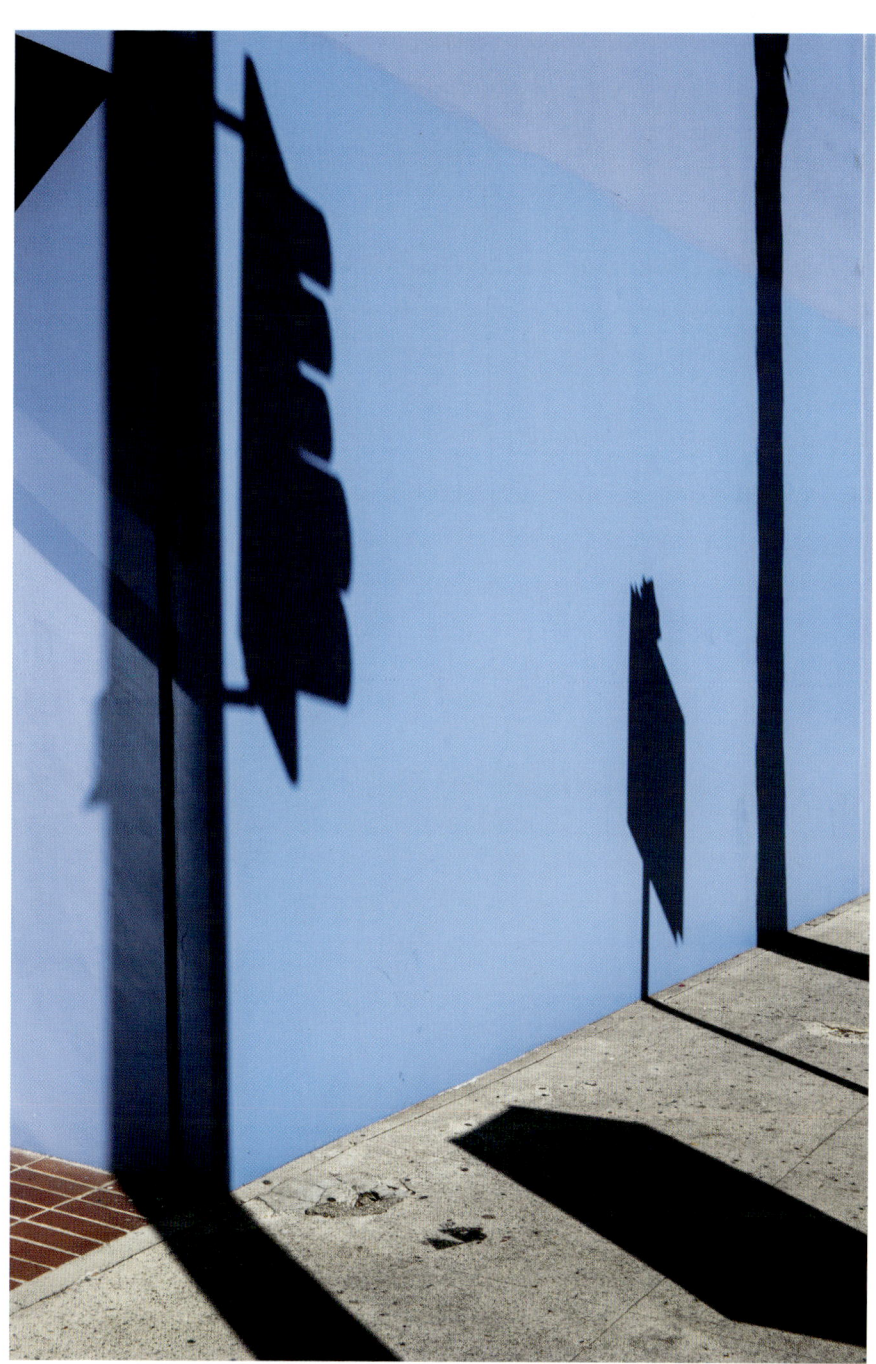

just a leg or a shadow? When I went with the vertical composition, I worked on how much of the triangular shadow to include in the upper-left corner and how much spacing to allow on the right edge of the frame.

This image was the result of a series of microadjustments, some so small that one frame is almost imperceptibly different from the frames just before and after it. But each choice was an important one for me and eventually led me to the final photograph.

Analyzing the Frame

Figuring out what to include and what to exclude from the frame is more than just settling on a subject. It is also a question of how everything that finds a home in the composition serves the photograph. I always ask myself whether the other elements within the frame serve my subject or story or detract from it. If it is the former, it stays in. If it does not, I find a way to get rid of it.

Once I have chosen a subject, I immediately assess what is behind and in front of my main subject. Are there things in either position that complement the subject or the moment? Are there elements that play off the subject in some way or help to provide some context, such as a sense of place or time? Does the light, shadow, or colors help to better define the subject? Or are these things making it hard to read my subject and the gesture? Do the elements in the background compete with the subject for the viewer's attention?

I ask these questions while looking at both the foreground and background, and also at the edges of the frame. I start from the 12 o'clock position and move clockwise around the frame, paying careful attention to elements that intrude into the frame and composition. I find that things at the edges of the frame often prove the most problematic.

"Everything that finds a home in your photograph is your responsibility, so own it. Own the frame."

This scanning of the frame allows me to avoid the mistake of being visually myopic, where my attention is solely on my subject to the exclusion of everything else. By paying attention to every millimeter of the frame within my viewfinder or LCD, I avoid those annoying surprises that are only discovered hours later when the image is pulled up on the computer screen.

This pattern of looking at the foreground, background, and periphery of the frame does not come naturally. We are used to seeing through the camera in the same way that we look at the world, with a democratic eye. But as the photographer that is trying to express something in a photograph, you have to be conscious of more than just your subject.

The nonprofit that I mentioned at the beginning of chapter 6 also teaches girls about organic gardening and working with farm animals. The photograph on the opposite page was an important part of the story that I wanted to tell. It includes the instructor teaching the girls about the plants they were growing, and also features one of the animals they were responsible for. The choice of where to stand for this shot was inspired by the story I was trying to tell with a single photograph. I was aware of the white lawn chair in the frame. Aesthetically, I did not love having it there, but I felt that it held little visual weight compared to the animal in the foreground.

Though this image is successful, I did notice later that on the far-right edge of the frame, I included the hand of one of the girls, and on the far-left edge you can see a portion of a white sheet of paper secured to the gate. Both are small distracting elements that I would normally hope to see and exclude from my composition, but which thankfully do not diminish the impact of the photograph. Though I would crop the image to eliminate those elements, it serves as a reminder of how I must evaluate the edges of my frame.

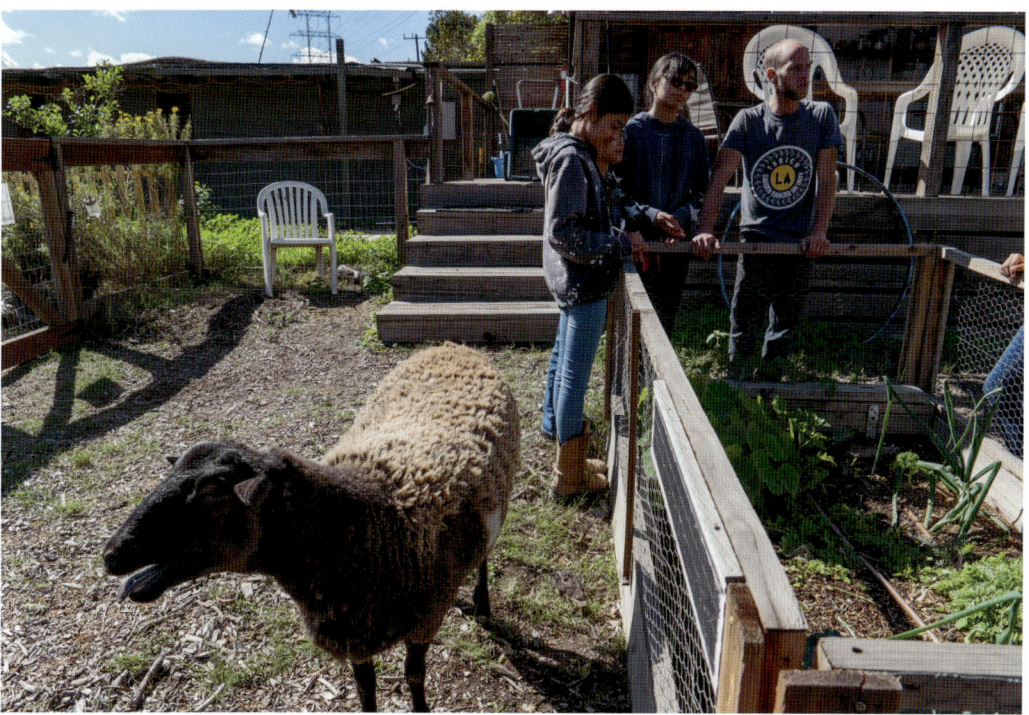

Identifying Distractions

A way to develop your sensitivity to potential distractions is to use your understanding of the visual draws of light and shadow, line and shape, color, and gesture. Just as you have learned that these elements can help you build your photograph around your subject, these very same qualities can weaken your photograph when possessed by secondary elements within the frame. The visual draws can draw one *in*, but they can also draw one *away*.

For example, I hate white T-shirts and white cars. They are everywhere, and I feel that they are always waiting in the wings, like some pernicious gremlins, ready to ruin my photographs. When they find their way into a photograph, that bright white element pulls the viewer's eye in its direction. It becomes the brightest element in the frame and subsequently competes with my subject for the viewer's attention. There ought to be a law against them.

That distraction could also be a strong saturated color or pattern or area of contrast. It is the tree branch intruding from the left of the frame creating a strong point of contrast. It is the store signage behind the subject with its vibrant colors and bold text. It is the complex lines and shapes created by the street scene itself. Sometimes it is one of these things and other times it is all of these things. Whatever it is, you have to train yourself to be aware of distracting elements when making the photograph and not place your hope on excising them later in Photoshop.

When I encountered this young artist in Johannesburg, it was at a busy street fair. There was an abundance of activity with vendors, locals, and tourists moving up and down the street. After I chatted with him, I asked him if I could make his portrait and thankfully he agreed.

If I had photographed him where I initially found him, the background would have been cluttered with numerous vendors, street signs, and people. I did not want this to be a storytelling image, but rather an exploration of this young man's strong features and style. I noticed a wall with interesting textures and colors and I posed him there, taking advantage of the two white rectangles that I made sure were positioned on either side of him. These helped to frame him within the composition.

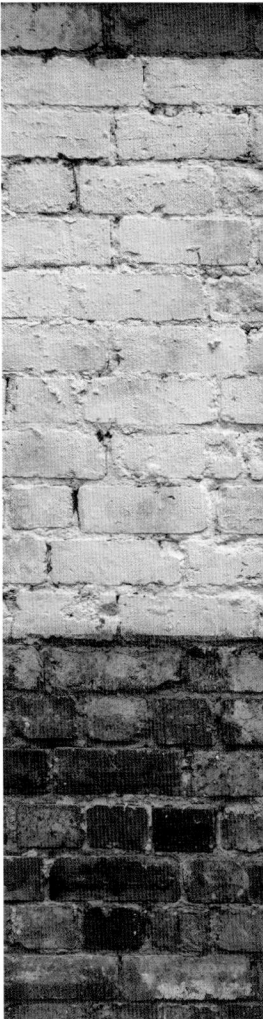

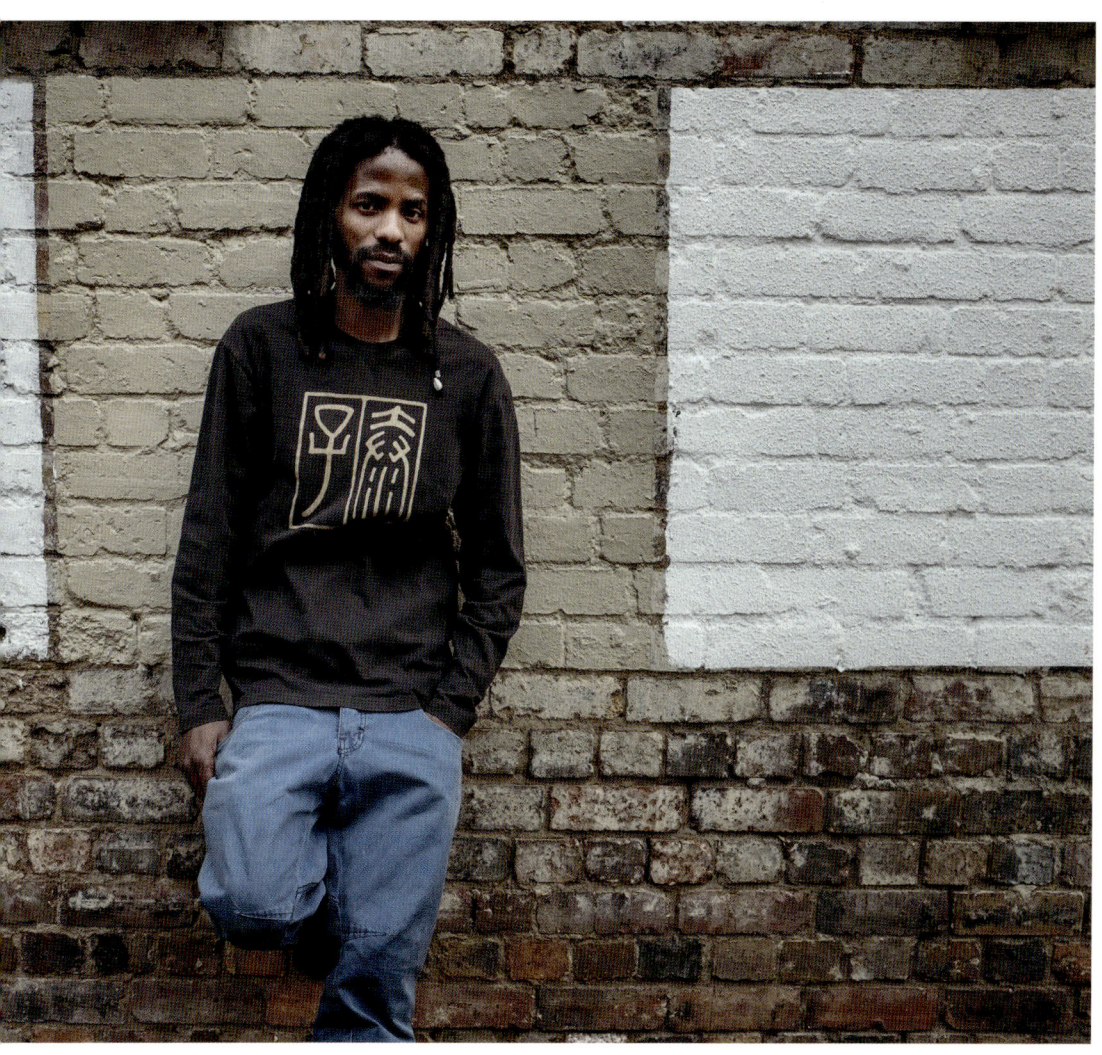

The strong repeating pattern of the brickwork provided an interesting setting for the portrait without being distracting. The color of his jeans provided a visual anchor for the composition and created some contrast that draws the viewer's eye to him. His body language and the slight lilt to his body delivered a relaxed and expressive gesture that helped complete the portrait.

Use Your Feet

Once I have determined what to include or exclude from the frame, I am moving. I am shifting the position of the camera in space and I am also moving my own body. I move my body to the left or right. I crouch down. I refine my frame by shifting myself at the waist in a myriad of ways that would make my yoga instructor proud (if I had a yoga instructor).

It is a little dance that I do as I constantly frame, evaluate, and reframe the scene, all in consideration of what to include or exclude from the frame. Because I rely on fixed focal length lenses, rather than zooms, it is necessary for me to move myself rather than adjust the lens's focal length. As versatile as zoom lenses can be, I feel I can achieve my visual goals faster and more easily by just moving my own body. I have something better than a zoom lens—I have my feet.

In the hours leading up to a wedding I had been commissioned to photograph, I observed the maids of honor preparing each other's hair in the kitchen. I knew that this interaction would result in some lovely gestures that would suggest the tenderness and care these women shared with each other.

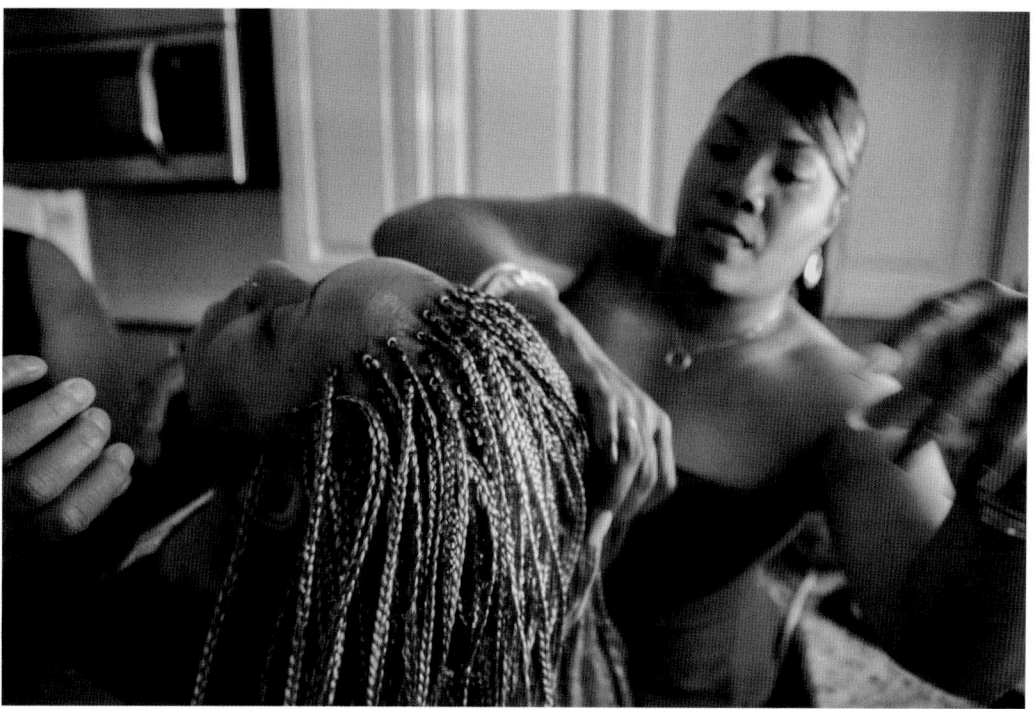

Rather than shooting from a distance, I moved in very close and composed the photograph with a wide-angle lens. The choice of a wide aperture of f/2.5 was both an aesthetic choice and a necessary one. The light levels in the kitchen were low, necessitating the use of an ISO of 6400. However, the wide aperture gave me the shallow depth of field that I wanted to emphasize the woman's braids.

As the woman's two friends tended to her, I adjusted my position, paying attention to the women's hands as they moved around the edges of my composition. The final result captured the intimacy of the moment and is a photograph that I consider to be strong aesthetically as well.

If I had photographed the women from where I initially observed them, the photograph would have less impact. It would have included the clutter of the kitchen and the other women in the room. Those many distractions would have taken away from the care that these women took with each other. The only way for me to make that image happen was to zoom with my feet, get close, and wait for the moment to reveal itself.

Do not make the mistake of making your picture from the place where you discovered your subject. That is likely not going to be the best location from which to make the photograph. You have to assess the scene, the subject, and the background and determine how to make them play well together. If you do not move and you just stay in place and do nothing more than adjust your zoom lens, you are likely just inviting disappointment. Get moving and earn that picture.

Go to a location where you have photographed before and reexamine subjects or scenes that you have captured previously. Consider the principles of the visual draws for your subject, background, foreground, and the edges of your composition. Try to improve on your earlier images by consciously deciding what to include and exclude from the composition.

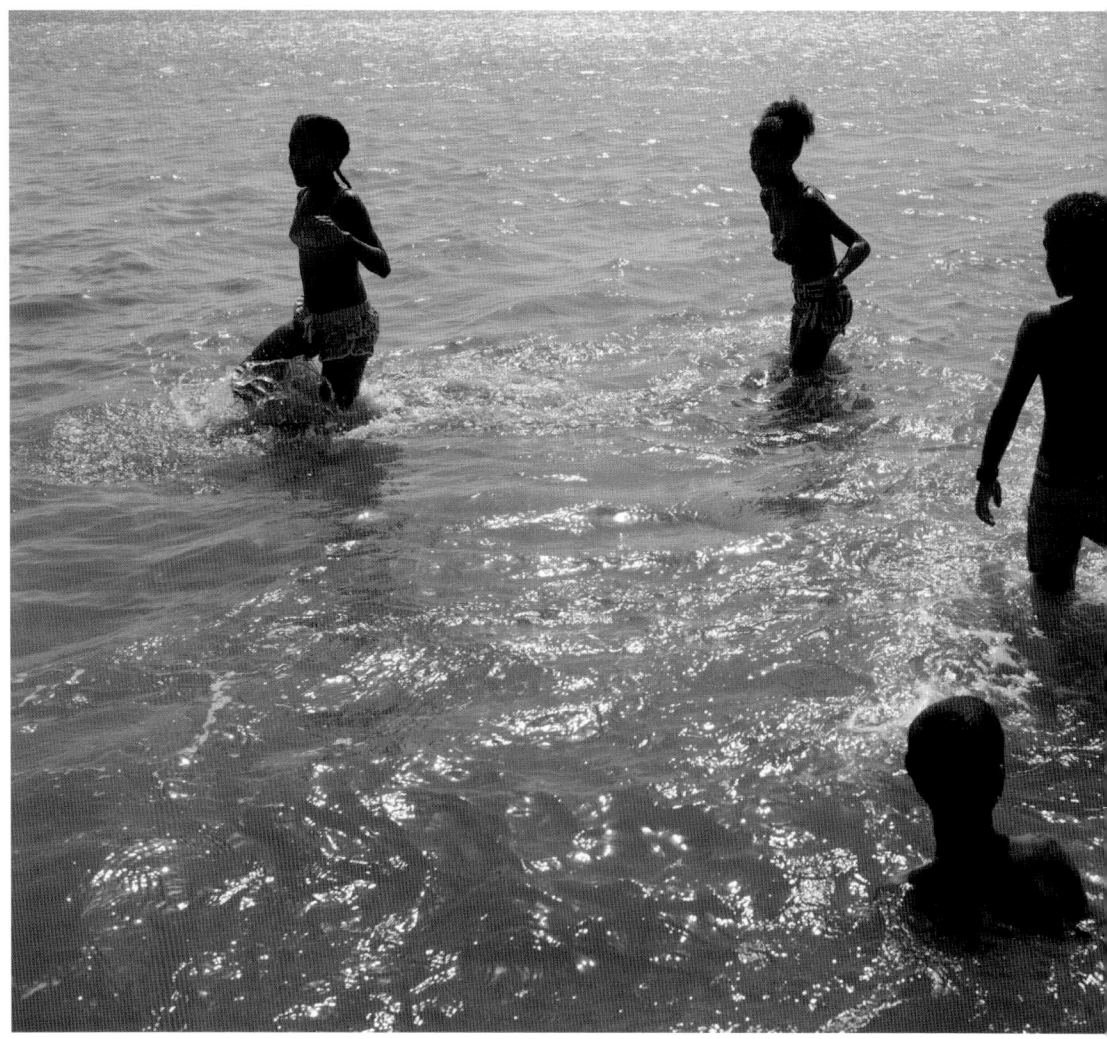

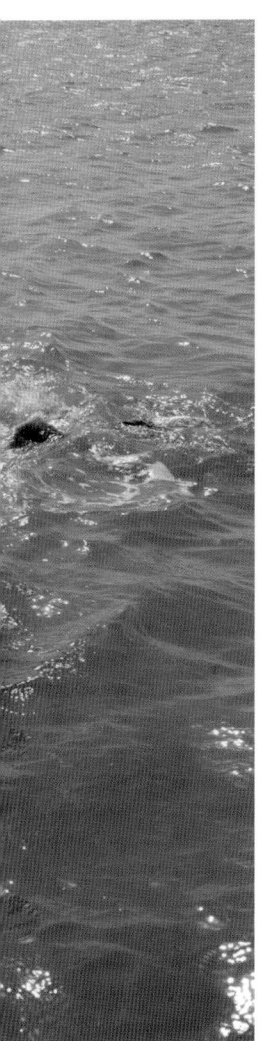

Composition

When it gets hot in my dad's hometown in the Dominican Republic, it is time to find shade or hit the beach. On this particular day, we headed to the ocean.

Though the Dominican Republic has become a popular resort destination, my dad's hometown does not draw many tourists. Sometimes I feel that my presence alone is the tourism industry in that small town. It is especially easy to feel this way when there are so few people enjoying one of the most beautiful beaches in the world.

We set up a large canopy and placed blankets in the sand. I opened a bottle of El Presidente, the country's most popular beer. I listened as the waves gently lapped against the shore and my sister's radio played bachata and meringue. It was a rare moment for me as I was not responding to emails, writing articles, or editing photographs. I just enjoyed the moment.

At some point, I noticed several kids playing in the water. They laughed and splashed around, reminding me of when I was their age enjoying the beaches of Southern California. I pulled out my camera and waded out into the water to see whether I might create an interesting image.

I noted the position of the sun behind the kids and the way the sunlight reflected across the surface of the water. It was a high-contrast scene. I would lose either highlight or shadow detail depending on how I metered. I decided to bias the exposure for the highlights and allow the kids to be rendered as silhouettes.

As I looked through the viewfinder, I did not include the sky or the horizon line in the composition. I wanted to use the water as the background. This allowed me to simplify the image and emphasize the figures of the children.

I tracked the children as they moved through the water. Some of them were passing a ball back and forth, while others splashed in the water. I did not want to focus on just a single figure. I wanted to include as many children in the frame as possible, but still have an image that felt balanced and read cleanly.

I moved along with them, slowly adjusting my position from moment to moment, taking great care to not lose my footing and fall into the water.

Finally, a moment revealed itself where each child was clearly defined within the frame and each offered an interesting movement or gesture. I liked how my eye moved naturally from one figure to the other, and after adjusting my frame ever so slightly, I made a series of photographs until I had my moment.

The Evolving Photograph

It is rare that I create a successful photograph with a single frame. Though I know that master photographer William Eggleston is famous for shooting only a single frame for each of his subjects, I do not try to emulate that aspect of his technique. I process my images and refine my compositions while making the photographs, making slight adjustments to each frame.

After I have evaluated a scene for the visual draws, I think about how I want to leverage all of those elements into a composition. The goal is to use those elements to my advantage, and to do so I have to consider the relationship between my subject, the background, and any and all elements that find a home in my frame.

For me the art of composition is about building relationships. At its most basic, it is the relationship between the subject and the background. Even when the background is a white seamless backdrop, as in the classic portraits created by Richard Avedon for his series "In the American West," there is a relationship between the subject and that featureless backdrop. It is the resulting contrast that leaves the viewer fixated on the face and body of the character in the photograph.

As demonstrated by the portrait of a stylish South African artist on the following page, the choice of what serves as a background for your subject influences the way the viewer reads the image. The choice to use this wall as a background was a compositional choice.

There were other choices that I made while photographing this man, including taking several steps back to capture more of his outfit and his amazing pants. When I did so, I included more of the wall with its patches of peeling paint. In some frames, I moved back even further to get more of the ground in the frame. Before ending my time with the man, I moved in closer yet again, producing an even tighter composition, which brought more emphasis to his round yellow earrings and other accessories.

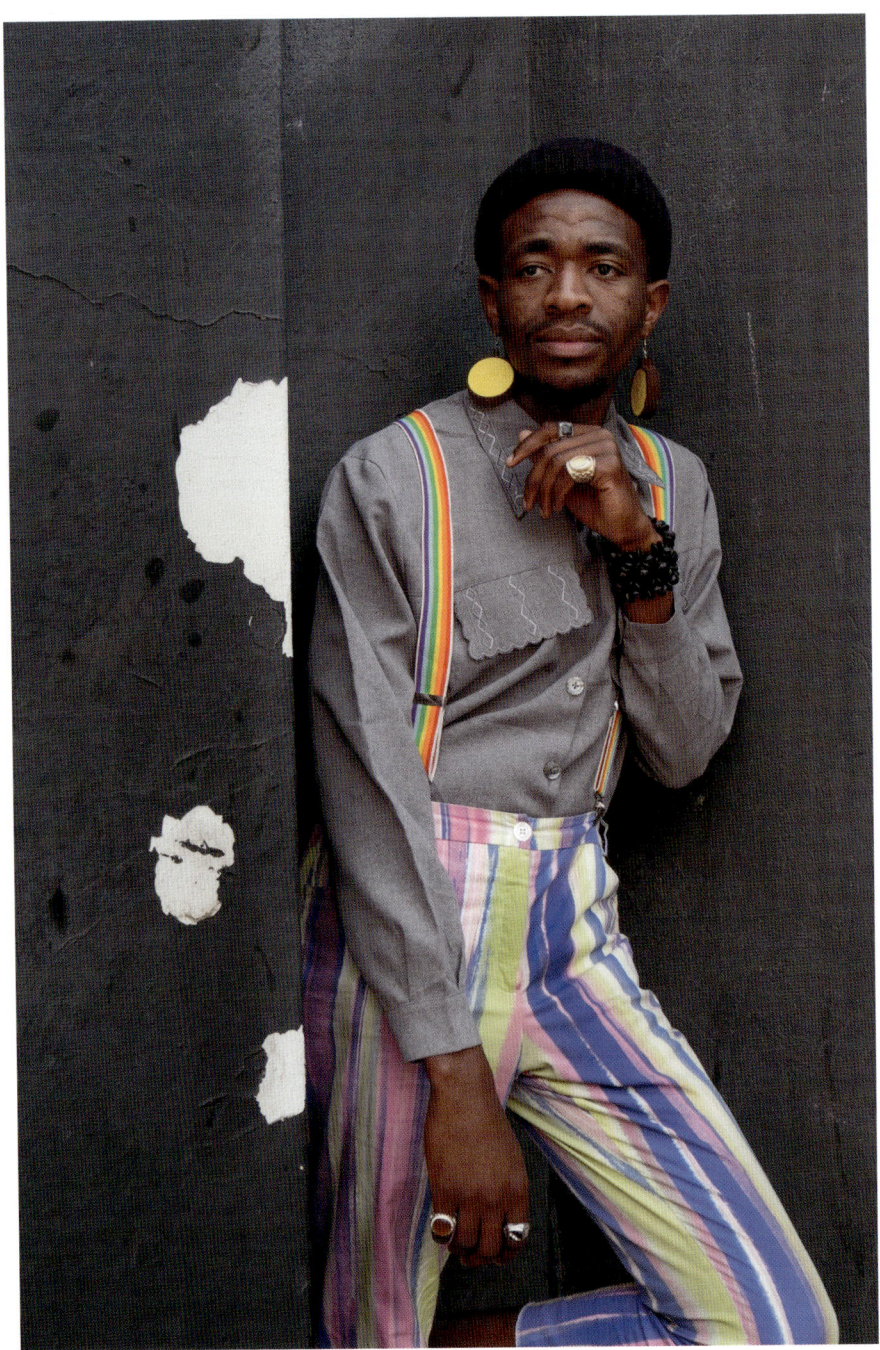

Even though the background did not feature a wealth of details, the amount of the background I included in the frame and where I placed the subject in relationship to that background created distinctly different renderings of my subject. This is why it is so important to try different approaches when photographing any subject or scene.

More Than the Rule of Thirds

You have likely heard about the rule of thirds, a compositional tool that is used by countless photographers to improve their compositions. It works by breaking up the frame into a grid of two equidistant parallel vertical and horizontal lines, which results in nine segments within the frame. The suggestion is to position your subject along one of those lines, or better yet, at a point where a vertical and horizontal line intersect. The result is hopefully an image that is not as static and boring as when you place your subject smack dab in the center of the frame.

The rule of thirds is an important tool that I often use to my advantage. However, composition is more than just using the rule of thirds. As helpful of a tool as it is, it can sometimes be a crutch that keeps photographers from seeing carefully and personally. It has its place, but it is not the be all and end all of composition. Just like any other tool, it has its time and purpose.

The rule of thirds is at its most effective when you are already thinking about what you want your image to be, what you want it to convey. Whether it is a portrait or a landscape, you identify what is important and what is not. You make the choice of what to include and what to exclude. You consider how you want to use light and shadow, line and shape, color, and gesture to build your photograph. And it is then that you can finally consider where you place those various elements within the frame. If you do not make all those choices before deciding on your composition, you are just framing blindly and will likely discover that you did not see things that were right in front of you.

"Composition starts when you begin evaluating how your subject relates to the space in which it exists."

Composition starts when you begin evaluating how your subject relates to the space in which it exists. You see how it plays off the light and the background. You see what serves your subject and what things are distractions. You actively think about the experience that you want to create for the viewer and the story you want to tell. Those are the building blocks of a composition.

During the same beach trip that begins this chapter, I spotted a bright-red gate across the road. When I saw it, I knew that it would serve as the perfect backdrop for a portrait of a family member who sported a wonderful reddish afro.

My initial image was a straightforward composition that positioned him in front of the gate and emphasized his curly hair, which was being blown this way and that by the warm sea breeze (next page). In this composition, he read cleanly. The gate's color and repeating vertical pattern served as a good stage for the portrait; however, I wondered if I could do more than this.

In the subsequent photographs, I included the roofline of the home behind the gate. At first, it was the very edge of the roof, but then I included more of it. I liked the yellow triangular shape and how it contrasted with the vertical lines and color of the gate. However, I realized that the image became more about the relationship between the gate and the structure and less about this young man and his hair. He was now a secondary element in the photograph. This change of composition transformed how the image read and transferred the visual weight to the background elements.

Wanting to still include the roofline, I moved in close, but this time only included the top of the building's peak in the composition so that the yellow triangle was juxtaposed atop the gate. This retained the interesting graphic elements that appealed to me, and because I moved closer, the young man became a more prominent element in the entire composition, which is what I desired.

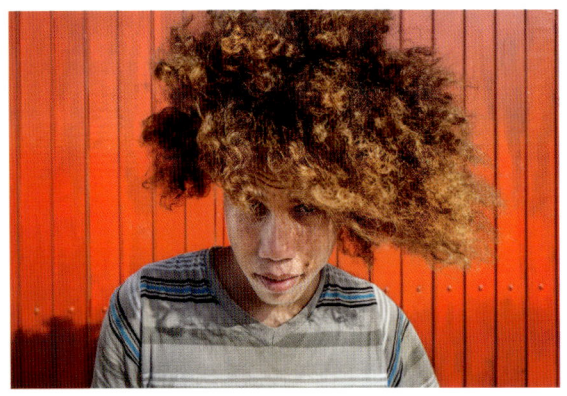

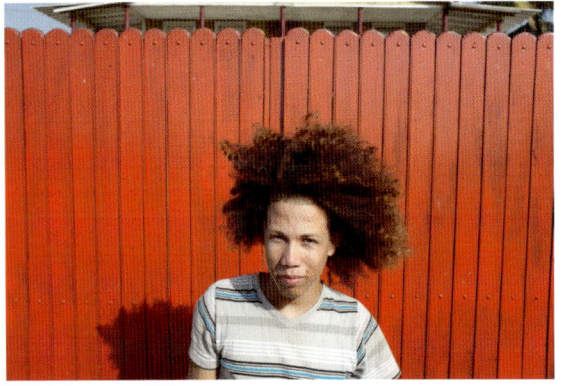

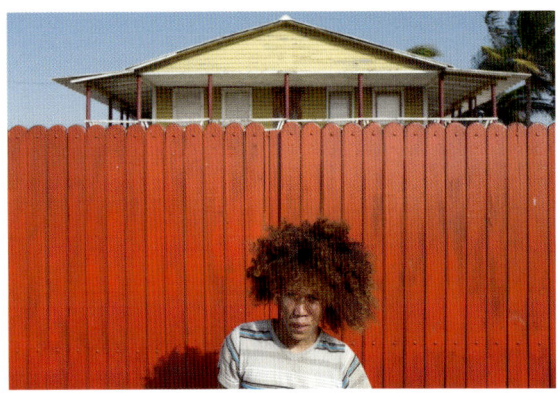

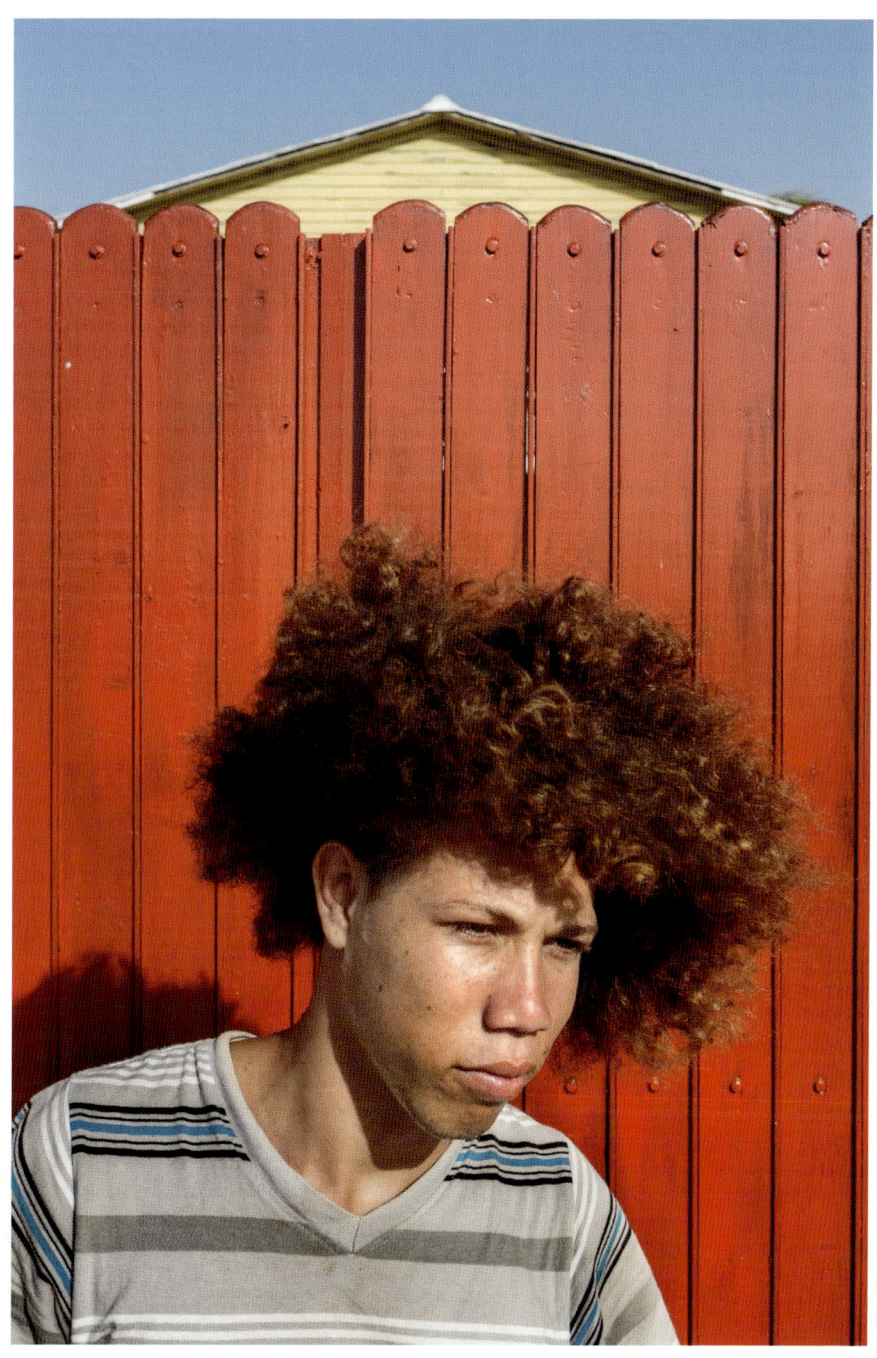

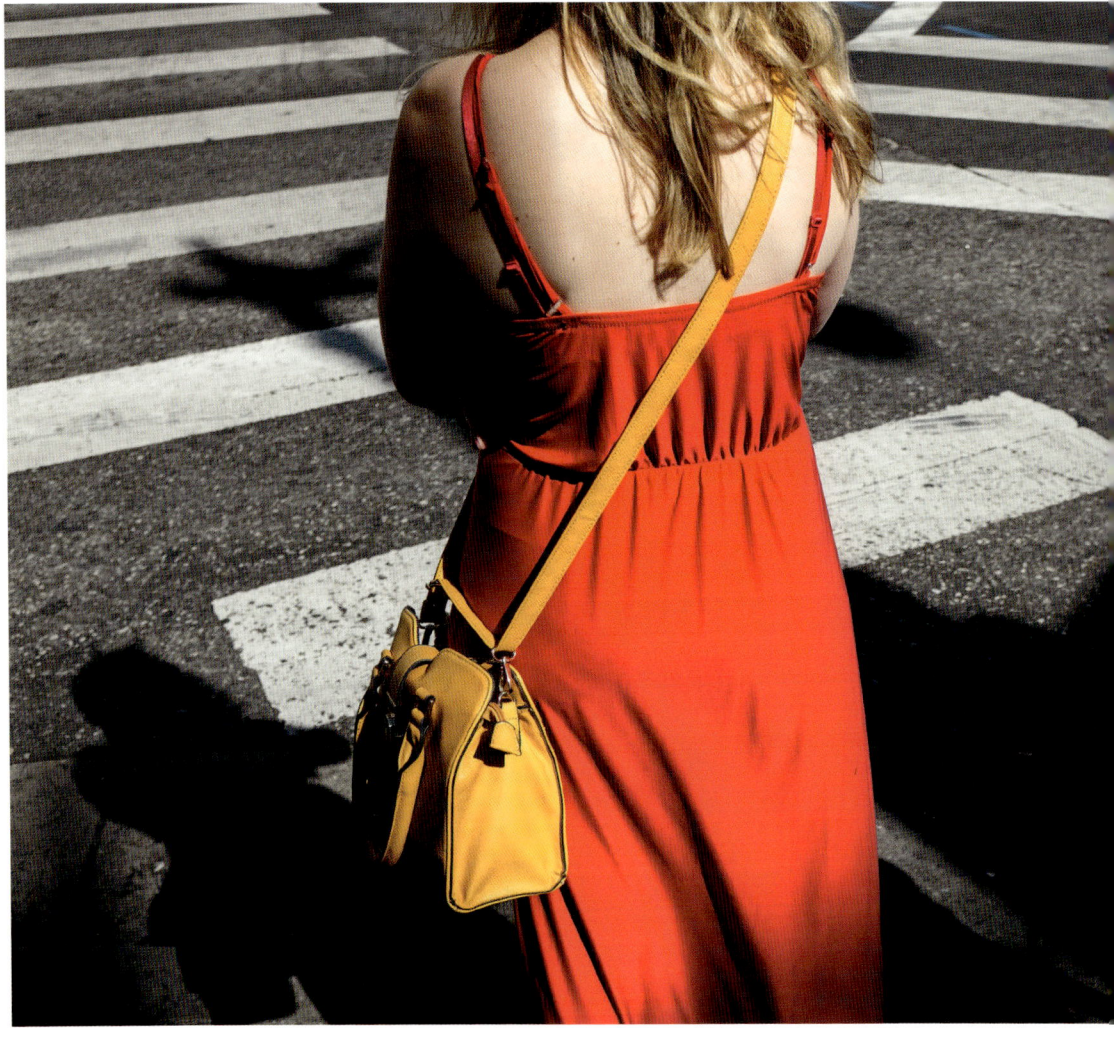

It then became an exercise in patience as I observed the wind whipping his hair about. I asked him to turn his face slightly in profile and I made a series of images, eventually settling on a photograph that provided a clear view of his eyes and his expression.

As this series of images shows, adjusting the relationship between the subject and the different elements in the background delivers very different results. In each image, we experience the subject in a different way as a result of not only what I included in the background, but how I built a relationship between each of those elements. That, for me, is at the heart of composition.

A Culmination of Choices

The consideration of what to include in the composition is at play even when I am working with the unpredictability and randomness of the street. Even though I may not have the ability to move the subject in relationship to the background, as I did for the portrait in the previous section, I am nevertheless observing the relationship between the subject and background and making choices about my camera position, which is something I can control.

When I was walking toward a street corner, I was drawn to a woman wearing a red dress and carrying a yellow purse that rested on her hip. The contrast between those two colors pulled me to her like a magnet.

As I got closer, I noted the quality of the direct sunlight and how it made the colors of her outfit and blonde hair pop. The elongated shadows cast by the woman and the street signs were cleanly defined against the repeating white lines that made up the crosswalks.

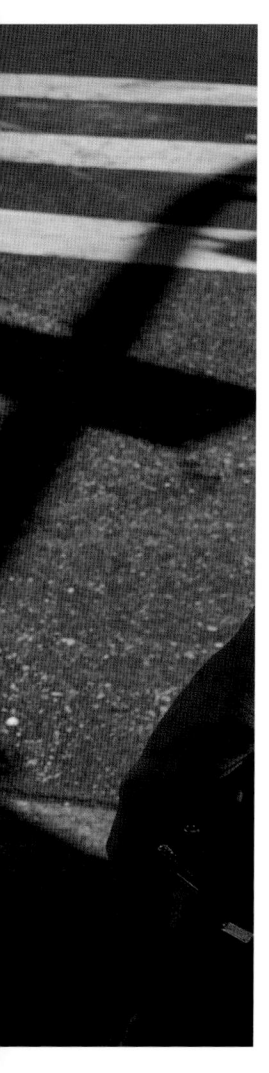

Though it had been the woman that had inspired me to make the photograph, I still evaluated everything else that would be included in the frame. I positioned myself so that I used the shadows and crosswalks as graphic elements that helped lead the viewer's eyes to her figure. I purposely cut off the top of her head because I did not want to include the cars that were moving through the intersection. There were other people waiting at the curb and I wanted to exclude them from the frame as well. There was one lone figure in the lower right-hand corner of the frame, but thankfully they were relegated to shadow. I used the rule of thirds to position her purse on the left vertical line and made my shot just as the light changed and she disappeared into the crowd.

As spontaneous and fleeting as this moment was, it was filled with numerous compositional choices: what to include and exclude from the frame, where I positioned the woman in relationship to the various elements in the background, and where exactly I wanted to position that bright-yellow purse.

Had I photographed from the initial spot from which I discovered her, I would have included cars moving through the intersection, other people on the curb, the McDonald's sign, and an assortment of other distractions. By thoughtfully considering my subject in relationship to the setting, I made compositional decisions that revealed to the viewer the very things that I found so interesting about the woman, the location, and the moment.

Layering

A challenge faced by photographers is translating a three-dimensional world into a two-dimensional medium. To evoke depth, we often use light, shadow, line, and shape. The juxtaposition of two elements, one close and one far, is a common method for creating that sense of depth.

A way to take this one step further is to compose an image using layers. This means that you are not simply placing a subject in front of a background, but are also including an element in the foreground. A composition with three or more layers creates a photograph that has more depth and potentially provides the viewer with more to explore. Layering is not adding just anything to the frame, but including elements that complement both the subject and the overall composition.

You most often see this technique practiced in landscape photography, where the photographer will use a prominent foreground element, such as flowers, rock formations, or a dead tree trunk, to complement the middle ground and background.

For this image of the Monte Cristi Bay, I included the corrugated steel roof as a foreground element, resulting in three layers (the roof, sea, and sky). An image of just the sea meeting the sky would have been lackluster. In this image, the strong pattern of the roof leads the viewer into the frame and provides an excellent point of color contrast.

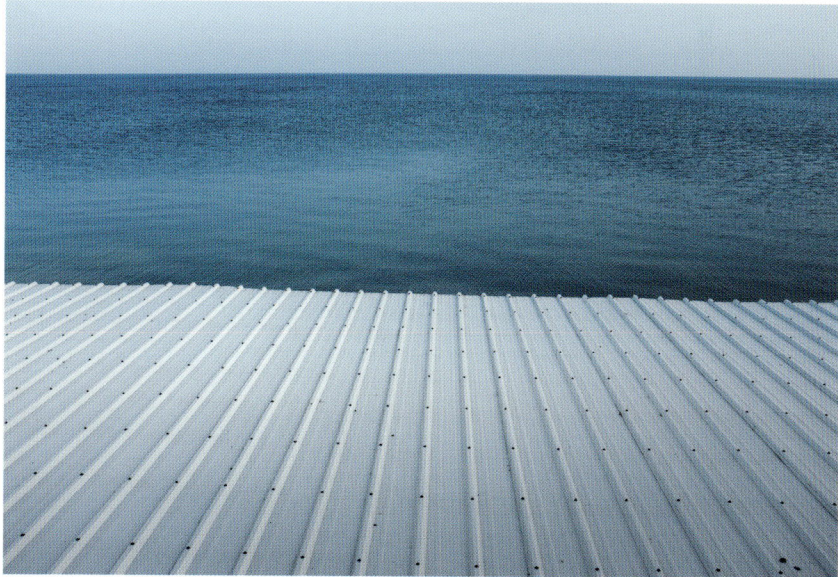

This approach to seeing is more demanding because you have to consider elements at varying distances from the camera as their own unique thing, while also considering how each element plays off of the others.

For this photograph of young cheerleaders preparing to march for a Black History parade, I composed a layered image with multiple subjects occupying separate planes of the composition. In the first plane is the young girl who stands in profile. Behind her is another layer with two girls, one with her hand to her mouth and another stretching out her arm. Additional layers include their coach and behind her another young girl. This layering creates a more dynamic composition, allowing the gesture of each person to play off of one another.

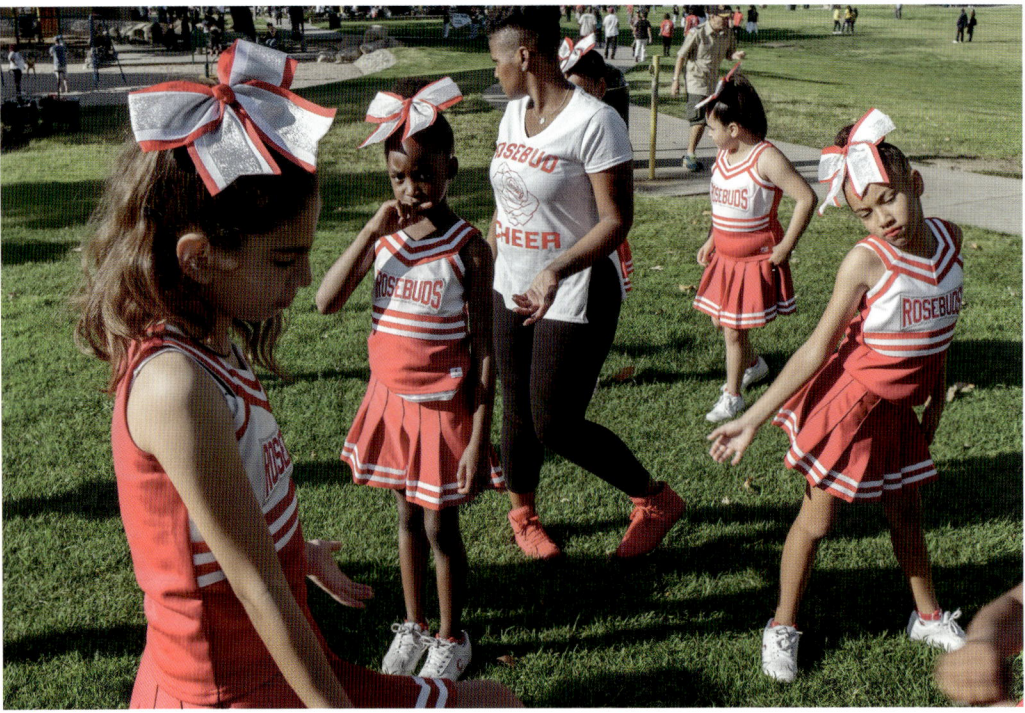

Layered photographs do not happen by chance. They are built by the purposeful inclusion of subject, background, and foreground. It is a skill that I am always trying to hone and develop, and I draw great inspiration from photographers such as Alex Webb and Sam Abell, who are especially adept at creating such compositions and are artists well worthy of your attention.

Turn Down the Noise

If you have ever photographed in a location that is busy with activity, you know how difficult it can be to figure out what to shoot and how to create an effective photograph. As a street photographer, I face this issue on a daily basis. It becomes all the more difficult when it is a completely new environment, such as a city I have never traveled to before. Suddenly, everything is new and seemingly deserving of a photograph. And if I am not too careful, I make hundreds and thousands of photographs that are nothing more than glorified snapshots. I may associate wonderful experiences and feelings with being there, but that does not mean the photographs captured any of that.

This is why being thoughtful about how you see is so important. Just as negative thoughts can pollute your way of seeing, so can the excitement and thrill of so much visual potential. Both produce a lot of mental noise that hampers your ability to see in a way that results in making a great photograph.

It is important to restrain yourself from blindly releasing the shutter. Instead, use that moment when you are triggered to make a photograph as the opportunity to begin your visual workflow. Analyze the scene, take it apart, and slowly put it together with intent rather than impulse.

That is what I did when I made this photograph of a bench amid a gathering of wet fall leaves. I was in Seattle, Washington, which has a variety of things to photograph, including several iconic locations. But it is this quieter moment that I prefer from that trip. Rather than photographing the obvious, I chose the simplest of moments to build a composition that incorporates the bench, the leaves, and the trunks of the trees.

My process of using the visual draws influenced my reading of the scene and what I included and excluded from the frame. It helped me to create an image that I was proud of.

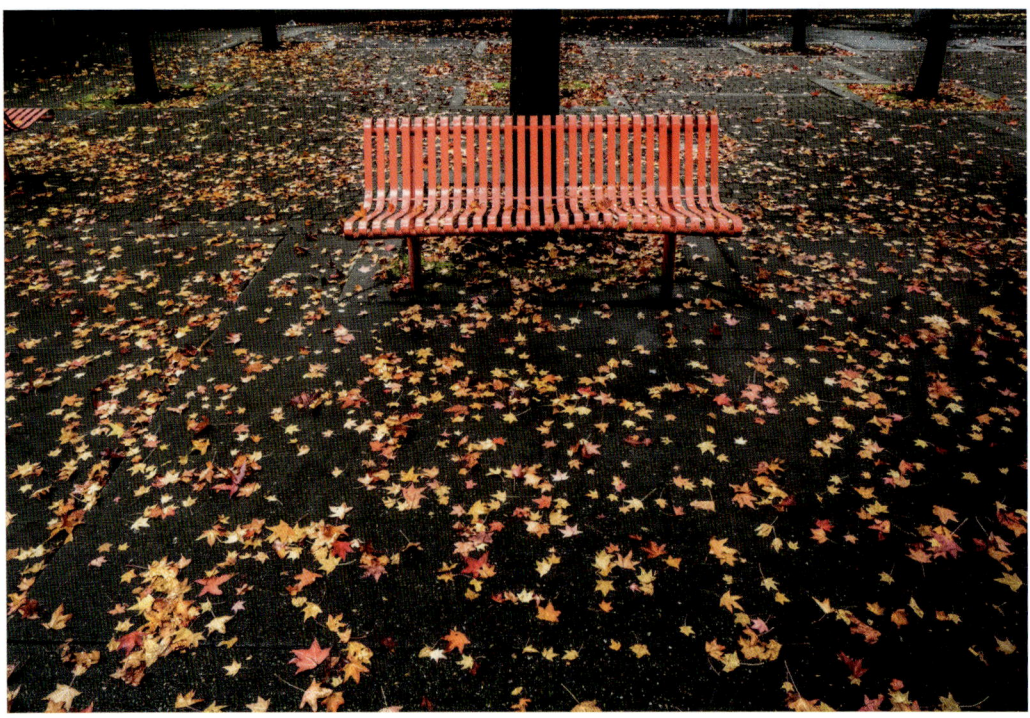

Go to a location where there is a variety of subject matter, such as a garden, a street corner, or a farmers' market. Choose your subjects and consider how your choice of background impacts your subject. Use the principles of inclusion and exclusion to refine your composition, and experiment with changing your camera position to change the relationship between the subject and the other elements in the frame.

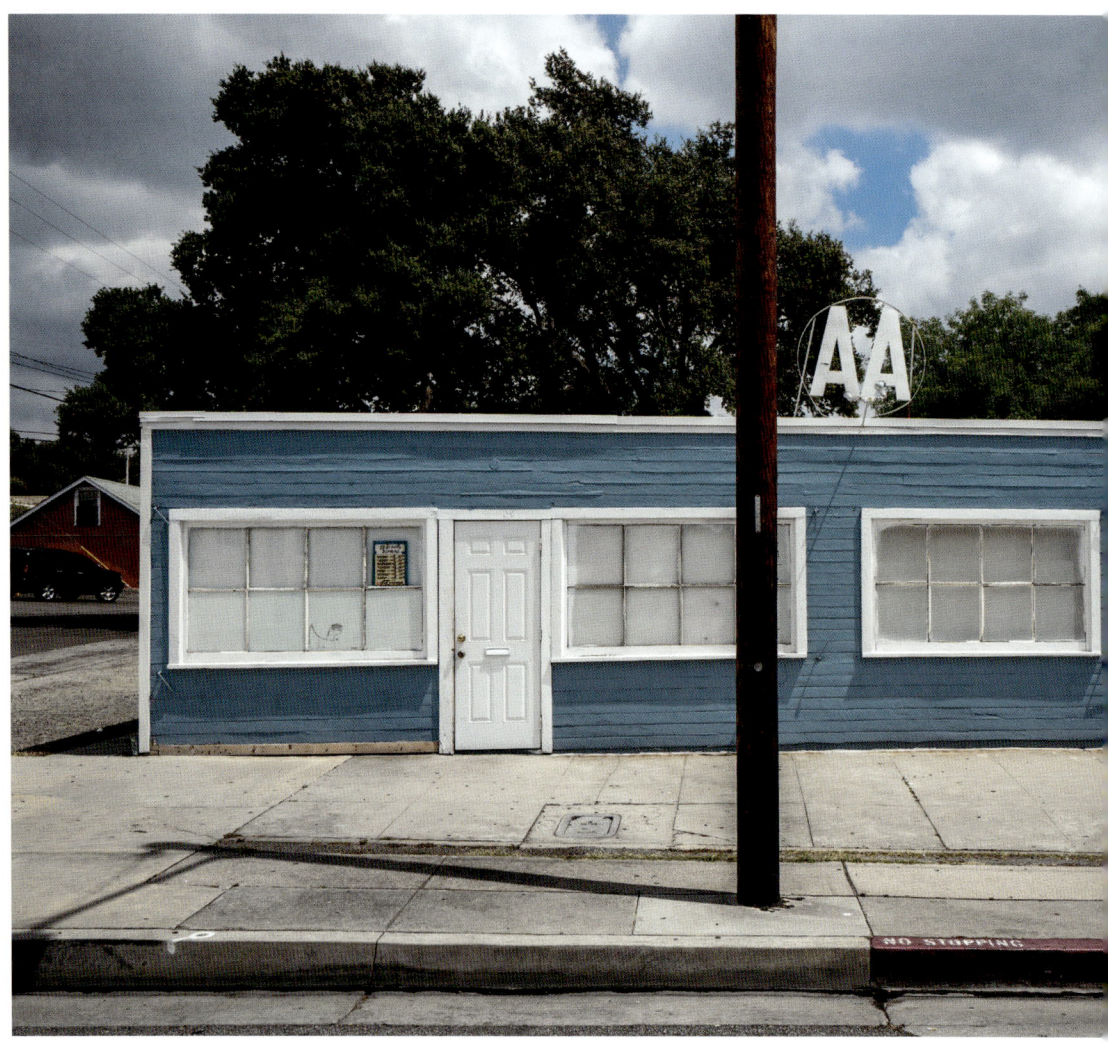

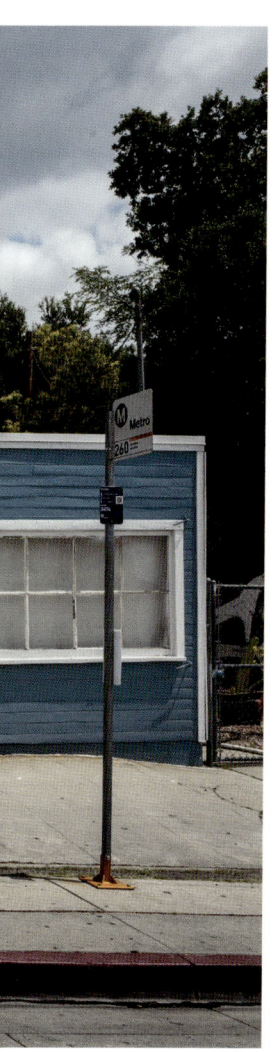

The Role of Emotion

Some weeks are busier than others. There are weeks when the calendar is full of appointments and events and what seems like an endless list of to-dos. In some ways, weeks like that can be good. It means that a lot of seeds that were planted took root. But sometimes, it means that I am so busy I am not getting out to make my photographs.

My usual approach is to wander with little to no agenda and get lost. And when I have not had the chance to do that in a while, I get frustrated and antsy. I am always thinking of my next best picture, of finding something that will challenge me and allow me to take my photography to the next level. While this is a good thing, it also means that I am hypercritical of the images I have already made. As good as those images may be or have been, I am always on the hunt to do one better. More accurately, I hope to discover a different way of seeing. I do not want to repeat what I have already done. To do this I have to rediscover the world around me in a slightly different way. It is not about what camera I use or the post-processing I do; rather, it's a slight shift in my perception that reveals something old and familiar to me in a distinctly different way.

I was returning home when I drove past a building where Alcoholics Anonymous meetings are held (previous page). I had driven past the building countless times before. The simple wooden structure had stood out to me with its blue color, white accents, and prominent AA on the rooftop, but I had never thought of making a photograph of it. On that day, something clicked and I saw the building for the remarkable thing that it was.

However, at that particular time of day, the light was lackluster. If I made an image of the building, the resulting photograph would not reflect that revelatory feeling I had experienced in that moment. I made a mental note to return to the spot when the light was favorable, which would be easy enough since it was just a short drive from home.

A week later, I was sitting on the couch reading a book when I looked up and gazed at my backyard through the sliding glass door. It had rained that morning and the sky was overcast, but the sun had just broken through. The overgrown bougainvillea on my fence glowed brilliantly in the sunlight. The greens and magentas took on a new vibrancy. I knew that it was the perfect time to photograph the building.

I grabbed my camera and drove to the location. I knew where I needed to position myself to make the image, which was unfortunately partway into the street, and at that moment, it seemed that everyone within 30 miles had to drive past me on that patch of road. As I waited, the cloud cover returned, and I saw the luminousness that had spurred me to get out disappear.

I looked at the sky and tried to gauge in what direction the clouds were moving. It was hard to tell, but I knew I just had to give it time. My patience would eventually pay off. The sun broke through again, the traffic eased, and I walked into the street and composed and made the photograph.

It was the only photograph I made that day, but I felt a wonderful sense of exhilaration. It was not just about the image I had made; it was more about the fact that I had experienced a visual breakthrough, whereby I was able to move past my filters and judgements of what was ordinary. I was able to move beyond that to see and create an image that I would not have made before.

Feelings and the Voice

My feelings are inexorably tied to my image-making, sometimes for good and sometimes for ill. While I am often in pursuit of the moment of creative gestalt, I frequently struggle getting there because of feelings of self-doubt, insecurity, and fear.

In the past those negative feelings severely hampered my creativity. They often dissuaded me from making time to make photographs or take on new challenges. Negative feelings also led me to be unreasonably critical of my work, which admittedly is something I still contend with. Such negative feelings colored my perspective on what was really good work. My hypercritical eye did not always allow me to see that. It was as if one aspect of my emotions led me to make the photographs, while another prevented me from fully appreciating what I had accomplished.

Although people whom I respected and admired would say good things about my work, I often focused on what I thought my photographs lacked, rather than what was good about them. I began to see that the harsh critic whose voice I heard in my head was not always an accurate barometer of what I was doing with my camera. I had to learn to trust the feelings that often surrounded my picture-making, especially when I was in the zone, and not always give credence to my own unforgiving criticism.

Rather than fixate on some level of unreasonable perfection, I looked for ways to see and photograph differently. Even if the images did not fully succeed in the ways that I hoped, my measure of them was instead based on where I felt my photography was taking me. If I saw evidence that I was taking greater risks and discovering new things about how to make a photograph, I gave less weight to the voice that insisted on perfection over progress.

As a result of challenging my way of seeing, I was rewarded with photographs that reflected a growing sensibility. I saw that I did not simply produce the same images over and over again, but was discovering the world with evolving eyes. My photographs demonstrated my progress and my improvement.

This layered composition of a young woman practicing gymnastics on parallel bars is an image for which I felt I explored new territory. Along with building a composition using multiple layers, I challenged my observational skills. Besides the obvious elements of the young woman, her boyfriend, and the young boy, I had to observe the other people walking and riding down the boardwalk, the horizon line, and even the swinging gymnastics rings.

It was a situation where I added more and more to the composition and succeeded in not having the entire photograph fall apart due to the inclusion of distractions. It is a sort of additive approach that I am actively practicing, and it frequently results in a failed image, but when it succeeds it is incredibly satisfying. The joy is derived not so much from my successes, but from the fact that I am doing what I love and can see evidence of my improvements.

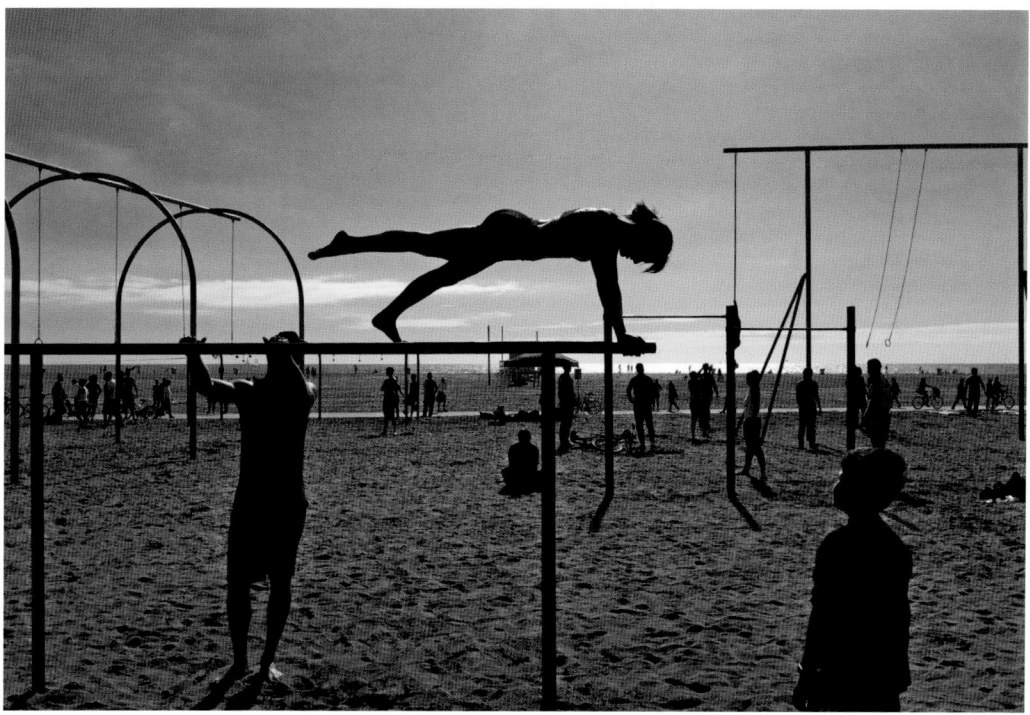

A Regular Practice

When I was a young photographer, I waited for inspiration. The thought was that the heavens would open up, inspiration would strike, and I would be impelled to create wonderful photographs. More often than not, inspiration did not come knocking and I settled for whatever excuse or distraction was convenient.

Then I heard a quote from the photographer and artist Chuck Close who said, "Inspiration is for amateurs. The rest of us just show up and get to work." The simple honesty and clarity of that statement cut me to the quick. I realized that I often allowed my feelings to create excuses for my lack of creativity. It was only going out and making an image that provided me the solution I desperately craved.

I began to have a camera with me every day. I did not relegate my creativity to the weekend or a special trip. The art of seeing and making photographs became an everyday occurrence. I could no longer end the day with the excuse that there was nothing of interest to photograph. Instead, I developed a new sensibility for observing the world. It was time to take the blinders off.

With the goal of making a good image every day, I reconsidered what was photo-worthy and what was not. I realized how many things I disregarded because of their ordinariness. I would raise the camera to my eye, but even before making a photograph I rejected its possibility and walked away. I could not continue that kind of mindset and hope to create a photograph, especially if I only had 15–20 minutes to photograph that day, which was often the case.

Much of my photography occurred during those in-between moments: leaving home to drive to work; parking my car and walking to my office; during my lunch breaks; and running errands. There were these windows of time when I was transitioning from one activity to another that were my only time to make photographs. And rather than using that time to daydream, listen to music, or browse the Internet, I used it to go and find something to photograph.

This became a daily practice that eventually transformed me as a photographer. Because I was so committed to discovering something new each day, regardless of what little time I had, I was forced to reexamine the world in a nonliteral way. This is how I came to observe the world based on light and shadow, line and shape, color, and gesture. If I just stood around waiting for something interesting to happen, the photographs rarely came. The world did not need to change—I needed to.

I had to make the time to make photographs, even if they were only captured with my smartphone. It did not matter what camera I used, it was about practicing my way of seeing. Much like a regular exercise regimen conditions the body, the daily process of seeing developed my ability to discern the extraordinary from the ordinary.

Seeing with New Eyes

I was walking to the bank to make a withdrawal and as usual I had my camera over my shoulder. I was about to ascend the handicap ramp leading to the bank's entrance when I looked down at my feet. There on the concrete were thick blue lines leading up to blocks of yellow. I saw two distinct shadows that added weight to those shapes. As I looked at the ground, it was like I could hear the synapses in my brain firing away. There was a photograph here.

Yes, I was busy running errands, but everything could wait until I figured out how to make a good image of this scene. I raised my camera to my eye and moved around the elements, shifting back and forth trying to determine what to include and what to

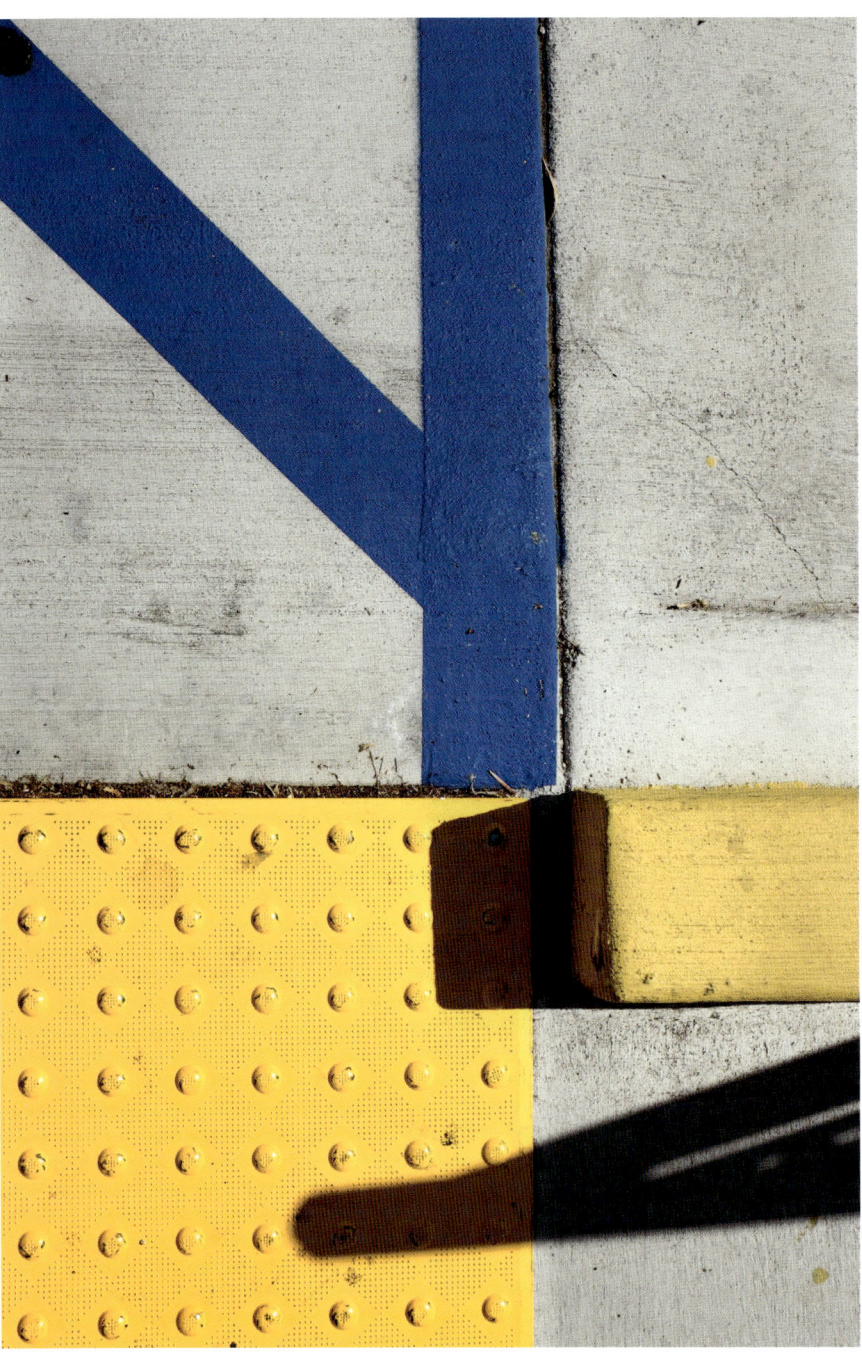

exclude from the frame. I saw a few people looking in my direction trying to figure out what the heck I was doing, but I ignored them and maintained my focus. I made several photographs, refining the frame until I was satisfied with what I had created.

When I pulled the image up and displayed it as shot, I was less than impressed. It did not work for me. But just as I was ready to give up, I rotated the image 180 degrees so that it appeared upside down. Suddenly, it worked for me and it took on the feel of an abstract painting. I was more than pleased that I had had my camera with me.

It is moments like this that have made the difference for me as a photographer. It is not that I wanted to make a career of photographing parking lots, but rather that I learned to become so attuned to my own process of seeing that something as ordinary as a handicap ramp provided me with the raw material for an interesting photograph. I came to learn that if I could discover the beauty in something as simple as this, I would have the skills to observe more complex and fluid scenes in an exacting and precise way.

When I was at the Grand Central Market, I saw a neon sign on the wall (next page). I knew I wanted to photograph it, but I also knew that I did not want to simply document it. There would be no challenge in that. As I moved closer to the wall, I caught the reflection of the neon sign on the surface of an empty table. The mirroring of the scene is what I needed to take my observation of the sign to another level. Thankfully, I was there early enough that there was only a single figure seated at a table situated between me and the sign. I lowered my camera so that the reflection dominated the foreground and I built the rest of the composition from there, creating a photograph that was not just about the sign, but that revealed how I saw the scene.

As I continue to photograph, it becomes clearer to me that it is not the technical knowledge that makes the difference in my photography. It is my application of that knowledge on an everyday basis that has led me to become a better photographer. Everything else is just excuses.

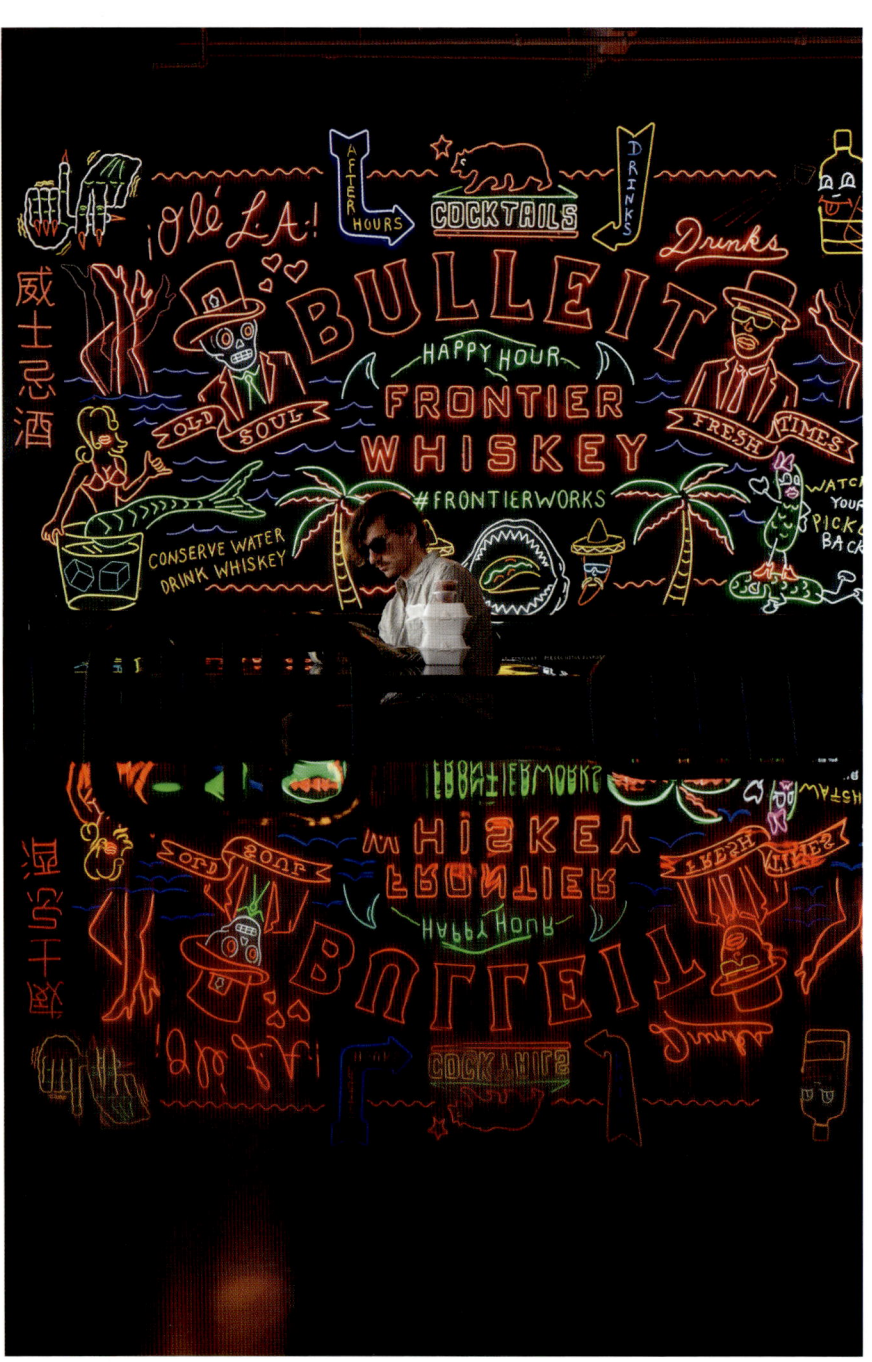

Try shooting for a minimum of five minutes a day using your camera or smartphone. Choose different subjects on each day that you can examine and photograph. Consider how you feel before, during, and after each daily photo outing, and observe what emotional changes occur throughout the experience. Examine when and how negative feelings threaten the process and what you do to surmount them.

Keep It Simple

We were in Monte Cristi in the Dominican Republic for my sister's wedding. It is the town where my father was born and where he built a family home that he would return to each year. It was while he was vacationing there that he passed away. He was buried in the town that he loved so much. On this trip, I was glad to return under happier circumstances.

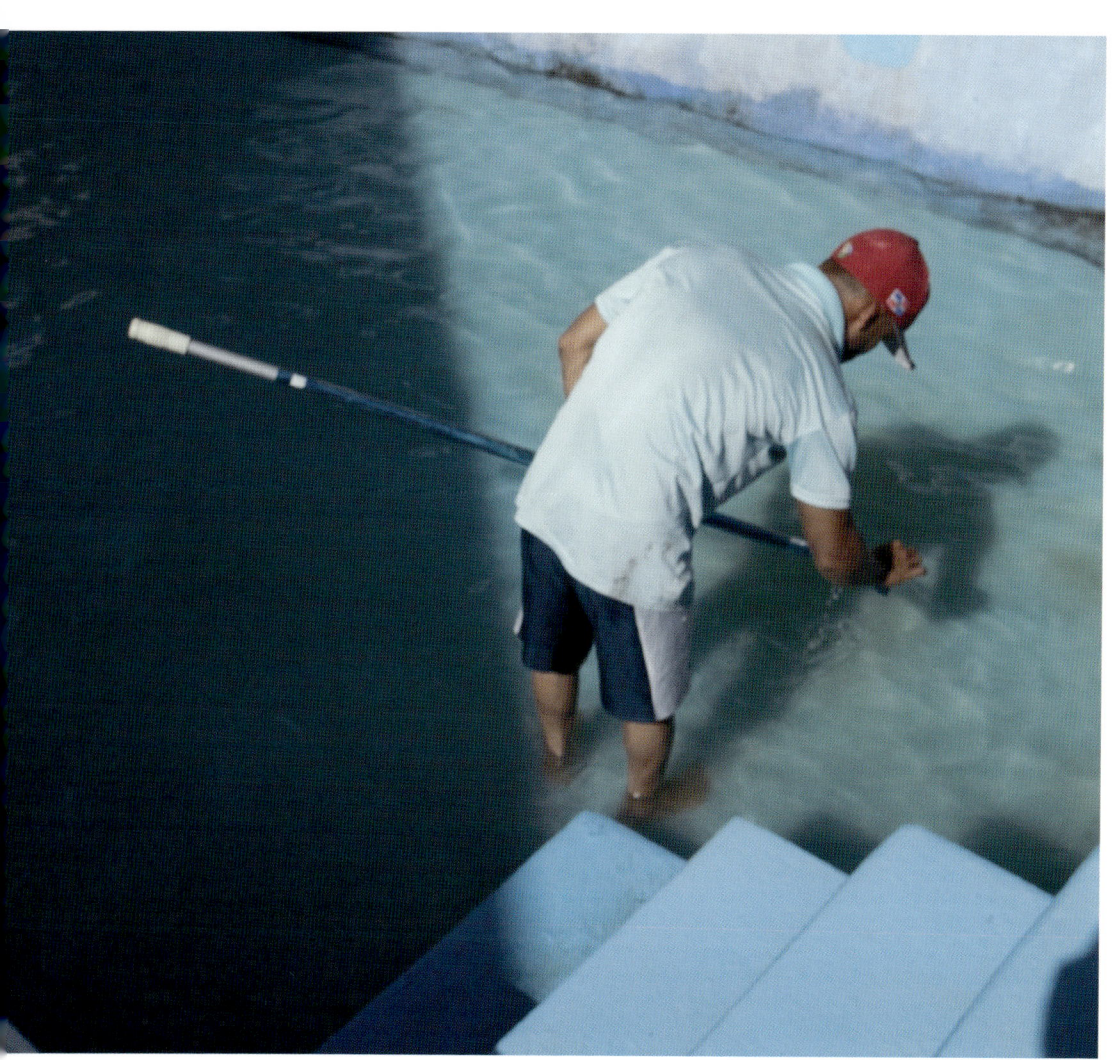

Because the house was occupied with other family members, we booked a room in a small modest hotel by the beach. The door to the balcony opened up to the bay with its clear blue water and view of El Moro, the small island that is just a short boat ride away. We awakened to the sound of the waves lapping against the shore and children chasing each other in the sand.

We walked down to the patio where we ordered breakfast: fried eggs, mangu (mashed plantain) with sautéed red onions, longaniza (Dominican sausage), and coffee. I rarely get to eat this way back home. Unlike in New York and Miami, there is no centralized Dominican community in Los Angeles, and there certainly is not a Dominican restaurant to be had. So each meal in Monte Cristi was special, a taste of home and a reminder of my youth.

As we waited for our food to arrive, I spotted a hotel worker cleaning out the pool filled with water that was about calf-high. I noticed how the morning sunlight was cut off by the roofline of the hotel and wondered whether I might find a photograph there.

I excused myself from the table, grabbed my Fujifilm x100s, and made my way poolside. It was there that I realized the potential of the scene. The transition between light and shadow created a pleasing graphic, and the blues and greens of the steps, water, and the man's outfit played wonderfully against each other. But it was his bright-red hat that provided the gesture that really set this moment off.

I stood near the top of the steps that led into the pool, wanting to include their descending pattern in my frame. I composed the scene to include the edges of the pool at the top and bottom of the frame, sandwiching the man in between. I made images as he dutifully scrubbed the bottom of the pool. His body and arms rocked back and forth in a rhythmic fashion as he slowly navigated through the water. I followed him with my camera, waiting for him to move into the right position and provide the right body language to complete the photograph.

The man moved out of the shadow and into the sunlight, and the color of his clothes and hat came to life. I timed the release of shutter for when he pushed the scrubber forward, pulling the white-tipped handle out of the shadow into the light.

When I returned to my table, my breakfast awaited me. I bit into its deliciousness that seemed all the better because of the photograph I had just made.

Have Your Camera Ready

That moment by the pool was made easier by having a camera at the ready. As much as I enjoy my smartphone, I prefer using a "real" camera when I'm making photographs, especially one as small and compact as my x100 series camera. Its fixed 23mm lens (35mm equivalent) eliminates concerns of what lens or focal to use in creating a photograph. That is all I have, and I just have to make it work.

You have likely heard the phrase, "the best camera is the one that you have with you," and there is great truth to that. Though I have my preference, it is my hope that you find a camera that makes it practical for you to always have a camera by your side. Though you may desire or already own an assortment of lenses, I recommend keeping your everyday kit as simple as possible. You want to make it something you always carry with you and that is neither intrusive nor a burden.

In the end, you want to have a camera that allows you to practice and develop your process of seeing on a regular and consistent basis.

A Simple Wedding

When my sister told me she was getting married in our dad's hometown, I knew I would be the official photographer. I rarely photograph weddings, much preferring to be a guest than the photographer. However, there was no way I would deny my sister's request to document her and her husband's special day.

As our travel day approached, I deliberated back and forth about what equipment to take. Though I primarily shoot with my x100s, I still owned a DSLR kit complete with an arsenal of fixed focal length and zoom lenses—a heavy bit of kit stowed tightly in a backpack.

I thought of all the shots I might capture and how I would need this and that lens, flash, battery grip, extra batteries, laptop, etc. However, when I picked up the bag, I was reminded of how heavy it was to carry. It was especially onerous walking through airports, where the weight of it all made the travel itself all the more exhausting. I knew from my assignment work that having all this gear would make the job that much more demanding. Putting down and picking up the bag throughout the day, moving gear in and out of it, was an additional task that I had to concern myself with as I made photographs.

Then I thought about how this was my sister's wedding and I wanted to be able to enjoy it, too. If I took all this equipment with me, I would be working, and working hard. I would be more focused on getting photographs than enjoying the wonderful memories that were being created. I did not want to travel all that distance to treat my sister's wedding as another job.

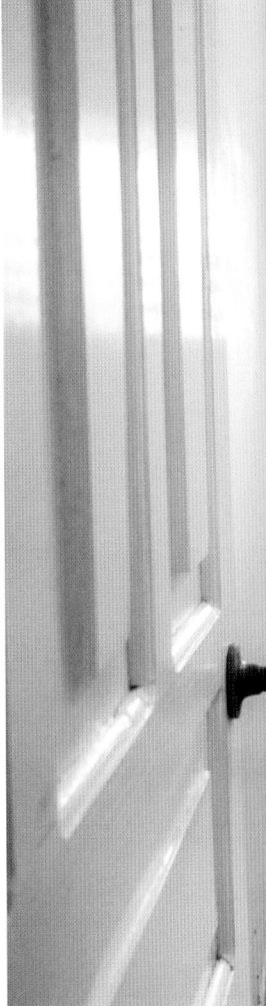

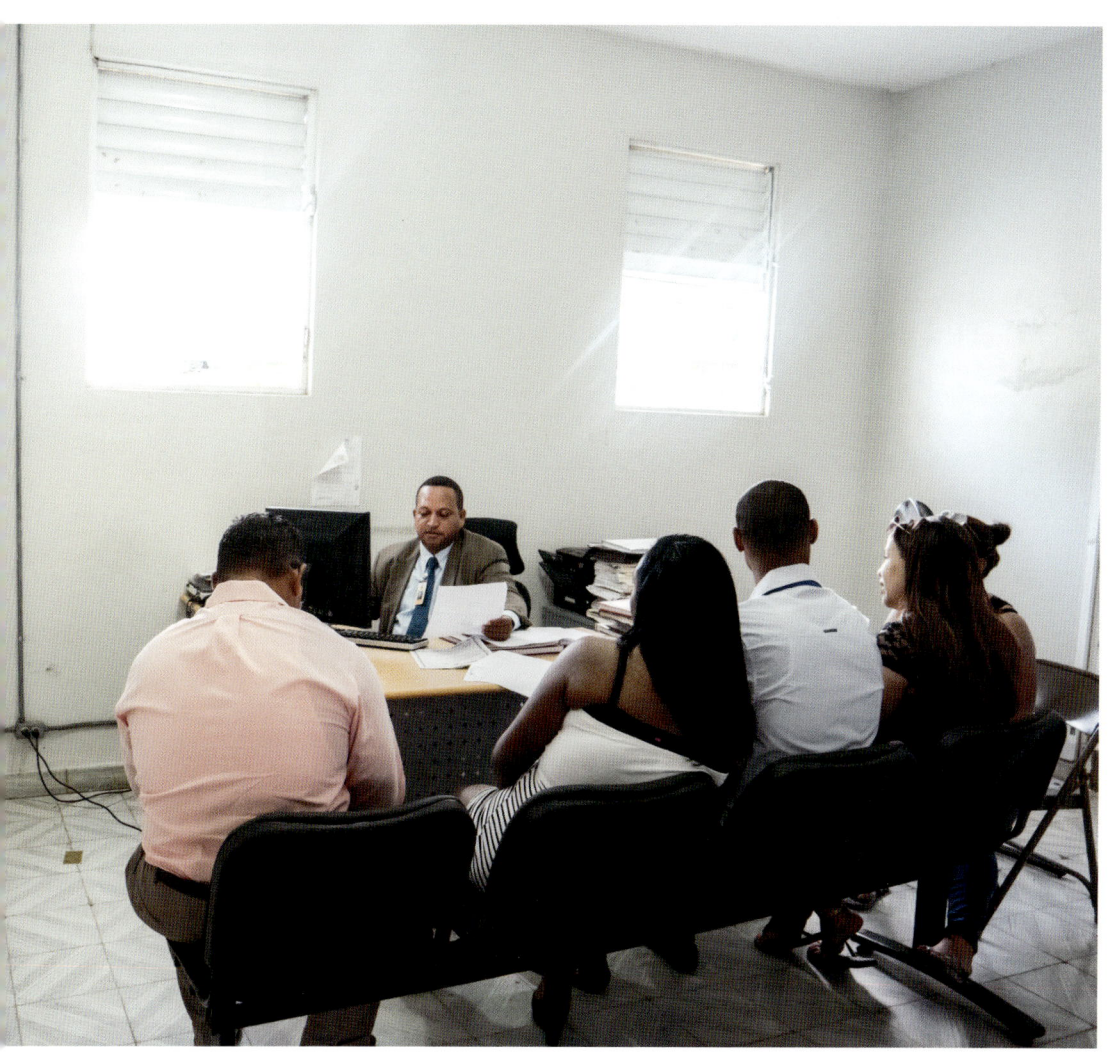

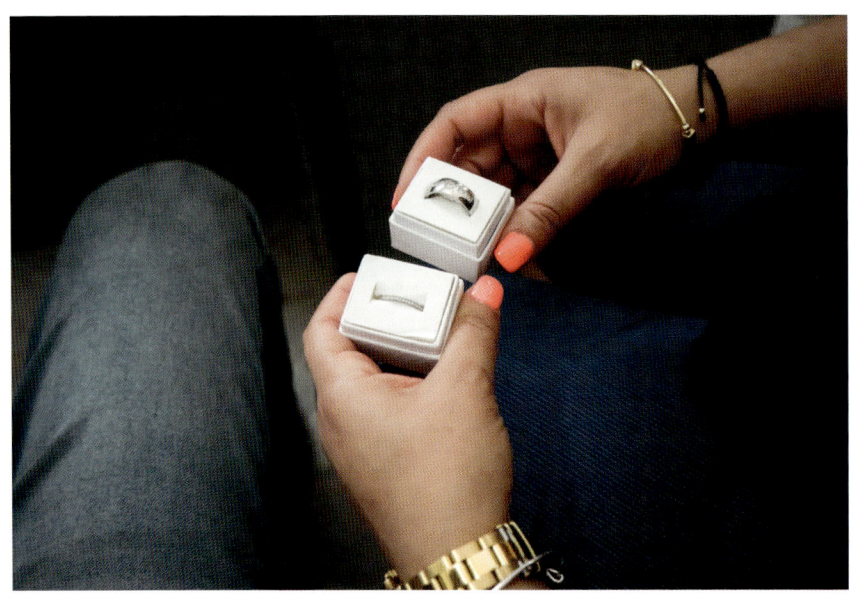

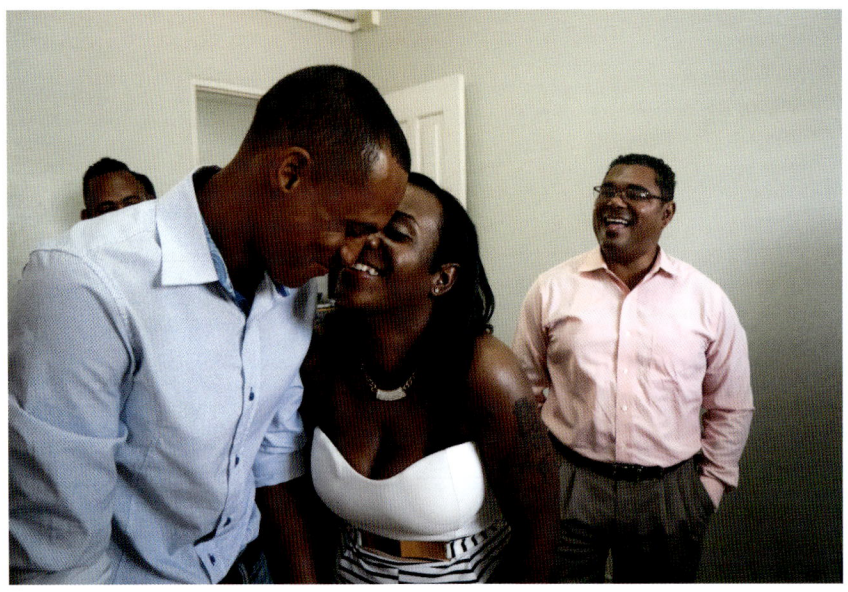

So I left the DSLR kit at home and took only my x100s with me. I had relied on that camera as my one piece of kit when vacationing, and I knew that it was more than capable of producing wonderful imagery. It was small and compact; it would free me of the burden of weight; and it would allow me to enjoy moments as a participant and not just a documentarian.

All the images that I produced of their wedding at the justice of the peace and at the reception afterward where made with the one camera. I did not miss leaving all the other equipment behind. Along with making photographs, I ate, drank, and danced, and had a wonderful time. I swapped my hat between photographer and brother-of-the-bride seamlessly, all the while using my skills of seeing to capture the moments I knew would be important to my sister and my new brother-in-law.

A Simpler Approach

I do not believe that every photographer should pare down to a single camera and lens. Each photographer has to determine exactly what type and what amount of gear they require to make their photographs. The needs of a wedding photographer or a nature photographer are completely different than those of a photographer who practices street or macro photography.

However, I have often succumbed to G.A.S. (gear acquisition syndrome), as have many other photographers. We have accumulated thousands of dollars of photographic equipment and software that did not result in a significant improvement in the quality of our photographs. As I have matured as a photographer, I have discovered that it is often limitations that serve to inspire me and propel me forward, rather than an abundance of the latest photographic innovations.

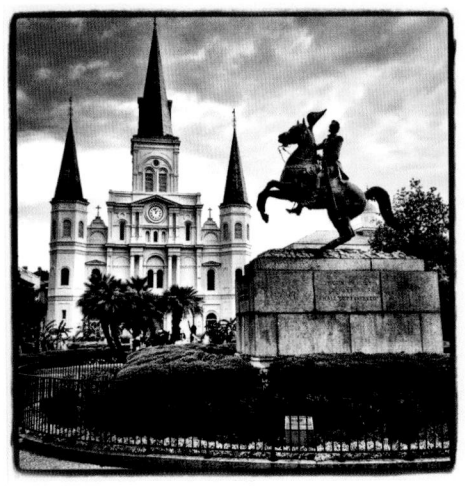
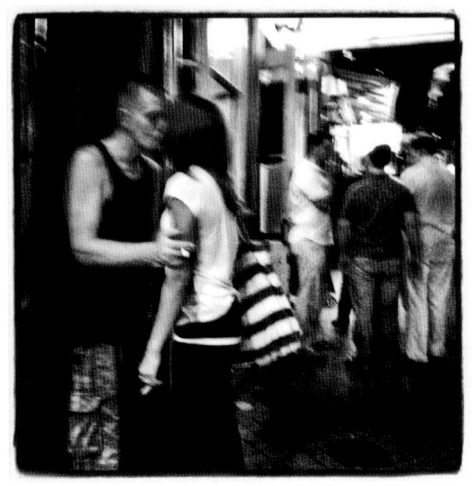
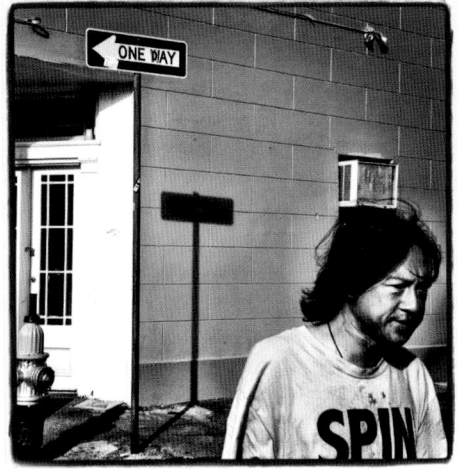
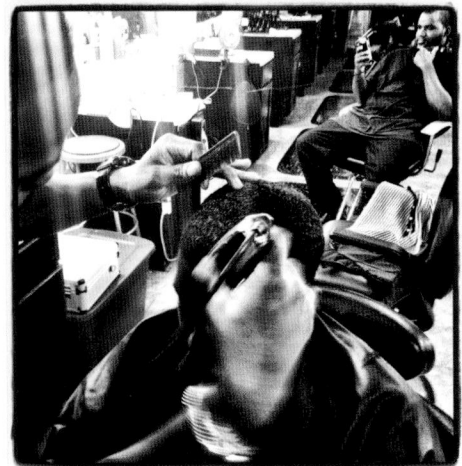

This began for me when I took a trip to New Orleans. I arrived there with my standard pack—a DSLR with five lenses, including two f/2.8 zoom lenses. After only two days, I became fatigued carrying that equipment all over the Big Easy. Not only was it heavy, but I was often focused on the security of my bag when I set it down to make photographs or eat. It got old very quickly.

I had just purchased my first smartphone and I made the conscious choice to leave my gear back at the hotel and make photographs with just my phone. It was incredibly liberating. I was no longer concerned with the weight and the bulk of a photo backpack, and I was free to be impulsive and spontaneous with my image-making. I found myself taking more risks and playing in a way that I was not accustomed to with my DSLR.

The small form factor of the camera phone gave me the freedom to move significantly closer to my subjects, as well as position the camera phone at distances and angles that would not have been feasible with a bulky DSLR. The resulting images were significantly different and more inventive than the photographs I had been making up to that point. I discovered a spontaneity that was lacking in much of my work until then.

After that I invested in my first mirrorless camera and it soon became my everyday camera, making it all the easier to always have a camera with me. The mirrorless camera and my smartphone made it possible for me to photograph anytime and anywhere.

Though I still owned my DSLR kit, I relied on it less for my day-to-day shooting. And when I did use it, I found myself relying less on my selection of lenses to do the work. I paired down my lens choices for an assignment to a 35mm and 85mm lens and I was surprised at how much I was able to produce with just those two fast primes. I did not miss using the 70–200mm, which I rarely used anyway.

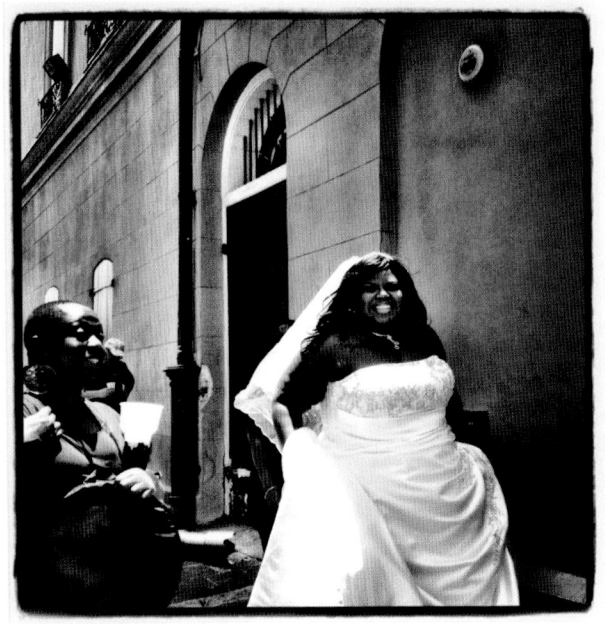

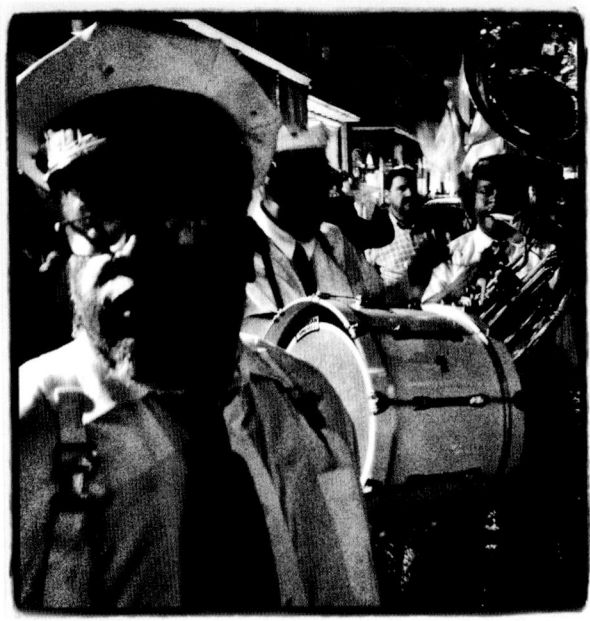

By limiting the amount of equipment I used, especially with respect to my lens choice, I became intimately familiar with how the world looked through a 35mm. Over time, I saw how a subject or scene would be rendered with a single focal length, even without bringing the camera to my eye. As I produced countless photographs, I became more attuned to how a scene would look in my frame, and it informed how close or how far I would need to be in order to capture the image I saw in my mind's eye.

My familiarity with a single focal length and not having the option to dig into my bag for another lens eliminated a big distraction. I needed to make the image work with the lens that I had with me. I would not miss a moment trying to find the right lens or zooming my lens back and forth trying to find the sweet spot.

Though I still relied on my zoom lenses for assignment work because of the versatility that they provide, I found myself relying more on fixed focal length lenses. I had trained myself to see the world from those specific fields of view.

More choices do not equate to better photographs for me. It is actually working within limitations that provides the greatest degree of creativity.

What Do You Need?

Many people pull out their credit card with lightning speed to purchase the latest version of a camera or lens in the mistaken belief that owning it will lead to a significant improvement in their photography. And while the lens may provide better bokeh or the camera may provide a new picture style or higher resolution, the images often look pretty much the same as the photographs made with their old equipment.

When it comes to determining what you need as a photographer, it is important to ask yourself the right question: "Is the equipment that I currently have preventing me from making the image that I aspire to make?" This is a much different question than whether the new version is considered "better" in some form or fashion. Your existing bit of kit does not become obsolete, as so many photographers declare when a new model arrives. It is just as capable of making great pictures as it ever was. And while the new equipment may offer more options, those new options do not necessarily result in better photographs.

It is important to consider your current choice of equipment and think about how it helps and hinders your productivity. Most of today's cameras, even those that are several years old, can produce amazing photographs that can be printed and displayed as exhibitions-size prints. They provide photographs that deliver incredible color, relatively low noise at high ISOs, and sharp images. So if you are less than satisfied with your current imagery, it is important to consider whether the camera is really the solution. Maybe the money can be better spent on creating time to practice your photography during a vacation or a workshop. The time you dedicate exclusively to producing photographs will more clearly help you to discover what it is you need to become a better photographer.

Pare your kit down to a bare minimum—a single camera body and single focal length. Minimize it as much as possible to make it feasible to have it with you every day.

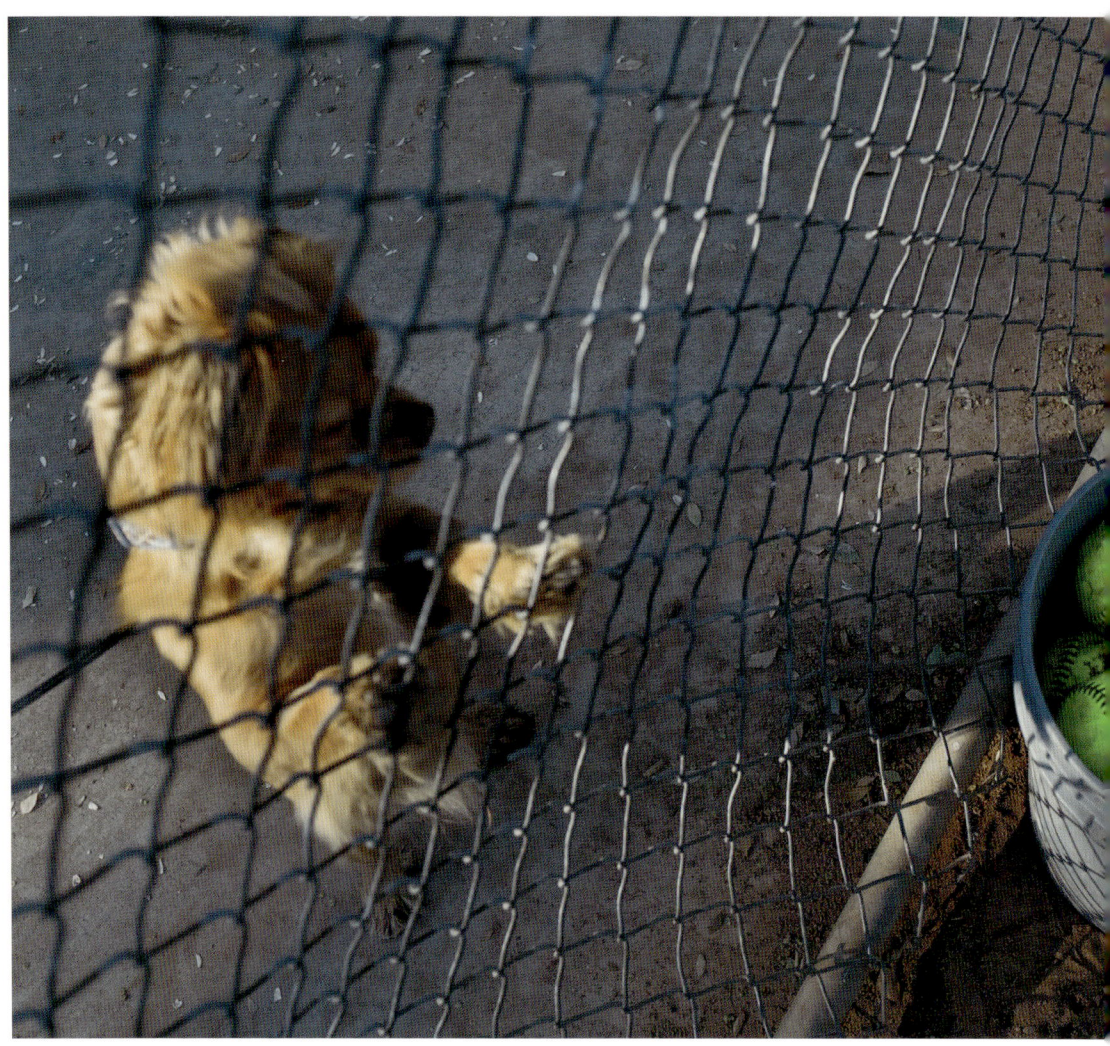

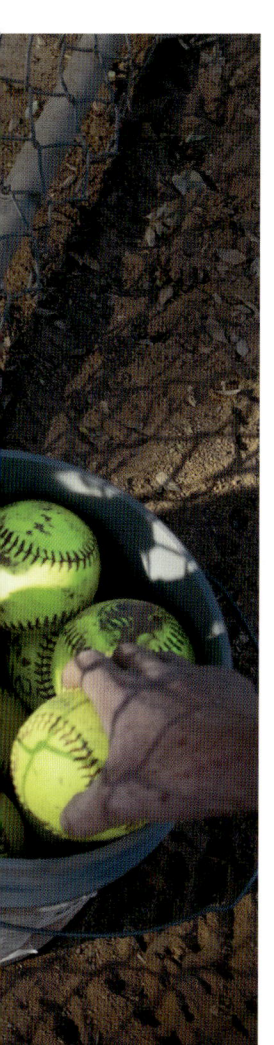

Practice, Practice, Practice

If there is one activity I love more than photography, it is playing softball. I joined a 50 and over coed league and we practice Monday mornings at a nearby park. The athleticism and camaraderie are a wonderful start to the week.

As always, the activity begins around 9 a.m. with cars pulling into the parking lot, the bases being put out, and teammates stretching and warming up. On this day, like many others, the morning light stretched across the field and illuminated the peaks of the Angeles National Forest that overlooks the park. Some of us stretched out within shafts of sunlight for a few extra degrees of warmth.

I am never without my camera, so it accompanies my mitt, bat, and cleats to practice. Though the priority is playing softball, I always look for opportunities to make a photograph. I do so because on some days it may be the only time I will have to make pictures. There are just days when I am going to be tied to the desk chair trying to make things happen and meet yet another deadline.

My x100s possesses only a fixed 23mm lens, which performs as the equivalent of a 35mm focal length. So I am not shooting from a distance with a telephoto lens to capture action. The images I create are more intimate and capture the small details of sports and friendship. These are not images of anonymous strangers on the street. I look for moments of personal interaction and telling details. I want images that my friends will recognize as part of our time together, but seen through my eyes.

On this day, I was in the queue to practice my batting when I saw another player's dog at the fence. I noticed the light illuminating him from behind as well as a plastic bucket filled with softballs. I liked how the sunlight produced a circle of edge-lighting around the center of the fence that the dog was looking through.

I made several frames of the dog, fence, and balls, but I knew the photograph needed a little something more. That little something arrived when a hand reached down and grasped a ball. I had everything I needed.

It was a quiet and simple moment, but this is an image that helps to tell part of the story that we share every week.

Finding the Time

Though I have made my living as a photographer and a writer for decades, that has not meant that I am always out in the world photographing. As anyone who is self-employed knows, much of my time is spent drumming up business, networking, organizing paperwork, and handling whatever personal business arises during the day. There is no shortage of things to do, and having the time to photograph continuously for a couple of hours is more the exception than the rule. Such times have to be planned and will hopefully not conflict with those unexpected and almost inevitable occurrences of life that eat away the hours and minutes of the day.

This is the reason I always have my camera with me. It keeps me from falling back on the excuse that I do not have time or the equipment available to practice making photographs. Whether I have minutes or hours, I am always on the hunt for an opportunity to practice seeing and making photographs. Even if I only find one scene to photograph in a day, I completely dedicate myself to those moments, because I know it is not how much time I have to enjoy photography that day, but how well I utilize the time I do have.

One of the habits I practice is arriving early for appointments. Not only is it a smart thing to do with Los Angeles's pernicious traffic jams, but it also gives me time to wander and look for photographs. I usually do not have to go far to find a scene to photograph. Using the principles of the visual draws, I often discover a scene that has potential.

This proved to be true when I came upon a scene in an alleyway just half a block from where my morning appointment was scheduled to take place (next page). I walked past it and saw the shadow of the street sign against the white wall. The graphic qualities of the sign and diagonal metal pole against the repeating pattern of white brick drew me in. I composed the photograph, making small refinements with each frame until I was satisfied.

Those 15 minutes provided me with a wonderful image to start the day and satisfied that daily craving to be creative. Even if that were the only photograph I made that day, I still felt a sense of accomplishment.

I used to beat myself up for not getting out to shoot for days and even weeks, but I rarely experience that now. With my camera at the ready, I always find time during the day to practice seeing and making photographs. It is not essential that the images be exceptional or great. What is important is that I am practicing seeing and creating opportunities for myself to grow and develop as a photographer.

Exhaust All the Possibilities

When you make time to photograph, you have to make the most of it, and to do that, you have to leverage the scene and the moment for as much as you can. It is often not enough to make a couple of photographs and move on to the next opportunity. If you measure your time practicing photography only by the number of images you create, you are poorly served. If, instead, you examine how carefully you explored a scene visually, you are ahead of the game.

If you come upon a moment, stop, raise the camera, and make only one or two photographs, you are not seeing. You are snapping pictures. You are not examining how all the disparate elements in front of you relate or do not relate to each other within the context of the photographic frame. This is this kind of picture-taking that leads to so much disappointment because the photographer is relying on the camera itself to work some form of

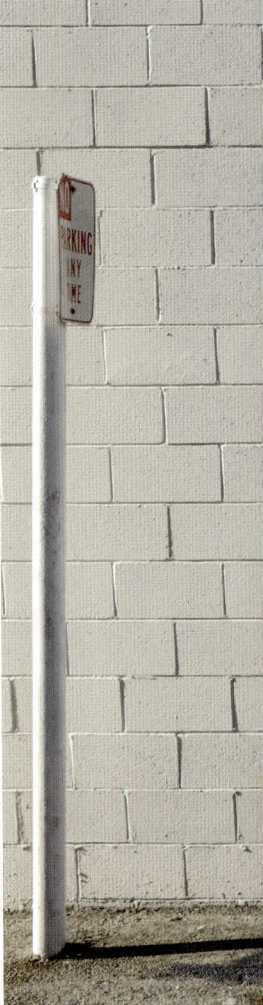

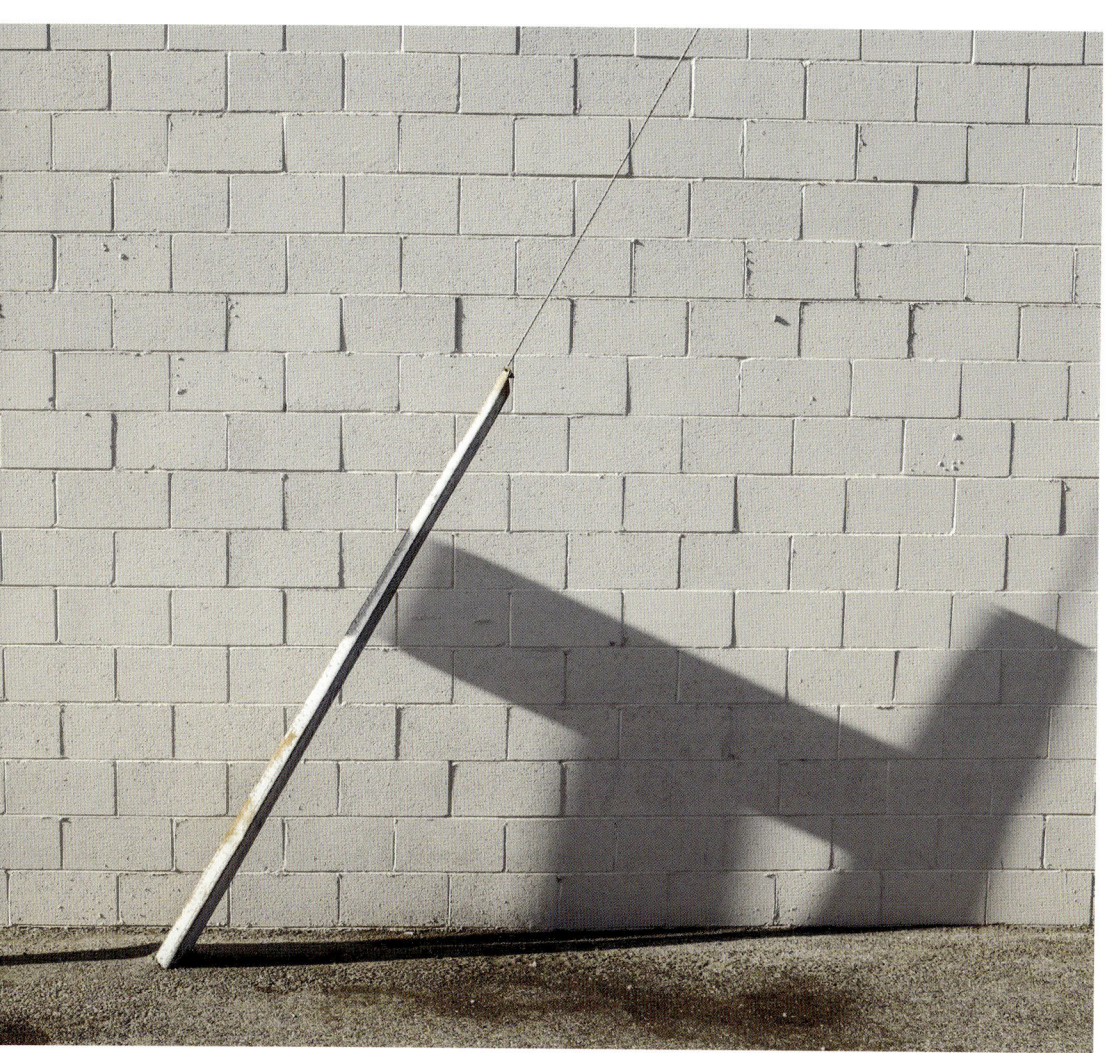

magic. This results in images that are more appreciated for the sharpness of the lens or the low noise of the camera's sensor than for the content of the photograph.

Exhausting all the possibilities means moving beyond that first photograph. It means considering more than just the subject, but also the foreground and background, as well as those elements located at the edges of the frame. It means evaluating the scene using the principles of the visual draws—light and shadow, line and shape, color, and gesture—and considering how they may strengthen and weaken the image. It means seeing the potential of a scene and recognizing that it needs a little something else in order to elevate the photograph to something special.

When I was photographing these two young boys, dressed for a wedding at a downtown church, I wanted to use the graphic shadows in the composition. The sun created a triangle of light in the center of the frame where I wanted the two kids to be. I wanted to leverage the shadows of the boys themselves as they moved through the scene.

I positioned myself on the overlook and worked on refining my overall frame, always keeping an eye on where the boys moved through the scene. They ran back and forth in and out of the shadows. I made several frames of them, many of which did not work because of their relative positions. I wanted each boy and his respective shadow to be cleanly defined against the ground. With each unsuccessful frame I made, I also practiced patience, believing that I would be rewarded for it.

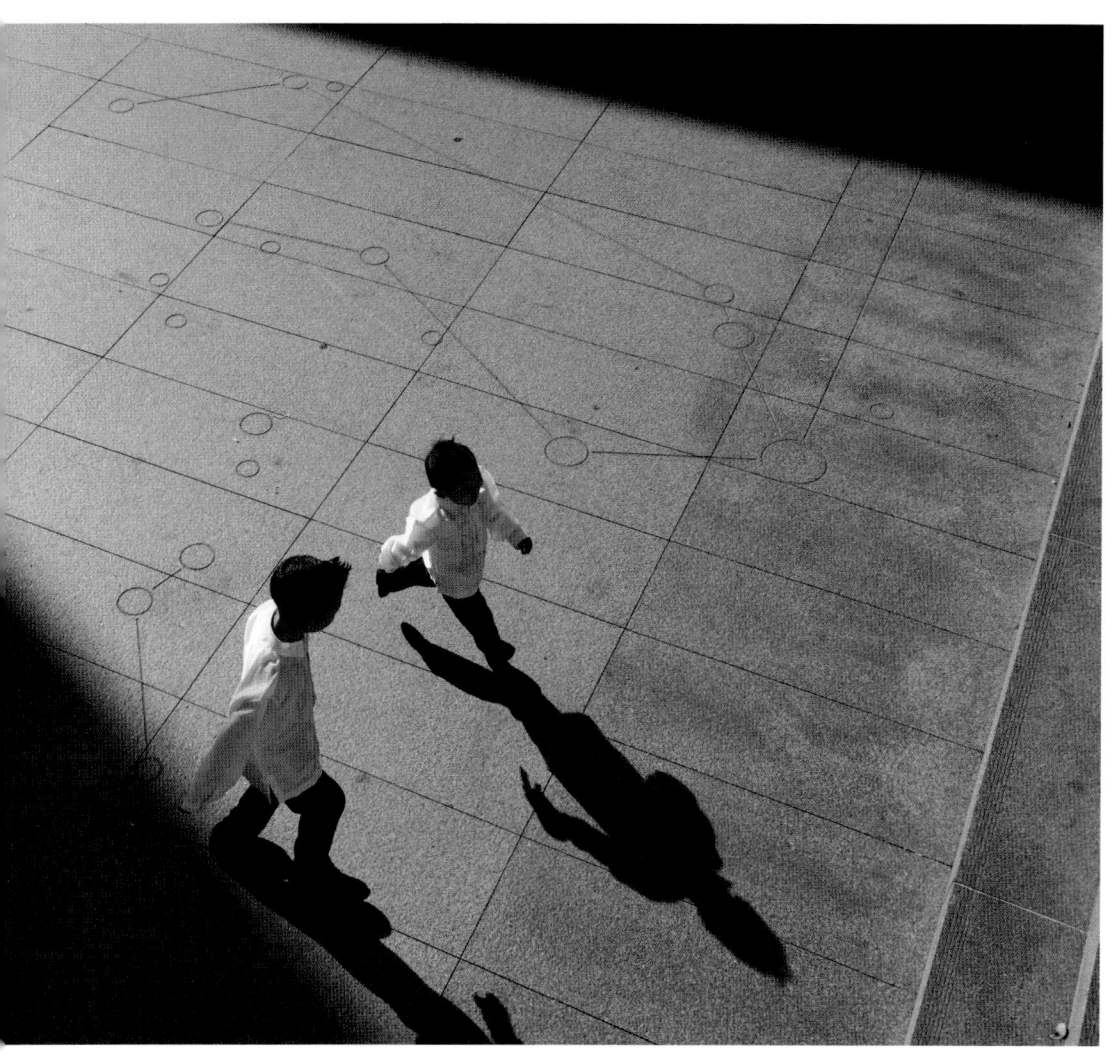

The moment happened when the younger boy dashed across the courtyard as his brother stepped out of the shadows. I saw the clear definition that I had been hoping for and I pressed the shutter-release button at the moment the younger boy's feet left the ground.

I was able to capture this photograph and so many other scenes like it not only because I parsed the scene using the visual draws, but also because I had the patience to let the moment play out. Sometimes the best photographs happen not because the photographer has catlike reflexes, but because they have the foresight and patience to allow the world to culminate in a moment that can only be captured in a photograph.

In the age of digital cameras, you can make as many photographs as you want. You are no longer restrained by the cost of processing film and creating prints. However, you cannot absently take photographs hoping to get a "good one." It is the choice to actively see and pick your moment that increases the likelihood of making a good photograph.

Making different choices, including changing your focal length or perspective, orienting your camera vertically or horizontally, moving closer to or further away from your subject, under- or overexposing the photograph, or adjusting any other variable, provides you with the opportunity to see, revaluate, and make a conscious choice as to how you want to make a photograph. It is this skill that makes you a photographer, and as you will find in the next chapter, it is the creation of these variations of a subject, scene, or moment that helps you to identify the images that work better than others.

Embrace the Failures

One of the reasons it is so important to practice photography on a daily basis is that it lessens the burden of always having to knock it out of the park. When I was not photographing on a regular basis, I created an unrealistic expectation for myself that the images I created on a given day had to be great. I had to make exceptional photographs in order for the time to feel justified. If the images were lackluster, I grew frustrated and questioned my abilities and talents.

When I did that I was not being fair to myself. The creative process is not about perfectionism, but rather the acceptance and even the embracing of failure. This is especially the case with photography, where the great majority of images that a photographer makes fall short of the mark. Failure is not an absolute. Failure is merely feedback.

When a photograph does not succeed, it is a learning opportunity, a chance to examine and reassess what we are doing with the camera and how we are seeing a subject and a scene. Each image that does not completely work—whether because of a technical issue, the composition, lighting, or timing—provides the photographer with valuable information. Each of those images, compounded several times over time, offers a lesson that should inevitably inform the next photo opportunity.

The image of the white wall earlier in this chapter is a perfect example of this idea at play. Because the scene was predominately white, the camera's metering system would have metered that as 18% gray by default, and the resulting image would have been underexposed. I had photographed similar scenes in the past that were dominated by white and had seen the resulting underexposure. I knew from experience that I needed to apply some exposure compensation so that the white wall would be rendered as white in the photograph. With this particular camera, I knew that a +1 compensation would be more than adequate. I did not need to correct for it after the fact in Lightroom.

Each error, mistake, or missed opportunity has proven more valuable to me than my successes. As pleased as I am with a great photograph, it is the many times that I have fallen short that have helped to shape me as a photographer. And this has only been possible by ensuring that I make time for my photography on a consistent and regular basis, even if it is as little as 15 minutes a day.

Combining Two Loves

Six months into playing in the softball league, I began to bring my camera to practice. At first I was tentative about making photographs, but people soon became accustomed to the camera's presence.

I noticed during our early morning practices and games that sometimes the light was beautiful. On clear days, the sun provided strong directional light and long shadows. It was something I wanted to take advantage of because I knew that the only other time I might have an opportunity to shoot would be in the middle of the day when the light was less ideal. The field featured the precise chalk lines of the game and I could see that the location offered a variety of graphic elements that I could use for compositions.

As I began to squeeze in a few photographs each practice or game day, I found myself looking for details and moments that captured the experience of being out in the field twice a week. Though I still wanted to create a good photograph that leveraged as many of the visual draws as possible, I was much more interested in creating images that told a facet of a story.

On such days, I might make no more than 15 images, but with each one I was thinking as thoughtfully as I could about composition and story. Though I limited the time I dedicated to photography during our practices and games, I was nevertheless applying a careful method of seeing. I found that the regular practice, especially with the same subject matter each week, provided me with more than I could have imagined when I first began bringing my camera.

Whether the images were of people at bat, tossing a ball, donning a glove, writing on the roster board, embracing, laughing, or yelling, they each exhibited an informed way of seeing that I had practiced and honed over years. It was not that I was specifically thinking of each of the visual draws every time I made a photograph, but later I could see how my awareness of them informed each photograph.

The sequence of images on the following pages illustrates a frequent moment in the dugout when my teammates were anxiously observing the action at home plate. It is a scene that I have witnessed often while sitting on the bench waiting for my turn at bat. I saw one of my teammates moving to take his position on deck while another stood at the opening of the dugout. Our manager was doing something at the roster and another person sat immediately to my right.

I saw the possibility for an interesting layered composition. I also observed that because we were in the shade, I risked underexposure due to the brightness of the background. I increased my exposure compensation by one stop and then brought the camera to my eye.

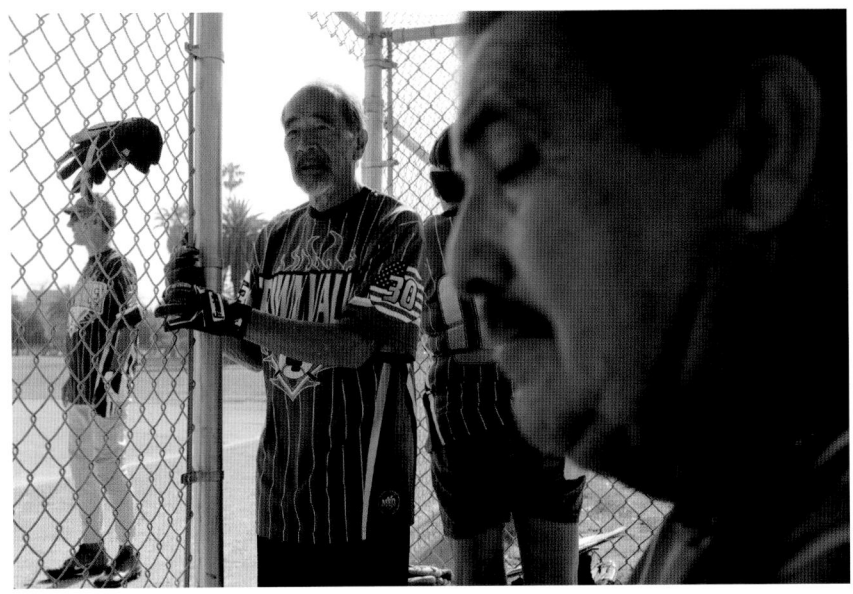

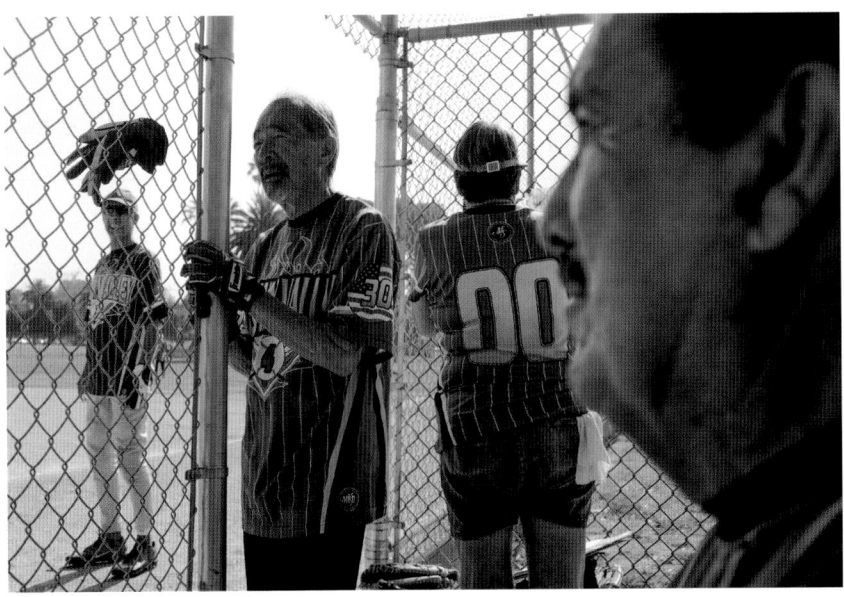

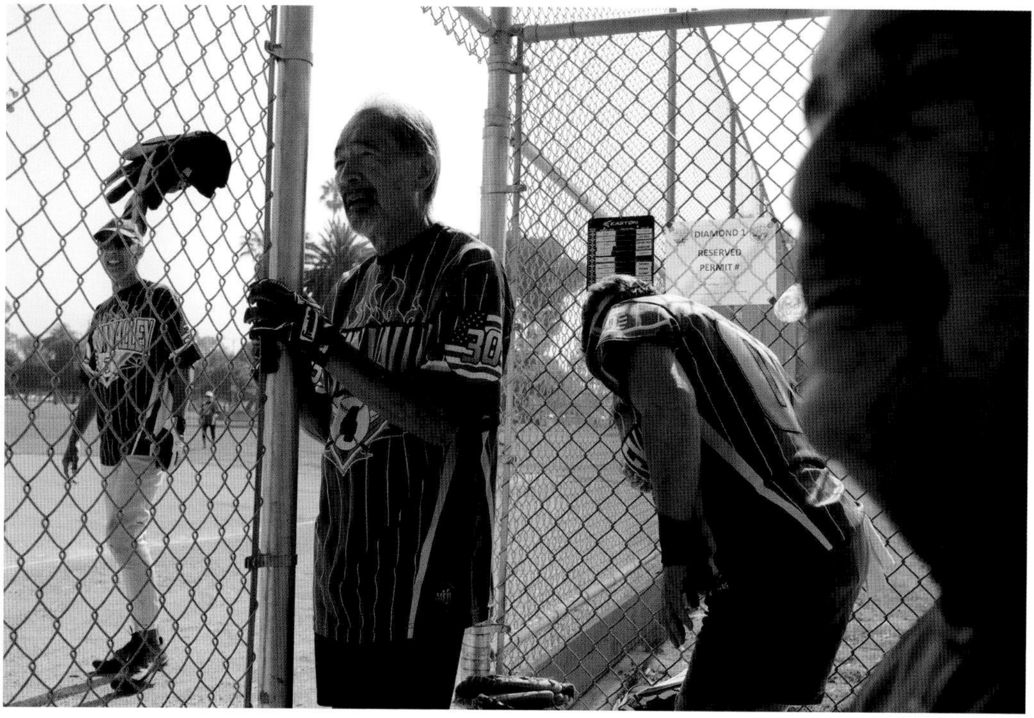

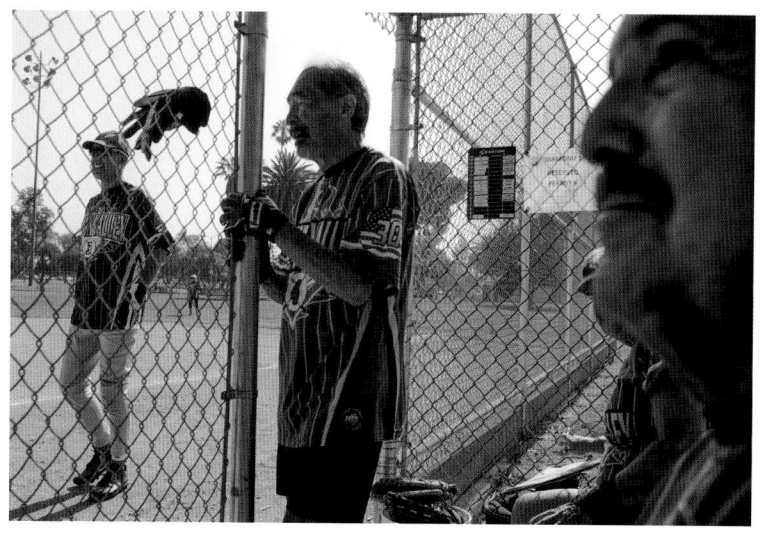

As the scene played out, I composed the photograph, including all four people in the frame. I only had time to create four photographs, each distinctly different from the next. The most successful of the four images is the one in which the manager is bending over to sit down. The first and second photograph do not work for me because the face of the person sitting next to me takes up too much of the frame. In the fourth, the manager is seated and is no longer an element in the frame. The third is the best image of the sequence.

This is not a perfect image. Compositionally, I should have shifted the camera down slightly to create greater separation between the glove in the fence and the player standing behind it. And in an ideal world, I would have loved to have a clear emotional reaction to what was happening on the field. But even with those qualifiers, I consider this a successful image because it tells an important aspect of the story. It also demonstrates my increasing awareness of scenes that can be transformed into strong and effective layered compositions. Though I only had four frames to play with, I recognized the natural intuitiveness that I was developing.

I imagine that this is much like when a seasoned guitarist plays a song. They do not have to think about exactly where to place their fingers to create a chord, their hands just automatically know what to do as if they had a mind of their own. That is the kind of intuitiveness that I have found myself practicing, and it only comes as a result of years of photographing every day.

These images are likely the beginning of what will be a long-term project. I derive a special kind of joy combining my two loves at least twice a week.

Make a commitment
to photograph for at
least 15 minutes a day
for 7 consecutive days.
Choose a scene or subject
that you can return
to regularly during
that period. With each
subject, make a variety of
photographs while trying
to exhaust all the visual
possibilities. Examine
the images later to see
what small changes exist
between each image. See
if you can identify what
small qualities make the
difference between a
successful image and a
failed one.

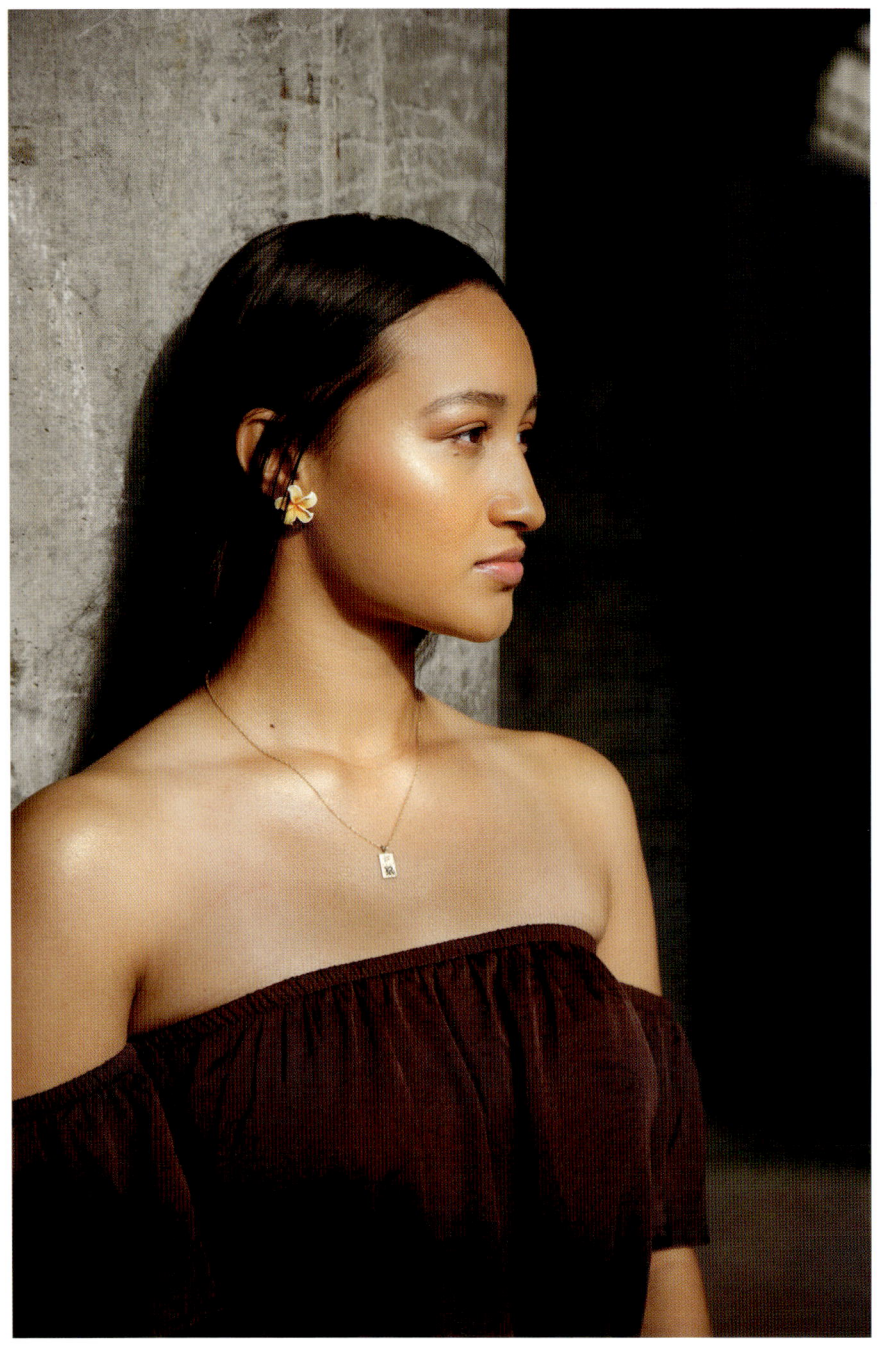

Evaluating Photographs

When I realized that my goddaughter Maritza was graduating high school, I let her know that I would be making her senior portraits. I playfully told her that I would be the photographer, or else there would be some serious consequences. I had made photographs of her throughout her young life, but I had never done a proper portrait sitting with her. I knew that at this pivotal moment I wanted to do that, and I wanted to do it right.

When I thought of the photographs, I immediately knew what I did not want. I did not want to create cliché graduation photos with her in a cap and gown in front of a white seamless backdrop, or with cheesy poses in the park. When her mother suggested a nearby park for the photographs, I immediately nixed the idea.

Unfortunately, they lived in a community largely made up of residences and strip malls—not the most inspiring locations for an outdoor portrait session. Though I knew beaches offered the possibility of their own cliché imagery, I agreed to just such a location that allowed us to take advantage of the late afternoon light.

I had to admit I was a bit nervous. Though I had photographed countless people over the years, including a number of celebrities, I wanted these images to be special. I knew that Maritza and her family would look at these images years from now. They would be an important way of remembering this time in her life. For myself, I wanted to create more than just pretty photographs. I wanted a series of portraits that captured not only my goddaughter's natural beauty, but the strength and character she embodied. I wanted photographs that reflected how I saw her as a young woman.

When we arrived at the beach, I was thankful to see a pier and an area just beneath it where we could begin to work. One of my big concerns was finding nothing more than the open beach with which to work. As beautiful as that could be at dusk, I wanted more to work with and the pier provided that.

Despite my nervousness, I fell back on evaluating the scene using the visual draws. The familiar workflow of evaluating and parsing a scene put me into a groove that raised my confidence level.

The area beneath the pier produced elements of light and shadow that I am always looking for when searching for a photographic setting. I do this all the time for my street photography, but it is especially important to me when making portraits. I have learned that the setting is often as important as the subject itself for a good photograph.

The sky was partly cloudy, making the late afternoon light relatively soft. However, the sun was strong enough to produce pronounced shadows. I noted how the light illuminated some of the pillars and then fell off into shadow further along beneath the pier. The lines, shapes, and textures of this area added a wonderful presence to the composition.

I asked Maritza to pose against a pillar and relax. I did not want her to force a smile or affect a pose. I wanted her to be present with me and not think that she had to force anything for the camera. I directed her to look off-camera and to relax.

When I reviewed the initial images on the camera's LCD screen, I knew that this was going to be a good session. Even though these were the very first images of the afternoon, I recognized that I would have all the elements I have come to rely on for making a good portrait. With my quick parsing of the scene and handling of my technical settings, I was able to focus my complete attention on her, offering subtle suggestions for her body language and expression.

As we found different locations and she changed her outfits, I fell back into my visual workflow of discovering the setting first and then figuring out my technical settings. Each new location resulted in very different photographs that took advantage of different background elements including color, tones, and details. As I shared the images with her, she shook off her nervousness, becoming more relaxed and playful as time went on and the quality of the light improved.

It was a time that was more than just an opportunity to make nice photographs. It was a wonderful moment for us to get to know each other as adults. The images represented more than just a landmark moment in her life—they also represented the beginning of a change in how we saw and related to each other.

The Greatest Challenge

Though it may surprise many, the greatest challenge a photographer faces does not involve the creation of images. The real challenge begins when the photographer looks at the hundreds, if not thousands, of images that he or she has created and tries to figure out which ones are the best. It is this time that is especially critical for the photographer, because it is through this culling process that the photographer gets to truly define their vision.

This is a skill that few photographers learn. Though there are endless books and videos on the use of cameras, lenses, and Photoshop, there is very little on the subject of culling and editing images. So it is no surprise that many photographers struggle when it comes to looking through their day's shoot to try and figure out what images deserve the attention involved with post-processing, printing, and sharing.

Part of the difficulty lies in the fact that people are never taught how to critically examine a photograph. They know what they like and what they do not like, and the critique often ends there. Ask them to explain why they appreciate one image over the other, and they will respond with a comment about liking the color or the lighting. Ask them to compare two similar images of the same subject or scene, and the decision becomes all the more complicated and difficult. It is not so much that the person does not know what they like or dislike, but rather that they lack the vocabulary to explain why.

The concept of the visual draws provides you the means to do this. Just as legends help you to read a map, the visual draws provide you with the vocabulary and understanding to read and evaluate a photograph. The very qualities that helped you to make the photograph are the same things that help you to cull, select, and eventually edit your photographs.

While walking on the Hermosa Beach pier, I saw a young woman wearing stylish sunglasses (next page). After introducing myself and asking to make her portrait, I positioned her at the center of the pier facing the late afternoon sun. I framed her using the implied diagonals of the pier, which guide the viewer to her in the center of the frame. The color of her skin, sunglasses, and red lipstick contrasted nicely with the clear blue sky behind her.

Both she and her friends were caught by surprise by the idea of a stranger asking to make her photograph and they started laughing. In that moment, she turned in their direction. I dropped my camera position slightly to eliminate the presence of my shadow on her. I captured the genuine reaction to this awkward situation in which she found herself.

Both of these images have a lot in common with respect to the visual draws of light and shadow, line and shape, and color. But the thing that creates the biggest difference is the gesture. The first shot is a more straightforward portrait that is composed in a more balanced, critical way. The second image is a lot looser and, most importantly, captures a more genuine expression of spontaneous feeling and emotion. Though not as "perfectly" composed as the first image, I prefer the latter image because of that genuine expression of emotion.

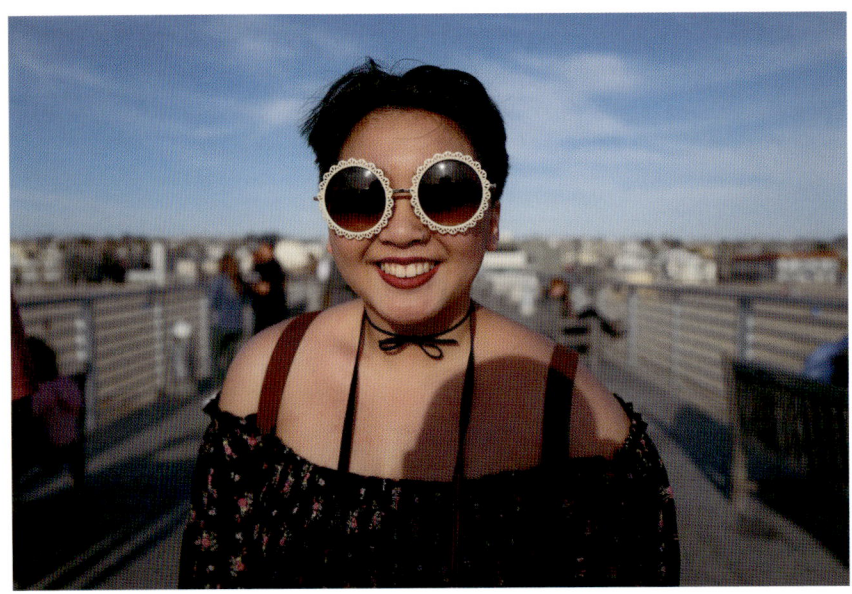

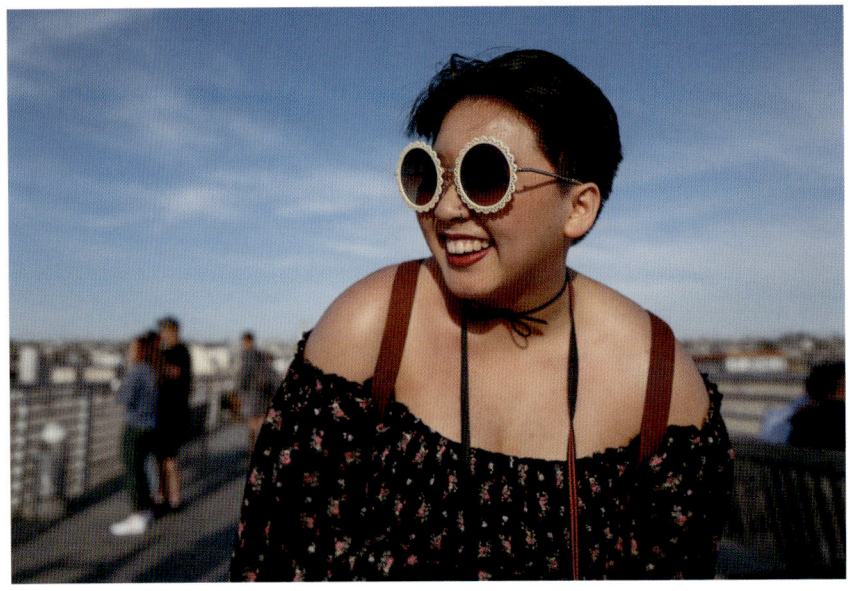

I had done much of the heavy lifting in figuring out the composition of the shot even before I asked the woman to make her portrait. I had considered where I wanted to place her in relation to the light and the pier. I chose a wide aperture to reduce the depth of field, emphasizing her and blurring the background. What followed was my effort to build rapport and watch for a sincere and honest expression. When it unexpectedly arrived in the form of her reaction to her friends, I was ready for it.

When you compare both images, you see a lot of little differences, even though the subject and the setting are exactly the same. Things such as the camera position, the relationship between the woman and the background, the turn of her head, and the reflection in her sunglasses all combine to create a very different experience of her in that moment, resulting in distinctly different photographs. Those little differences, however minor, are the qualities I often look for when comparing similar images and working toward the goal of finding the one image that works best.

Having Enough to Work With

Creating variations of a subject or scene sets the stage for successful culling of your photographs in the editing stage. You want to have a good number of images of the same subject or scene to compare and contrast so that you can determine which images work best. If you have just one photograph, that sole image is your only opportunity to succeed or fail. If my experience is any indicator, the greater the variety of images that I have of a moment, the greater my chances are that I have captured a worthwhile moment in a wonderful way.

To have a sense of what your approach is, you need not look any further than your digital contact sheet. As you look through your thumbnails, examine how many images you made of a given subject or scene. If you made only one, two, or three images before you moved on to the next moment, you are not seeing carefully enough. And I can say with all confidence that if you have been frustrated with your growth as a photographer and the quality of your images, your problem has nothing to do with the equipment that you were using. Your impatience and lack of careful seeing is what has really been hurting your growth as a photographer.

Having a variety of images to choose from provides you with your second opportunity to see the scene. The first time was when you made the photographs, when the whole world and everything in it was part of the moment. Your second pass has been filtered by your own seeing and when you pressed the shutter-release button. This paring things down from moment to moment helps you to find the gems in the rough.

Not every moment will provide you with the luxury of multiple takes, but many of the moments that are presented to us as photographers do. You have to learn to take advantage of them.

Combatting Impatience

We are incredibly impatient animals. In an age of microwave ovens, two-day shipping, and fast food, we have been convinced that fast and convenient is the best way to experience something. When it comes to photography, that is rarely true. A common mistake is made when we treat photography in the same way we order and eat a fast-food meal. It may be momentarily satisfying, but it rarely provides us with what we need over the long-term.

The importance of slowing down and exhausting the possibilities of a scene or moment are going to be clearly evident to you when you sit down to begin the culling process. Too few images, and you are simply on the hunt for the images in which luck was the real arbiter of whether or not you produced a good image. However, if you fully explore a scene for all its possibilities and make informed choices about how you compose each frame, you should be able to produce a series of images, each of which possesses major or minor differences that help differentiate it from the next. This increases the likelihood of producing an exceptional photograph. It is in this way you that you create photographs based more on skill and experience, rather than expensive technology and dumb luck.

This was the approach I took when photographing two young men passing a ball between one another in Hermosa Beach (next page). After initially evaluating the scene using the visual draws, I figured out how I wanted to render the scene as the young men played. I wanted to photograph their figures as silhouettes and enhance the colors and shapes provided by the late afternoon light. After setting my exposure and getting a rough sense of where I needed to photograph from, I began shooting.

My focus was primarily on trying to time the placement of the ball. I wanted it to be near one young man's head and to be cleanly defined against the blue sky. By keeping both eyes open, I was able to see the ball just before it came into the frame. More often than not, I was able to get the ball in a good place within the frame.

However, the other people that moved through the scene were another consideration for me. Because there were so many people in the background, there were many frames where the outline of the young man's body bled into another figure. Such juxtaposition took away from the gesture that his body provided each time he took to the air to head-butt the ball back to his partner. On top of that, the young men kept shifting position up and down the courtyard, forcing me to constantly change my position and reestablish my frame.

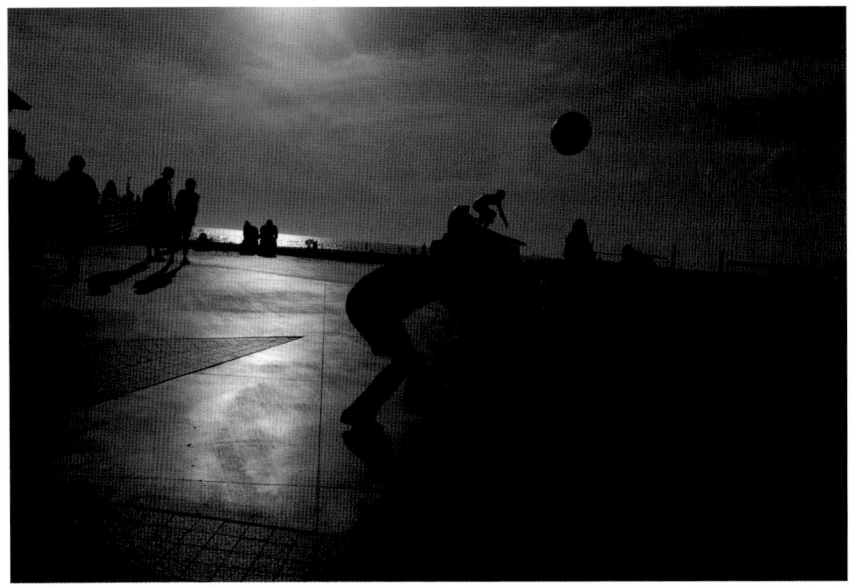

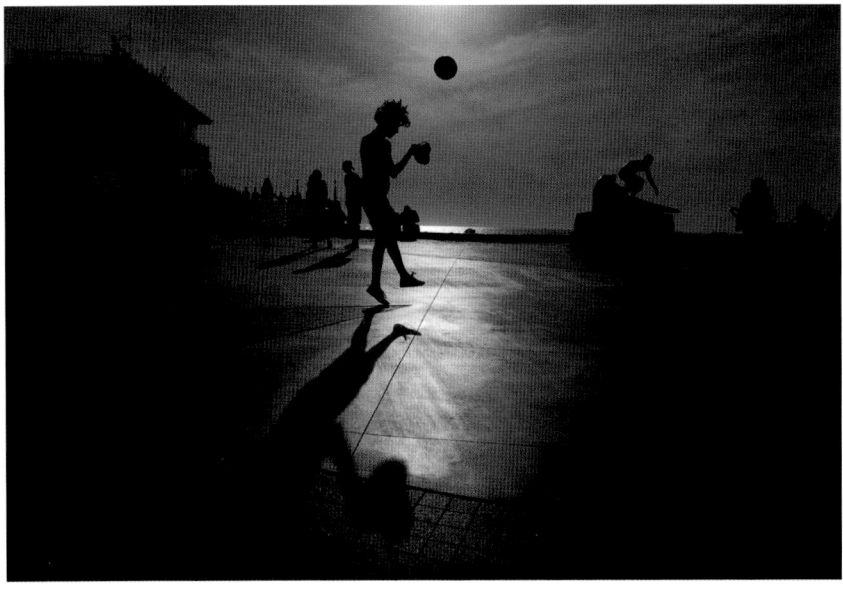

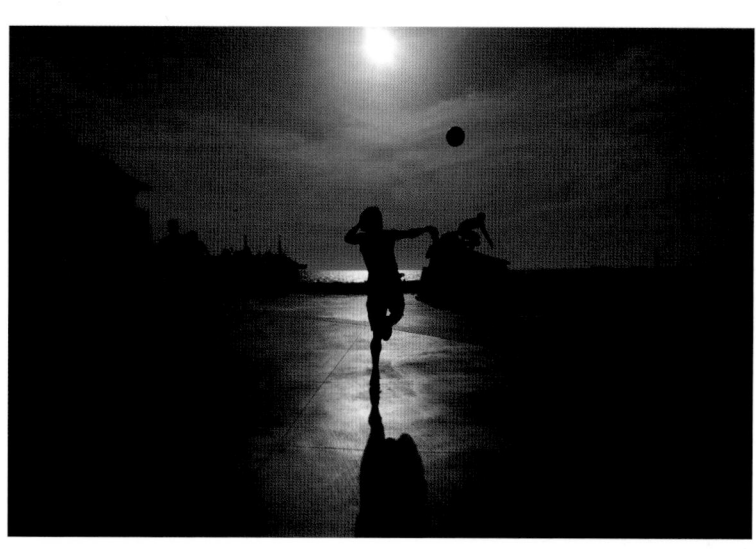

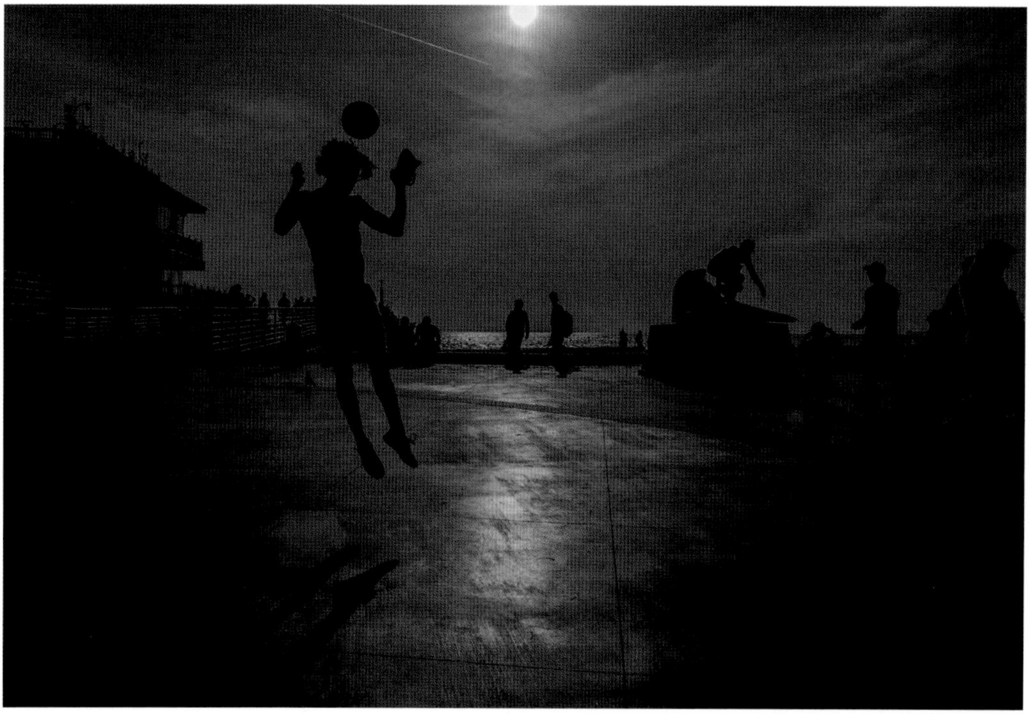

This dance that we were performing with each other made it a great challenge, but I persisted, knowing that there was a good shot to be had. As you can see in these examples, there were many images that came close, but because of framing or bad juxtapositions they did not work. However, I was able to finally settle on a single frame that I felt embodied much of what I was going for.

Like the photograph of the young woman with the sunglasses, the images of the ball players are similar. The light, shadow, and colors are relatively consistent. There are slight differences in line and shape due to camera position and framing. But just like the portrait, the critical elements that make the biggest difference for me are the gestures and the small details I described.

Succeeding in having that single frame would likely not have happened had I only made one or two frames. I understood that I not only needed to make a number of photographs, but that I had to be constantly assessing and reassessing my frame and making informed choices about what to change. If I were to succeed, I had to be completely focused on seeing with a keen eye and not giving up prematurely.

As much as embracing the concept of the visual draws help you to produce better compositions, it is going to be this process of exhausting the possibilities of a moment that helps you when evaluating your photographs. When you use the principles of the visual draws in the creation of your images, you begin the process of discerning the real potential of a scene and how it translates into a photograph. When it comes time to review the photographs on your computer, they will hopefully reaffirm those choices and free you to look for the small differences that bring a photograph to life.

Visual Stepping Stones

When actively seeing, you as the photographer are refining your vision. You are figuring out what elements need to remain in the frame and what needs to be eliminated. You are considering how light, shapes, color, and gesture help or hinder your ability to create the image that you have imagined in your mind's eye. You are leaving less to chance and increasing the likelihood that you produce exceptional photographs.

As the image that begins this chapter illustrates, I was able to produce a final image that I was pleased with as a result of carefully parsing the scene based on the principles of the visual draws. I slowly built my image by analyzing the elements that were fixed in place as well as the fluid elements that changed from frame to frame.

When I was evaluating each image of that series, I was not only looking for the one image that best represented the moment, but I was also confirming my thought process and the choices I made while I was shooting. Those "failed" images were valuable to me for reinforcing the ideas and concepts that have formed my beliefs about what makes an image fail and what makes another succeed.

Each photograph, especially those that fell short, reaffirmed the importance of the small details, those almost insignificant flourishes that allow a photograph to succeed. These are my visual stepping stones.

In the series of images on the following pages, I photographed a scene at the Goodwill Center in Los Angeles where customers were sorting through bins of donated clothes. Clothes that for a variety of reasons do not sell in the Goodwill retail store are offered to the public for sale at a discounted price. Many people sort through the bins looking for items they believe they can resell privately.

When a new bin is rolled out, dozens of people are waiting to dive into the bins looking for items they deem valuable. I intended to capture the frantic energy of that moment and positioned my camera with a wide-angle lens at about waist level.

I composed the photograph to include the pile of clothes as well as the people sorting through it. The overall composition included several people within the frame, but emphasized two figures that I framed in the foreground.

As I shot, I paid attention to the body language and gestures of those two figures as they dug through the clothes. I looked for a moment when both produced gestures that complimented each other and provided a nice graphic dynamic to the frame. I consciously exposed each frame, rather than riding the shutter-release button in a continuous-high drive mode. I wanted to anticipate the moment and not rely on the camera to hand it over to me.

When I culled through the images, I could see that I had correctly considered all the important elements. My camera settings and the compositional choices had gotten me the majority of the way there. Now I was looking for that final flourish that would make the image stand out, and it was knowing that I was looking for small gestures that freed me to readily recognize them when I saw them. The image of the man sending a piece of pink fabric into the air while the woman was doing the same with a blue article of clothing provided me a mirrored gesture that strengthened the core of the entire composition.

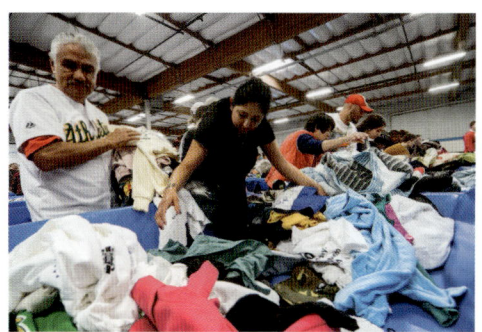
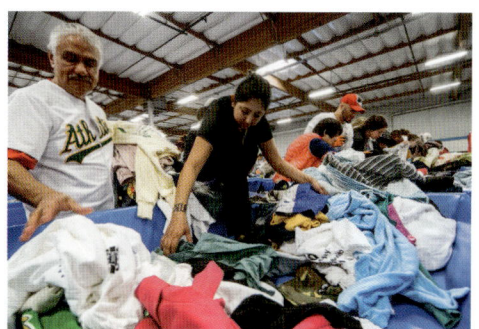

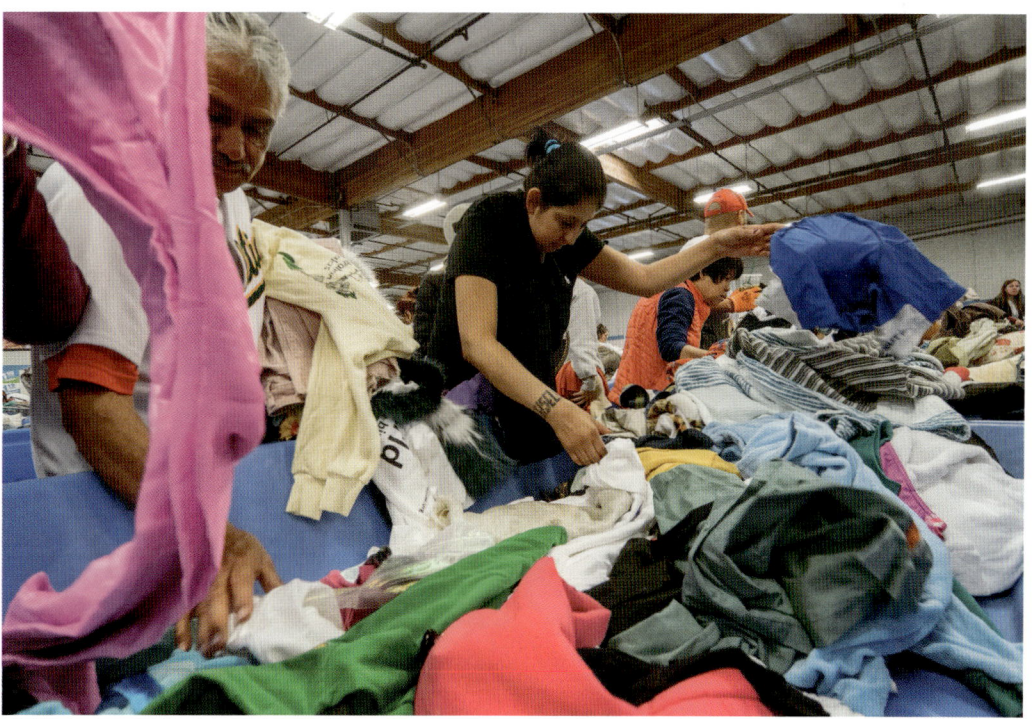

"Having a variety
of images to choose
from provides you
with your second
opportunity to
see the scene."

The Role of the Critic

Each person has the voice of the critic inside them. I am not talking about the harsh critic that tells us that our images suck and that we should never have picked up a camera in the first place. You should relegate that guy to the dust heap. I am instead talking about the informed critic, the fellow who carefully examines an image and judges its effectiveness based on solid and repeatable criteria. You may not be familiar and completely confident with this voice, but given time and practice, it will be a natural extension of your creative process.

There is one caveat, however. The voice of the critic, while important, should only be present when it is time to cull and edit your photographs. That same critic should not play a role when you are actively creating your photographs. If you are taking photographs and repeatedly chimping on the back of your camera's LCD, making judgements about the worthiness of your photographs, that is a mistake. You are introducing the critic prematurely and it will only succeed in interrupting, if not stifling, your creativity.

As the images of the two boys earlier in this chapter illustrated, I made a series of photographs, most of which did not work and did not fulfill my vision for the scene. I did not allow those initial images to dissuade me from shooting further. I did not use each unsuccessful image to question my skills as a photographer or to grow frustrated that the moment did not happen with a single frame. Instead, I focused completely on allowing the moment to play out.

Had I given up prematurely, I would not have that final image. If I had made one or two photographs, I would have a picture, but it would not have been an image that I considered successful. I was there to make photographs and make the best photographs I was capable of. It was not a time for making harsh judgements over how I was seeing and how I made photographs. Rather, it was about being fully in the moment and making changes and refinements as the moment changed fluidly and naturally in front of me.

The voice of your critic, if it is anything like mine, strives for perfection. However, that is completely antithetical to the creative process. When you are in the midst of creating, making your photographs, you have to be in a mental space where you embrace the risk of failure. You want to take chances, experiment, and do things that are uncomfortable, because those choices produce unexpected and welcome surprises that help spur your creativity even further. If you are simply duplicating what you have done successfully before, there is no creativity in that. There is no spark of inspiration or innovation. At that point, you are a technician rather than an artist.

So, remember to distinguish between the times when you welcome the critic into your creative process and the times when its feedback is a hindrance.

Take some time to go through some recent photo shoots and examine how long you lingered on a scene or subject. Assess how many images, on average, you produced when making photographs of a new subject. Also, examine what different choices you made in pursuit of your best photograph.

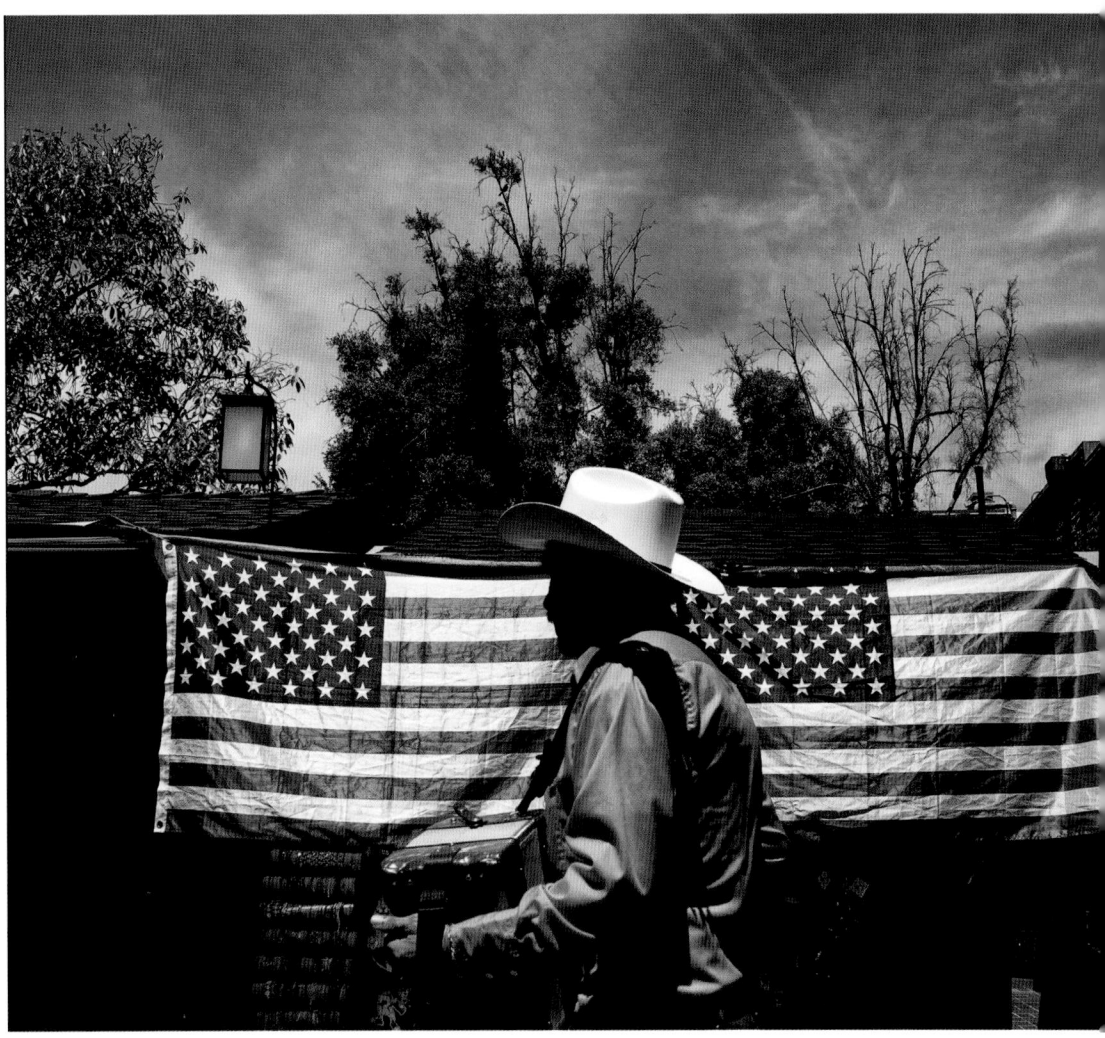

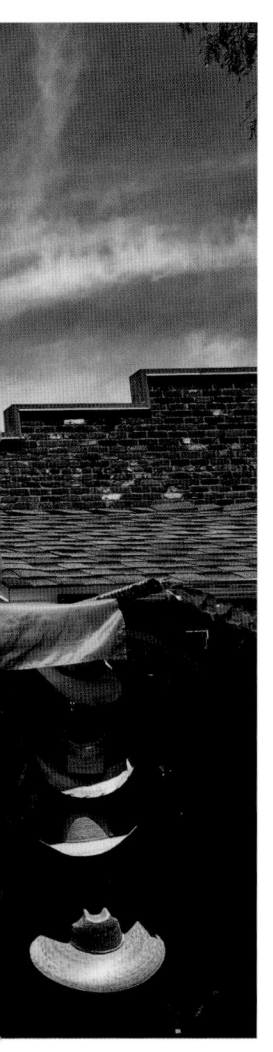

Culling

It was a day when I took several photographers out for a small photo workshop. Rather than drive, I decided to take the metro, which conveniently dropped me off at Union Station, a beautiful and iconic railway station built in 1926. It is located blocks away from City Hall, Little Tokyo, Chinatown, and Olvera Street.

I directed the photographers to wander about Olvera Street, which is home to some of the city's oldest buildings, dating back to when California was still part of Mexico. Though it caters to countless tourists, it is still a thriving community of Latino immigrants. In the neighborhood is a Catholic church with a beautiful courtyard, where I have witnessed many baptisms, weddings, and quinceañeras.

I was not feeling especially good that day as I was recovering from a recent flare up of sciatica. Though I was able to walk short distances again, I had not built up to my usual stamina. I almost cancelled the outing, but I knew that I would do myself no favors by staying home and working at the computer. It would be good to get out, socialize, and hopefully make a few images.

I walked down the center of the main corridor that is Olvera Street, whose spine is made up of vendors selling colorful piñatas, peasant garb, maracas, oversized sombreros, pottery, bull horns, and sweets. Aromas emanated from the several restaurants that are located there, triggering my appetite.

I felt the need to sit down and I found an empty bench. As I did, I saw a vendor across from me who had positioned two American flags hanging from the roofline. They were there to provide shade.

I noticed the clouds in the sky, the various rooflines, and a vertical row of hats. I was particularly struck by the quality of light. The sun produced strong, hard shadows. While they obscured the details within the vendors' stations, they made the shapes and patterns more pronounced. I fully recognized the potential of the scene.

Without rising from my seat, I figured out what my overall composition needed to be. I also determined that I wanted to purposely bias my exposure for the highlights and allow the shadows to go to complete black to emphasize the contrast. I was already thinking of the photograph as a black-and-white image.

Once I figured out my overall composition, I knew I needed some human figures within the frame to complete the shot. As peopled walked past, I examined how the light fell on them. I discerned that when people walked from left to right, their faces were better illuminated by the sun, and when they walked in the opposite direction, their faces were often obscured by shadow. I figured out approximately where I wanted a person (or people) to be in order to balance out with everything I had already positioned within the composition.

As people passed by, I made photographs, many of which did not work. Sometimes people were not in the right position; other times they were clustered too close together. Sometimes my timing was just off. But with each exposure, I had a keener sense of what I needed and where I needed it to be.

A group of mariachis walked into the scene from the left, but as much as I would have loved for them to complete my frame, they were walking too close together. The image I captured failed to clearly define them. It just did not work.

Moments later, one of those same mariachis walked back through the scene, now by himself and moving in the opposite direction. I knew he was exactly what I was looking for. I made two frames, the second of which perfectly situated him between the two flags. The strong graphic of his hat created a dramatic visual draw because of its brightness and contrast, and it served as the perfect anchor for the image. The presence of the accordion in his hands provided the gesture that completed the story of who he was and what role he played in this classic location.

My Personal Culling Process

Culling refers to the practice of browsing through images and selecting the best photographs from a shoot or assignment. Different photographers have different approaches for doing this, and the process I describe in this chapter is my personal approach. Feel free to adopt any or all of the steps that I explain here as part of your own workflow.

Adobe Lightroom, despite its recent improvements, can be slow to render images. So unless you have a newer computer that performs speedily, you may want to consider investing in Photo Mechanic, which provides the fastest means by which to cull through imagery. I find it invaluable when having to sort through hundreds of images from a shoot. Photo Mechanic can communicate with Lightroom so that your rankings translate from one to the other. The only exception to this is the pick flag, so if you do use Photo Mechanic, you should use a color ranking, such as green or yellow, to mark which images you have selected as part of your first pass.

The First Pass

Once I download my photographs to my computer, I sort through my images to determine which images have proved the most successful. Though I primarily use Photo Mechanic and Adobe Lightroom, the principles I share with you can be applied to any photo software that offers a ranking and rating system. As long as you can quickly move from image to image and rate them in one form or another, the information shared here should apply. The following instructions reference my approach using Adobe Lightroom Classic.

When I look at images on Instagram or on a photographer's website, I flick from image to image, waiting for something to arrest my attention. This is the same approach I follow when sorting through my own images for the first time. Using the Library module in Lightroom, I browse from image to image, assigning a rank to those that peak my interest. In Lightroom, I assign a pick flag by pressing the P key on my keyboard. I then move to the next image by clicking on my keyboard's right arrow key.

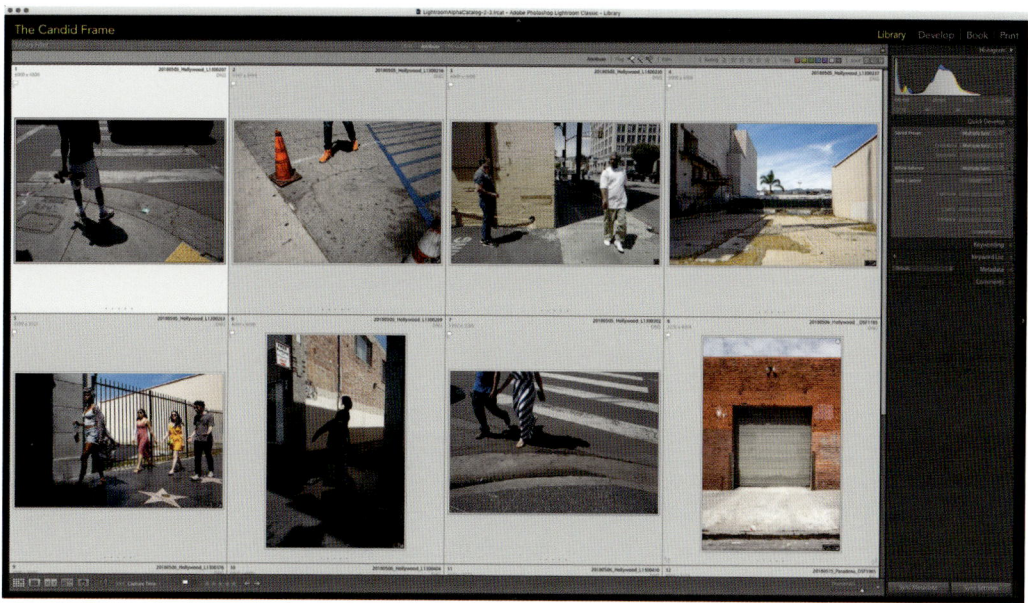

By quickly culling through the images in this way, I view my photographs from a point of view that is as objective as possible. I may want to linger and explore individual photographs, or even begin post-processing them, but I resist the temptation. I want to pare down my imagery to a manageable amount first, and this is just the first step in that process.

If I have practiced actively seeing while shooting, I usually know which images I want to initially consider. The photographs that I know do not work, I pass over. If there are images that are very similar, and I am not sure which is better, I simply assign the pick flag and keep moving through the photographs. I can determine which is the better image during a second or third pass. For my first pass, I want to get through all the photographs as quickly as possible.

Once I have completed the first pass through my images and assigned them a basic rating, I filter out the other images so that I see only my selects. To do this, I remain in the Library module and press the backslash key on my keyboard to open the Library Filter bar at the top of the screen. I then click on Attribute, which reveals the various rating methods including flags, stars, and colors. Because I used the pick flag for my first pass, I click the pick flag icon, which filters through all the images I am currently looking at and edits out all the images to which I have not assigned a pick flag. This is my first pass.

Before sorting through these images again, I create a collection of the first pass images. To begin this process, I remain in the Library module and move to the far left of the screen where my Collections tab is located. I click on the plus sign to the right of it, select Create Collection Set from the menu, and give the collection set a name that reflects the subject of the shoot. This creates a parent folder (collection set) where each pass of my images will be gathered into separate subfolders (collections), providing me with a single location to sort through the various stages of my culling process.

I will then select all (Command + A) the images that are currently in view and which are flagged in the Library module. I move the cursor to the far left of the screen where my Collections tab is located, click on the plus sign to the right of it, and select Create Collection. In the Create Collection dialog, I check the box next to Inside a Collection Set and select the collection set I created for this particular shoot. I will name this group 1st pass and click Create. This folder will contain all the images to which I have assigned a flag rating, and will be nested inside the collection set I selected.

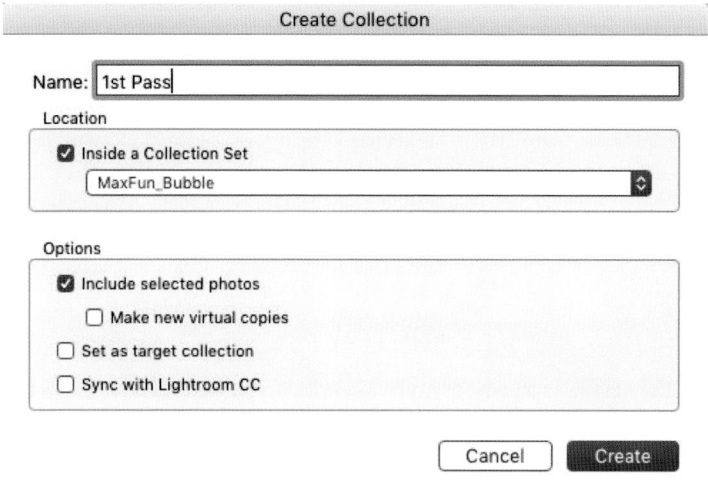

The Second Pass

It is at this point that I look through images from the shoot and select an anchor image. This is the one image that I believe is the standout image of the shoot. It is the photograph that I compare the other photographs against while considering another level of ranking.

After completing the first pass, it is relatively easy to find this singular anchor image, to which I apply a single star rating. The anchor image has then been assigned both a pick flag and a single star rating.

While still in the Library module, I select the anchor image, and then press the C key on the keyboard. This launches the Compare View, in which you will see two screens. The anchor image (the Select) appears on the left and the next photograph in the collection (the Candidate) appears on the right. Hitting the right arrow key cycles through each remaining photograph. I press the left arrow key to go in the other direction.

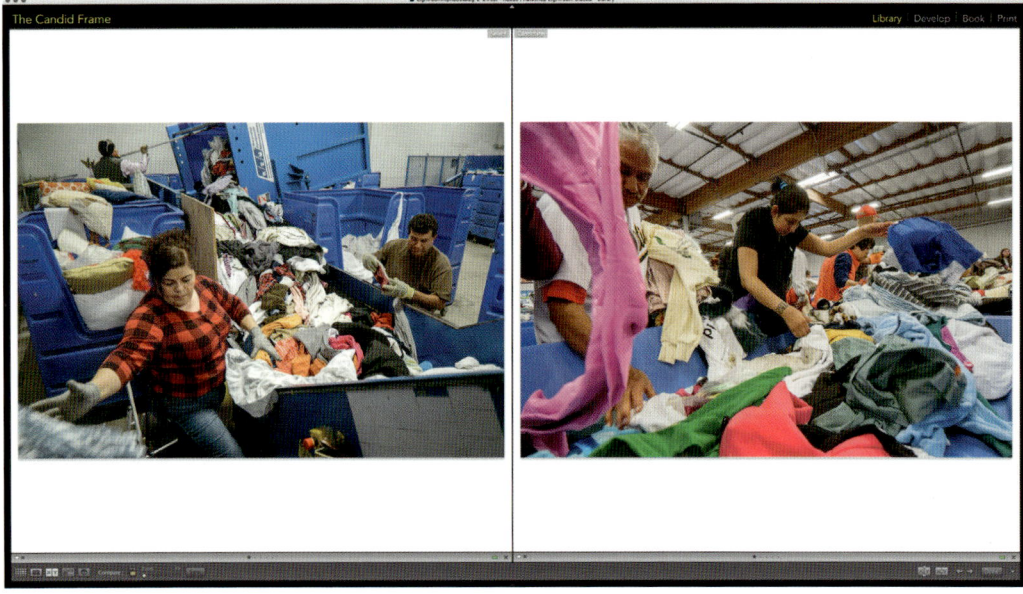

The question I ask myself at this stage of culling is whether the second image I am considering is comparable in quality and content to the anchor image. If the answer is no, I continue on to the next photograph. If the answer is yes, I will single-click on the image on the right and assign it a single star. Now two images have been flagged and possess a single star.

This is, of course, a very subjective decision that is based on more than just how effectively I composed using the visual draws or whether I captured a great gesture. I am now measuring the image in a more emotional, intuitive way. By comparing my images to the anchor image, which I know is the best image of the shoot, I have to consider more than whether an image is technically sound, which the majority of images in my first pass should be. This is more of a gut reaction to the photographs, made easier because I have pared down the images to a manageable amount.

Choosing Among Like Images

As I move through this culling process, I may find that in my first pass, I selected a sequence of images that are very similar to each other. They may possess only small differences in lighting or composition. To narrow my choice, I will return to the Grid View in the Library module and select all the similar images that I have flagged. I then press the N key to launch Lightroom's Survey View, which displays large thumbnails of the selected images.

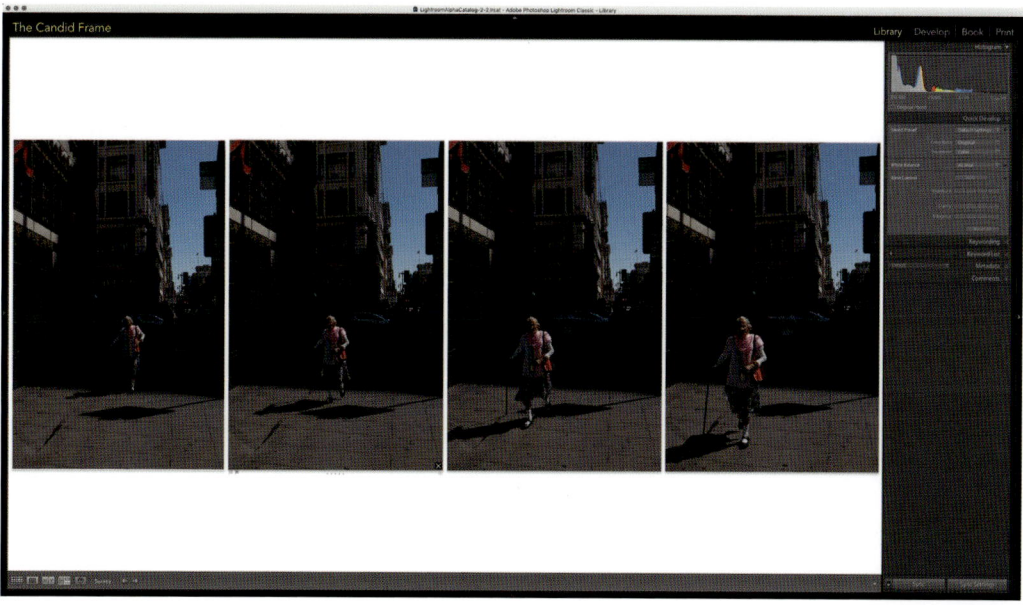

I evaluate and compare each version of the image and when I find the one that I believe is the weakest, I click on the X icon that appears in the lower-right corner of the displayed image. This image will be removed from the Survey View. The remaining images may shift slightly in position and possibly become larger in appearance. I continue to compare and contrast the photographs until I have selected a single photograph. I assign that final image a single star. Once I have finished evaluating this group of images and assigned one of the images a star, I move on to the next similar group of images and continue the process.

When I am finished assigning star ratings, I return to the Grid View, click on Attribute in the Library Filter bar at the top of the screen, and click on the single star icon. Only those images that have received a single star will be displayed. I then select all the thumbnails, create a new collection, and name it 2nd Pass. In the Create Collection dialog, I make sure to click on the checkbox next to Inside a Collection Set, and then select the collection set I created earlier from the drop-down menu.

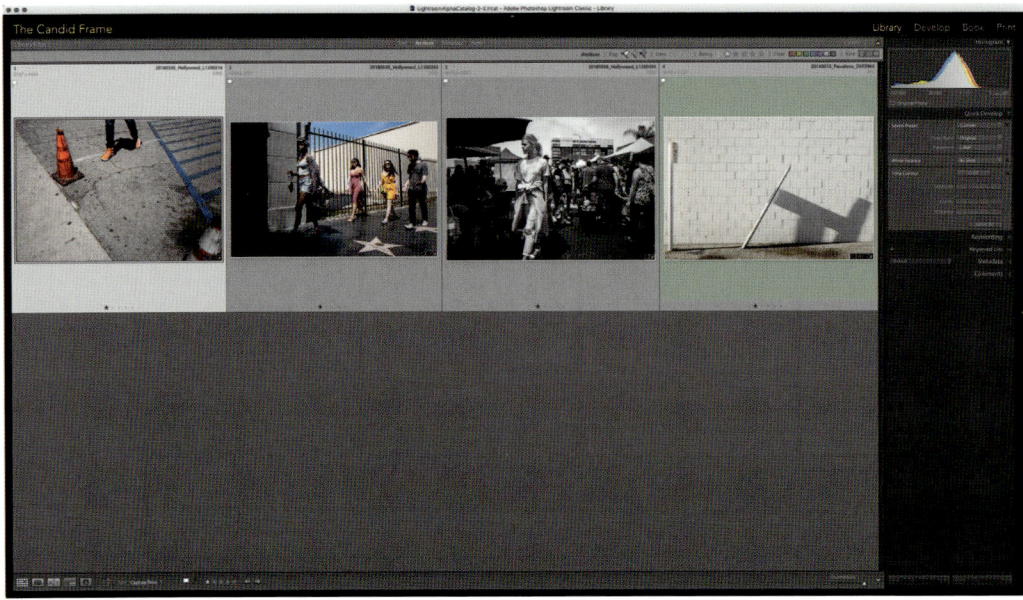

I now have both a first pass and second pass edit in my collection set. I will see an image count to the right of each collection and there should be a marked decrease in the number of images from the first pass to the second.

The Third Pass

Though I am sorting through fewer images on my third pass, I sometimes find this phase of the culling process the most difficult. This requires me to go deep into the weeds of what differentiates one image from another to settle on which ones are really the best. However, I avoid worrying about this too much. The great thing about this process is that I can always revisit my choices later. This is one of the reasons I create collections for each phase of my culling process; I can always return to any phase of this process and revisit the images to determine whether I made a mistake or overlooked an image.

That said, I challenge you to make those difficult choices and keep the process moving. If you make the mistake of getting stuck on an image for too long, you will likely not be able to get out of the hole that you are digging for yourself. Part of the culling and editing process is developing your ability to make these hard choices. Though you may not have a lot of confidence as you begin this process, your confidence will increase and you will develop a clearer vision of your own photography.

With this third pass, I will assign a second star to the images I choose and organize them into a collection of images that I label 3rd Pass. I again use the Compare and Survey Views in Lightroom to determine which images deserve a second star rating. I find that the Survey View is incredibly helpful when I am comparing one image against another.

By this time, my goal is to pare my images down to what I call the core eight. These are the best of the best. This pass really forces me to consider every aspect of an image, including the technical quality, the composition, and my emotional reaction to it.

I decided on eight images because I imagined laying out a mini portfolio with a lead image, a closing image, and three sets of paired images in between. I found that if I could create a strong mini portfolio with eight photographs, I could later expand from there to any number of images, but I would always reference back to the established strength of my initial eight-image portfolio.

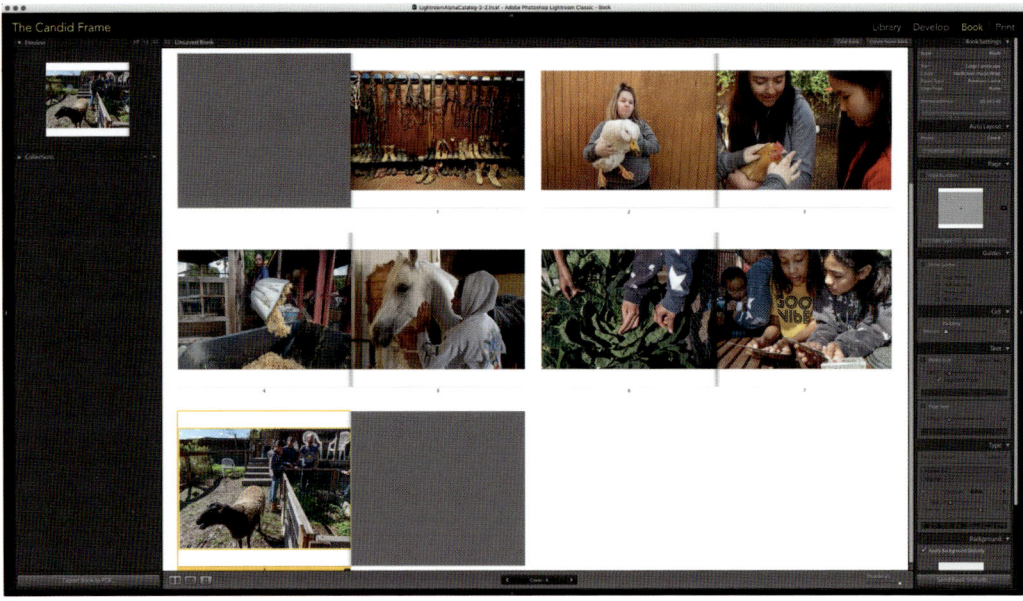

It is usually at this point that I begin to consider how well I did with my shoot. It is these select images that really reflect everything I was trying to do. These are the photographs that truly reflect my abilities, skill, and thoughtful seeing. If I passed judgement based on every single image I made, I would likely not think much of myself.

But by filtering through all the "work images"—the photographs that I had to make to get to the photographs that really worked—I am able to eliminate the wheat from the chafe. These final photographs are the ones that truly represent my vision and my skill.

When working for a client, these are usually the images that I suggest my client consider as the best from the shoot. They might not agree, which is usually the case, but I can confidently explain why I believe these images to be the best.

For my personal work, these are the photographs I choose from when making prints, posting on my website or Instagram, or using photographs in a book or magazine article. The rest of the images are relegated to a hard drive not to be seen by anyone.

If you find yourself having to go through a fourth or even a fifth pass when culling through your images, you are likely not making the hard choices. You are only making more work for yourself. You want to move through images as quickly and easily as you do when you're viewing other people's images on Instagram or Facebook.

Keep the Bad Pictures

Though I will delete images that are severely out of focus or badly exposed, I usually keep all the images from my shoot. I do this because these images provide me valuable information that helps me to improve my skills as a photographer.

As I go through the process of culling and comparing images, I am assessing photographs for what makes them work and what makes them fail. I am noticing the small and large differences relative to the visual draws, as well as my own critical choices at the moment of exposure. I am learning from my own vision.

Doing this has taught me valuable lessons, including the importance of sticking to a scene long enough to exhaust all the possibilities. Mistakes in exposure or focus have taught me the importance of nailing my technical settings before I expose a single frame. Even photographs that failed completely have a lesson to teach for the next time I go out to photograph a similar scene. The process of culling through my images demands that I evaluate the photographs with the care and consideration that I applied when originally making the images.

Go through a recent shoot using the process described in this chapter. Remember to create distinct collections as you move through each phase of the culling process. Examine how fully you explored a scene and note what choices you made in your effort to produce the best photograph.

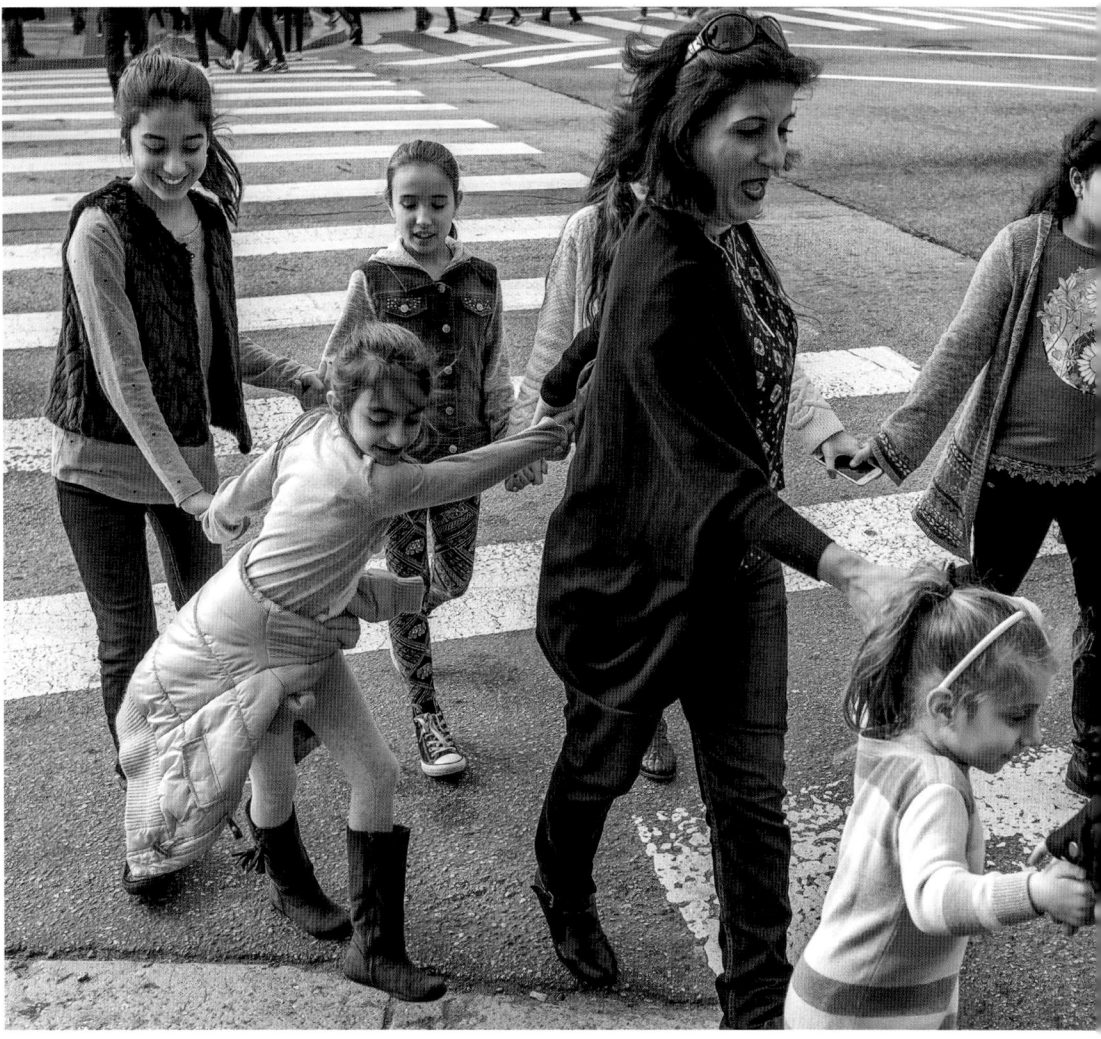

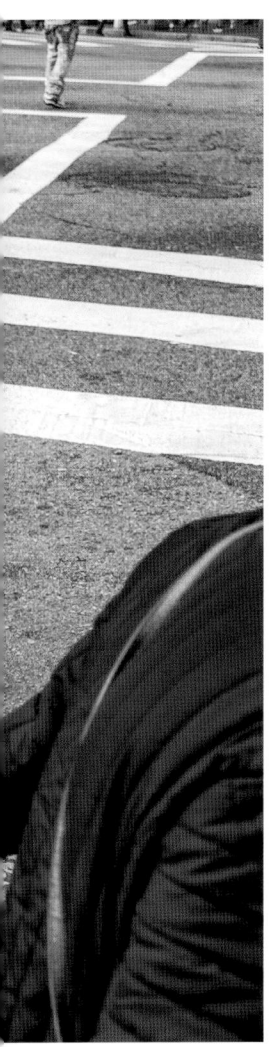

Collecting and Comparing

There are days when I am inspired to photograph because I want to see new images on my computer screen that are my own. I can quickly get frustrated when I see that my better images were created weeks or months ago. I do not just want to take photographs, I want to come back with images I've produced by challenging the way that I see.

On one of those days, I found myself in Hollywood, near the intersection of Hollywood Boulevard and Highland Street. It is a crazy location to photograph, largely due to the endless swarms of people, mostly tourists visiting this half-mile stretch of Los Angeles. It is home to the theater that hosts the Academy Awards, a portion of the Walk of Fame, and the theater that I still insist on calling Grauman's Chinese Theatre, though it has been known by several names since.

Being in an area with an abundance of people is often a good thing for the kind of photography I practice. However, the density of people in this small area makes it especially difficult to produce well-ordered compositions. Even with good light and an interesting subject, there is so much busyness that the likelihood of distracting elements increases exponentially.

As I had done previously, I staked out the intersection, which featured a diagonal crosswalk. Designed as a safety measure for pedestrians, these crosswalks allow people to cross a street diagonally as well as traditionally. It stops all automobile traffic while people make their way across.

I gravitated to such an intersection because it allowed me to produce photographs where the street itself would not be cluttered with automobiles, especially those white vehicles that I often find distracting in a composition. Most importantly, I could use the painted lines on the street as a graphic element in my composition. Even better, I could stake a claim on the sidewalk and allow subjects to come to me and to enter the stage upon which I intended to compose a photograph.

This is exactly what unfolded when I saw this group of women and girls entering the intersection. They were on the tail end of a wave of people crossing the street. They moved slowly because they were all holding hands as they crossed, creating an interlocked group. I loved the tenderness exhibited by the gesture and I wanted to capture that in a photograph.

I wanted to use the crosswalk pattern on the ground as leading lines for the composition, so I positioned myself near the spot where the group would step up onto the curb. I looked through my viewfinder as they were midway across the street and made the choice to tilt the camera down slightly to eliminate distractions at the top of the frame. I included the feet of the people who had already crossed the street, but I did not want see waiting cars or signage in the background.

As the women and girls moved into place, I made a sequence of images, observing each individual as they moved through the scene. There were eight of them in all, and I got as many of them as possible to be cleanly read in the composition. Their hands were of particular importance to me.

By the time they arrived at the ideal position, I only had time to make two frames. I could not resist the temptation to review my camera's LCD after I made the photographs. I needed to know that I had gotten the shot.

When I saw the image and realized that I had something special, I was both relieved and thrilled. I recognized that I had not only a good photograph, but a photograph that was much different than what I had created recently. It was a photograph that embodied the visual aesthetics I was always in pursuit of, but also revealed a moment of genuine human connection.

It became a benchmark image for me that year that I was always hoping to match or best. It was the kind of image that inspired me to get out as soon as possible to make more photographs.

Setting Goals

For years, I produced photographs for two primary reasons. The first was for the joy of making photographs. The second was to have images to illustrate the magazine articles and books I wrote. Both of these reasons provided me with the excuse to practice something I loved to do, but I did not give much consideration to the process beyond that.

I did have a desire to become a better photographer, but I did not think about how to quantify that. I might produce a truly exceptional image that I would sometimes use as the measuring stick for my improvement, but the reality was that I did not have a clear method for assessing my growth and development. Saying that I wanted to be better was not a clear enough goal.

One of my early goals was to become more adept at creating portraits of people. Though I had created street portraits of random strangers, I had little experience photographing a person for a formal portrait sitting. Rather than taking minutes to produce a portrait, I wanted to spend time with my subject and slowly draw them out for a more thoughtful and disciplined photograph.

The thought of this terrified me because although I had become adept at approaching strangers and producing photographs within a short period of time, I did not know how I would perform when I spent an hour with someone. Despite my fear, I knew I needed to do it.

So for a year, I solicited the help of friends and acquaintances to serve as my portrait subjects, often visiting them in their homes and studios to make their portraits. The aim was to create portraits in their personal environments using only available light. I wanted to use the sensibility I had practiced in the streets and bring it to my portrait sessions.

One of the photographs I made was of my friend Bill. We were attending a men's retreat when I spotted some dappled window light shining against a wall. He happened to pass by and I asked him to pose for me. During the short session, I directed him and tried to engage him, hoping to elicit something genuine from him in that moment that we shared together. I knew the light and the setting was good, but I wanted to be intentional about what I aimed to capture about him in that moment.

I have found Bill to be very sensitive and vulnerable, and I wanted to reflect that in some way in the photograph. He is a handsome man, but I did not want to rely on just his physicality to carry the photograph. As we were engaged with each other, I produced a sequence of photographs, and finally settled on the image on the following page, which I thought captured his complexity.

The images I produced throughout that year were about more than just aesthetics; they were about the experience I created for myself and my sitter. I wanted the images to reflect our time together and I wanted to feel that I had created more than just a pretty picture. This was a high bar that I did not always meet, but it helped me to maintain focus on what I was trying to do. My progress was not just measured by the number of images I created, but also by the increased confidence I felt when it came to this kind of photography.

In later years, I set many goals for my photography, with the most recent revolving around becoming more adept at creating more layered compositions. It is something I admire in other photographers and I have worked hard to achieve in my own work with a mixture of success. But as I evaluate my images over the course of a year, I have a keen awareness of whether I am being dutiful with improving my work in that way or if I am just repeating myself.

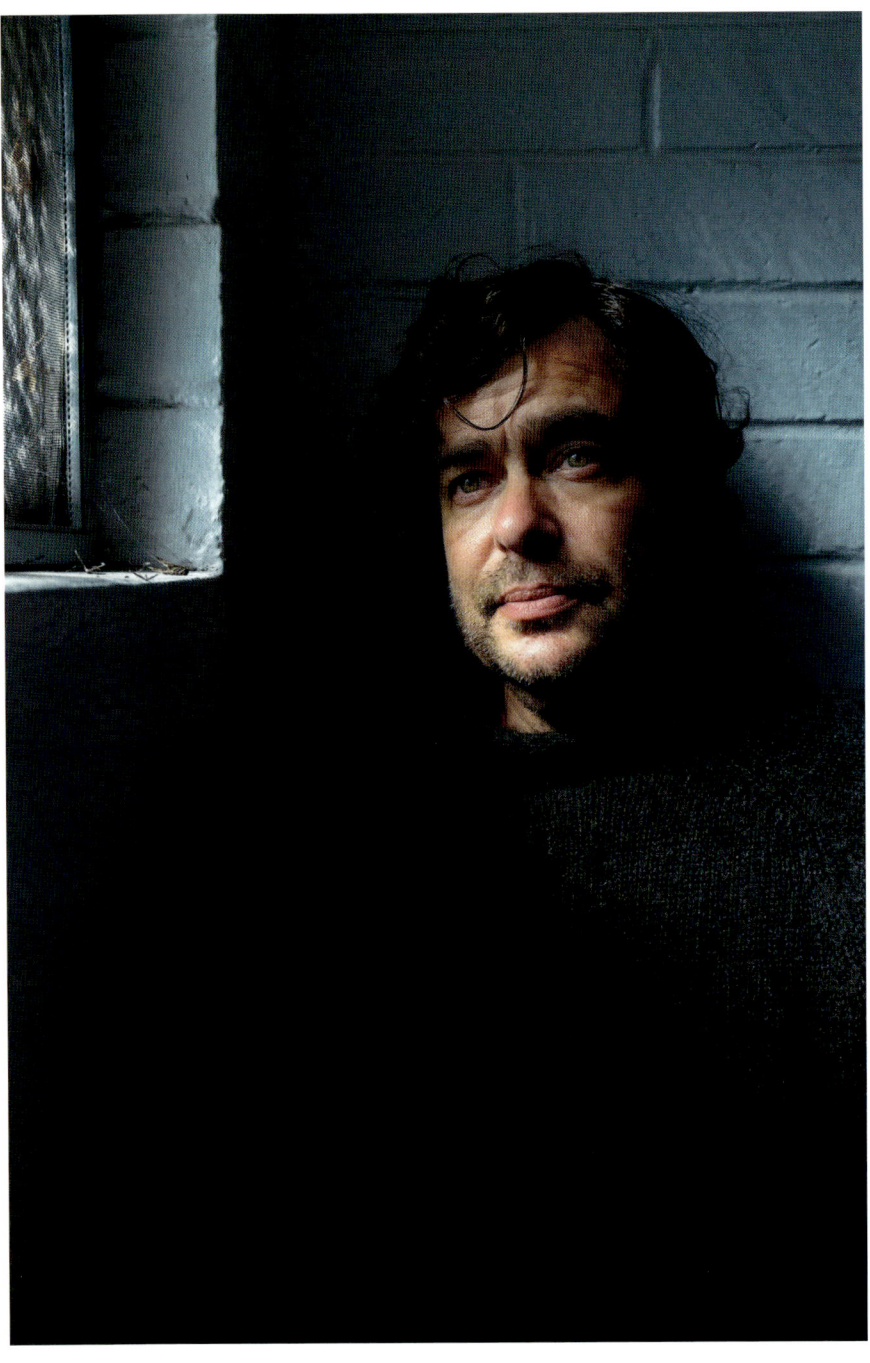

Measuring Progress

Whether they produce photographs consistently or intermittently, a question that each photographer asks themselves is whether or not they are improving. Am I getting better? Do I have talent? Am I developing a personal style?

The answers to these questions are often difficult ones because we are so intimately connected to the photographs we make. While it may be reasonably easy to turn a dispassionate eye to the work of others, it is an altogether different matter when it comes to passing judgement on our own photographs.

Nevertheless, serving as our own critic is an invaluable skill that each photographer needs to develop. Otherwise, we are subject to the taste and opinions of others, which can vary wildly. You need look no further than the Internet to see how a photograph you posted can evoke feelings of approval, dislike, or indifference, which often differs from your own feelings and opinions. Other people's opinions or comments can be helpful, but you as the photographer have to be the final arbiter of the photographs that represent who you are as an artist.

To do this, it is important to measure one's progress over time. By that I do not mean counting how many frames you have produced in a given year, but rather conducting a thorough assessment of your technical skills and your personal vision. This can be an incredibly difficult thing to do, but with the principles you have learned with respect to the visual draws, I believe you can begin to assess both individual photographs and a body of work.

It is important to schedule regular intervals during which you evaluate the images you have recently produced. By using the ranking system described in the previous chapter, you have the beginnings of a process for measuring both the quantity and quality of the photographs you have produced.

Organizing Images for Evaluation

People view and organize their images on their computers in a wide variety of ways. Some deposit all the images into a single folder and use keywords to find images, while others use a detailed folder structure that can include many subfolders. I currently use a hybrid of the two, but largely to take advantage of a system that allows me to evaluate my images throughout the year.

I organize my images by year and include subfolders for each month. Within those monthly folders, I create subfolders that represent the assignment or type of photography I practiced. I use a person's last name or the organization's name for the folder. If it is personal work, I create a subfolder identified as street photography, personal, etc.

Soon after the images are imported into their respective folders, I go through the process of flagging and rating my images. As described in the previous chapter, I favor using a picked flag for my first culling pass. I then sort through those flagged images to further refine my choices and assign a single star, thus reducing the total number of images. By my second and third pass, I have compiled a tight selection of images from the various shoots.

By culling my images and applying ratings to my favored photographs, I begin the process of determining which images represent my better work. And while some of those images may be printed or posted on social media, the real measure of them comes when I evaluate these photographs at the end of each quarter and at the end of the year.

After each quarter, I look at the photographs that I have favored in the previous three months and further refine my choices to select the best images. I have developed a particular method for gathering those images to help remove much of the heavy lifting when it comes to organizing and sorting them.

Using Lightroom Smart Collections

I have created an automatic process using Adobe Lightroom's smart collection feature to organize my images for evaluation. A smart collection is a collection of photographs that is compiled using metadata, keywords, and ratings. Rather than having to drag individual items into a collection, a smart collection does so automatically as I rank and rate images.

If you look in your Collections panel, you will see that Adobe has provided a few default smart collections in which images are collected because they have been flagged, rated with five stars, recently modified, or produced in the last month. You can also create new smart collections based on your own criteria. For example, I created a smart collection that is defined by images rated with two or more stars and a pick flag. Any image with these attributes will automatically be deposited into the designated smart collection.

The reason I find this automated process so helpful is that it is built on a process that I already practice when culling my images. I do not have to do additional work to organize these images; rather, it becomes a natural extension of what I am already doing. This is a big plus in my book.

Whatever criteria you use for creating smart collections is completely up to you. If you want to pull images that have three stars or higher, or have a particular color rating, or even those that possess particular keywords, you are at complete liberty to do so.

One of the ways I eliminate images that have been ingested previously is by creating smart folders for each year. This allows me to specify which folders are searched through when coming up with smart collections. This is especially important if, like me, you have tried a variety of rating systems throughout the years before settling on one. For example, I created a smart collection that collects photographs ingested into my 2018 folder, which have been rated with a pick flag and a single star.

I also created another folder where the criteria includes "has adjustments," which means that the image has been processed or edited in some way. Though I normally add an additional star rating to those images that I have processed, I sometimes forget to do so, making more work for me later. In this way, it is an automated process that reduces the amount of work I have to do to organize my images.

If you desire, you can further refine the selections to images that have been assigned two stars or a color rating. This system is completely flexible, and you should feel free to refine it in any way that works for you.

Quarterly Assessment

At the end of each quarter, I go through the images I have collected in that year's smart collection and begin to sort them. But before doing so, I select all the ranked images in that quarter and assign them a colored rating—e.g., green for first quarter, red for second quarter, etc. This helps me differentiate between the images that have been collected in that year's smart collection by quarter.

I then create collections that represent the types of photography I normally practice, such as portraiture, urban landscape, travel, or abstract. These are normal collections, not smart collections. I will organize these collections in a collection set called 2018 Culling, and I will precede the name of each one with the given year. This makes it easier should I ever use a keyword search.

I will then go through the new ranked images produced in that quarter and place them into the appropriate folders—portraiture, street photography, etc. So rather than just having all my ranked images in a single collection, I have them gathered in collections with like images. I do this for a variety of reasons. First, it gives me a sense of the kinds of images I have produced throughout the year. These categories reflect how I arrange the portfolios on my website, and since I am hoping to update my website at the beginning of the new year, this helps me to get ahead of the game with that.

Organizing my images in this way also gives me insight into whether I am actually meeting personal goals to produce particular types of images throughout the year. If I intended to produce more environmental portraits this year, a quick look at my portrait folder gives me important feedback as to whether I am meeting that goal or not.

As I look through these images and compare them, I can get a sense of what I am doing in each respective category. I can ask myself questions like: Do all these images look pretty much the same? Am I trying to push myself with my use of light, color, or composition? Am I seeing anything that surprises me? Am I not producing enough of a particular type of photography that I have been aspiring to do?

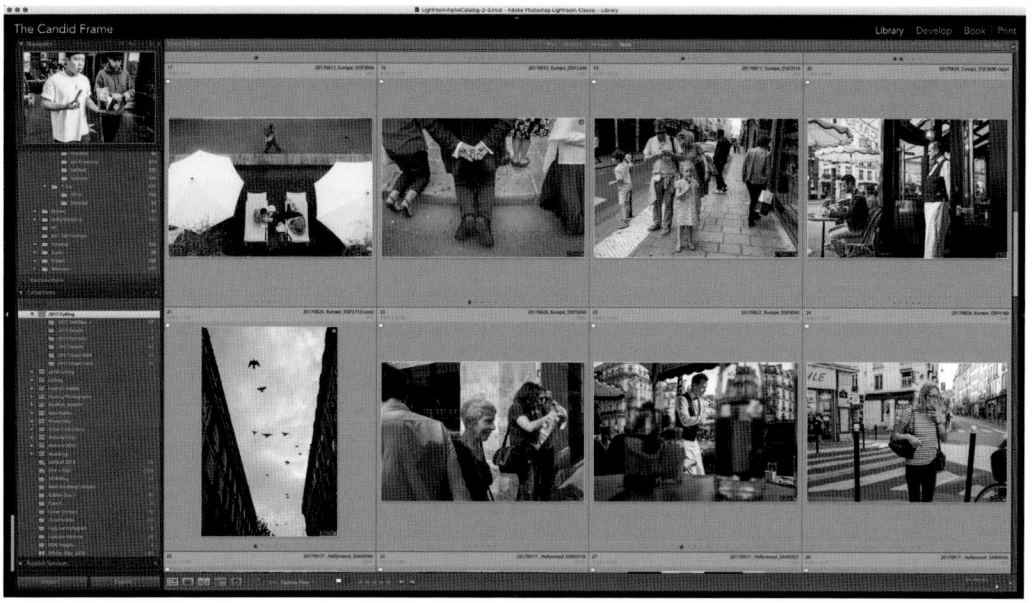

Looking at these categories at the end of each quarter provides me with a lot of information regarding the kinds of images I have produced, as well as whether or not I have met the goals I set for myself at the beginning of the year. I am often surprised midway through the year to see what I have been doing with respect to my photography. It can often light a fire beneath my butt to be more proactive about certain aspects of my work.

I will go through this process at the end of each quarter, giving me a solid foundation for assessing the best images of the year.

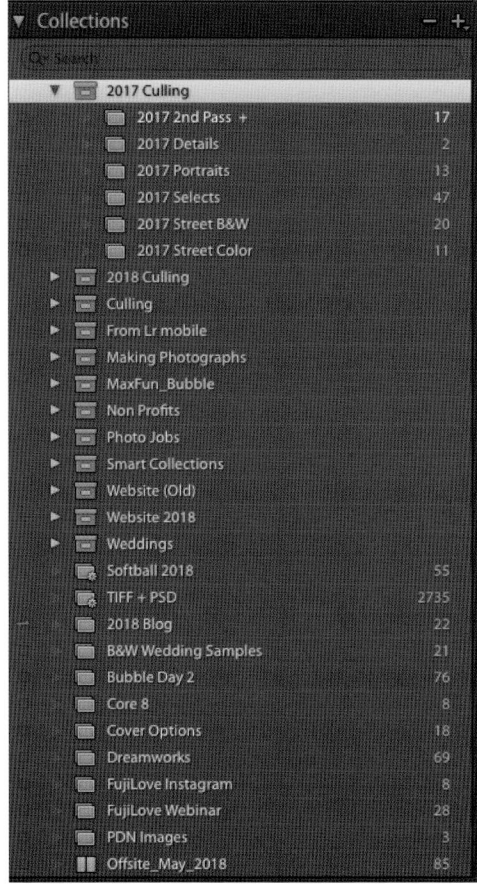

Selecting a Benchmark Image

After the year has ended, I will go through the images I have collected in these respective folders and further refine my ratings to determine which images will likely be included in my website update. To begin this process, I select a photograph in each folder that I describe as my benchmark image.

The benchmark image is the standout photograph, much like the anchor image used during the culling process. It is the image that I believe is the best photograph of its type that I have created and placed within this folder. It is the image against which all the other images will be compared. This is usually an easy thing for me to determine. Just looking through the thumbnails on my screen, I gravitate to the photograph that not only possesses almost all the visual draws to great effect, but that also resonates with me emotionally. I will assign that image another star rating. Depending on my culling process during the year, the benchmark image will have a total of two or three stars.

With my benchmark image selected, I will hit the C key on my computer to enter Lightroom's Compare View. My selected image (the benchmark photograph) will be displayed on the left and the other images in the folder will be displayed on the right, one at a time. I press the left or right arrow key to cycle through the other images in the folder so that I can compare each one directly to my benchmark photograph.

This is where I have to ask myself a hard question: is the image on the right as good or better than my benchmark image? I have to be brutally honest in my response in order to narrow down my selection of images. If I were completely in love with everything that I photographed, I would never get anywhere. This is really where the rubber meets the road with respect to my editing chops.

If the image ranks equal to or better than my benchmark image, I assign it another star by clicking on the image and hitting the 3 key on my keyboard. Now I have another image that has been assigned three stars. I go through all the images in that category and hopefully I'm able to pare down my images from their initial count.

Once I'm done, I go back to the Grid View, click on Attributes in the Library Filter bar, and filter my selection to those images containing three or more stars. I then select all of those images and create a collection called something like Portrait_2ndPass, Street_2ndPass, or Personal_2ndPass. I will repeat this process for each collection in which I have gathered images throughout the year.

Normally when I do this, I can get the number of images down to about a dozen in each category for that year. If not, I go through the images again until I have narrowed them down to a dozen. After this, I will do a final pass to select what I call my core eight images.

The Core Eight

Through my years of editing my images and helping others build their portfolios, I have felt that it is essential to build a body of work around a selection of core images. Core images are photographs that are the best of the best and have no agenda other than being exceptional photographs. In terms of my own work, these are photographs that I believe best represent my skills, talent, and vision.

These are not photographs that are meant to reflect my ability to produce a particular type of photograph. I have not selected images based on proving that I can photograph a specific subject matter in a particular way. Instead, these are what I feel are the best photographs I have produced in an area of photography for which I have a passion.

When I have edited each category of images down to a core selection of eight, I have a real sense of what I have achieved or not achieved over the past 12 months, especially when I compare these images to the images from the previous year. Most importantly, I can evaluate what progress I made with respect to the creative goals I set for myself the year before.

As I mentioned in the previous chapter, I settled on eight photographs because I imagined sharing these images as a printed portfolio, which would include an opening image, a closing image, and three sets of photographs that face each other on printed two-page spreads. This is something that I can easily create using the Book module in Adobe Lightroom.

When I view the images in this way, I simulate the experience of looking at these core eight images as if they were in a printed portfolio or book. And unlike just looking at the images on the screen, this method of display creates a very different experience for me. There is something about seeing this collection as a printed book or portfolio that gives me a greater sense of how the photographs work individually and as a group. More often than not, I affirm my selection by viewing the images in this way.

Another advantage of having this core selection of eight images is that it provides a foundation on which to build. If I know that the eight selected images work strongly together, I can begin the process of editing more images, and quickly assess whether the images maintain their strength as a body of work or whether the strength of the group is diminished. I have seen many photographers' portfolios weakened by the fact that they have some lackluster photographs mixed in with the great ones.

When it comes time to produce a printed monograph or portfolio, I create 4×6-inch prints of images that I have selected as my core eight, over multiple years. If my intent is to create a new portfolio of portrait images, I go through the process of culling by comparison, but this time physically handling the photographs, moving them around the floor or on a table. I find that this more visceral process of evaluating my images provides me insights that are just not possible when looking at a computer screen. I am frequently surprised by my choices and by how two images play off of each other during this process.

An Ever-Changing Process

The process that I have described in this chapter is constantly evolving and changing. However, its foundation has proven to be invaluable for measuring my progress as a photographer. It allows me to discern what images are my best, and also how I am progressing in terms of the way that I see and photograph.

I believe that if I did not make this a normal part of my creative process, I would simply produce a lot of photographs with no idea of what I was doing or where I was going. I might make some great photographs during the course of the year, but I would be left doubting whether I am growing and challenging myself in ways that are fruitful and fulfilling.

So whether you embrace this process as written or adapt some of it to your existing method of working, I encourage you to make any such process a part of your photographic experience. It will make all the difference in your ability to improve and fully enjoy your photography.

Begin to cull and organize your images using the principles described in this chapter. When creating genre folders, choose areas of photography that you currently have a passion for, as well as types of photography you would like to produce more of. If possible, go through a previous year's work and see what images rise as your core eight in your designated categories.

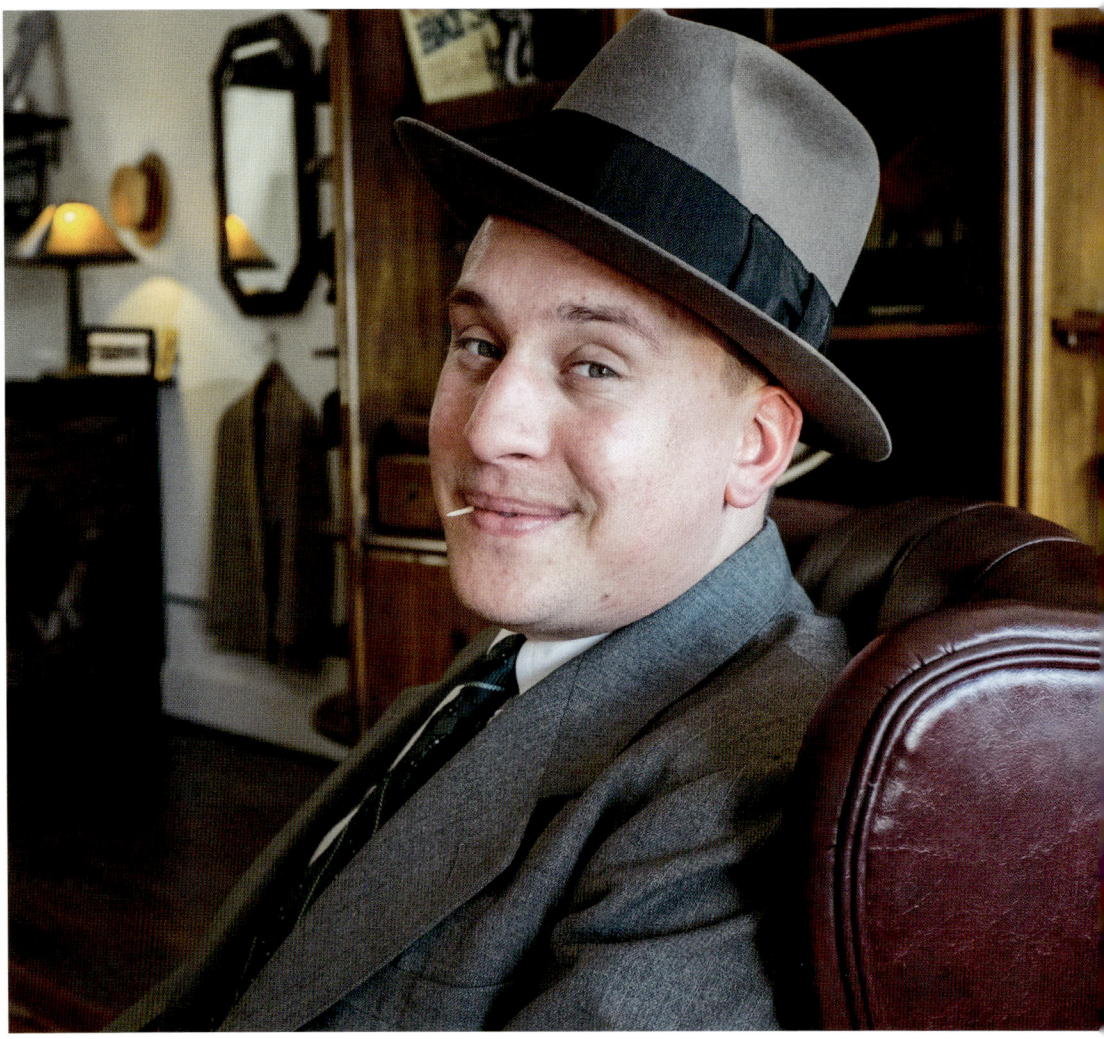

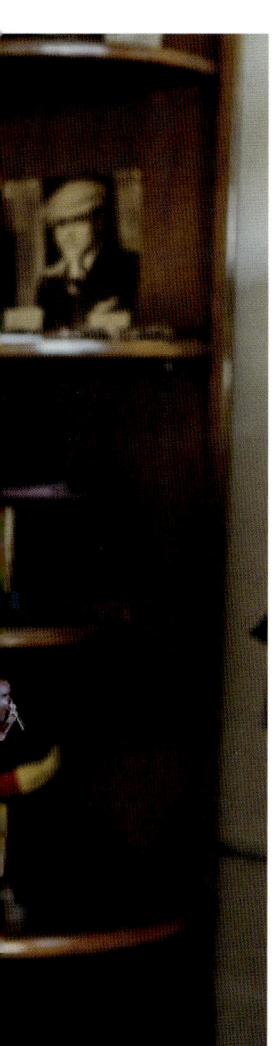

Post-Processing with Vision

Cody Wellema is hard to miss. He has affinity for vintage suits that make it appear as if he stepped out of a time machine. It informs his style of dress and has also inspired his passion for making custom hats. With much of our clothing coming out of major factories, it is rare to find a place that is so dedicated to handcrafting clothing, especially a character-defining article like a hat, but that is exactly what Cody has done for years at the Wellema Hat Company (wellemahatco.com).

I met Cody soon after he relocated to Altadena and I knew upon meeting him that I wanted to photograph him. We scheduled a couple of days for me to come by his shop to make photographs. What surprised me was that he used vintage tools for crafting his hats. Rather than using modern devices, he relied on decades-old blocks, steamers, and hand tools. I observed the weathering on all his equipment, including the blocks that he used to help determine a client's hat size. The shop was visually rich and provided much to photograph.

I put on my storytelling hat when making the various images of Cody and his workspace, spending as much time photographing the small details as I did capturing him at work. It was the accumulation of these things that helped create the entire visual story.

I had two qualities of light to work with. During previous visits, I had noticed that at a certain time of day, sunlight would shine through his front window. It cast a shadow of the store's lettering on the back wall. It was an element I wanted to include in some of the photographs, so I scheduled the shoot for around that time. There was also a back area that did not benefit fully from that sunlight and was illuminated by artificial light sources. I needed to be very aware of both my ISO and white balance for both of these conditions.

Whether I created establishing photographs, images of small details, or environmental portraits, I built each composition using the visual draws. I made each new frame after evaluating light and shadow, line and shape, color, and gesture. Though I knew that this self-assignment was going to take the form of a photo essay, I still needed the individual images to be as strong and effective as possible.

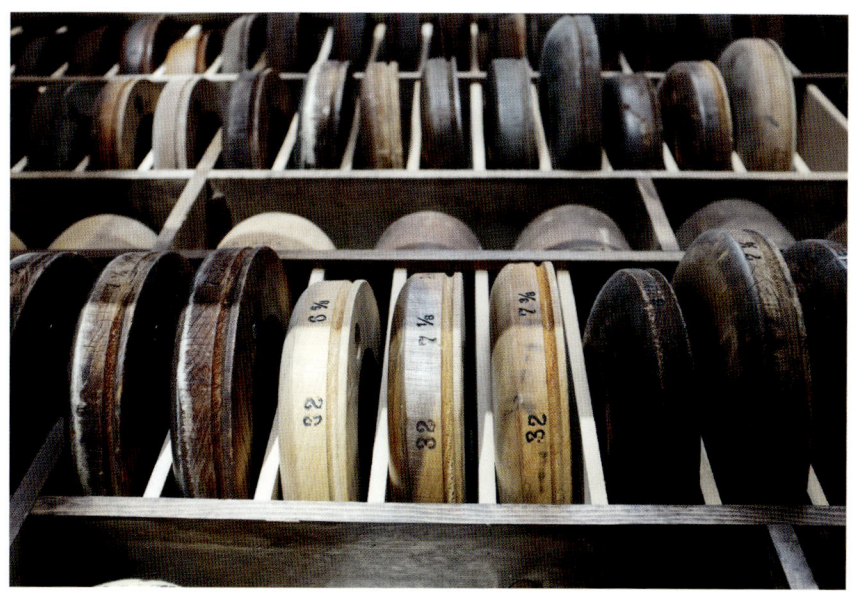

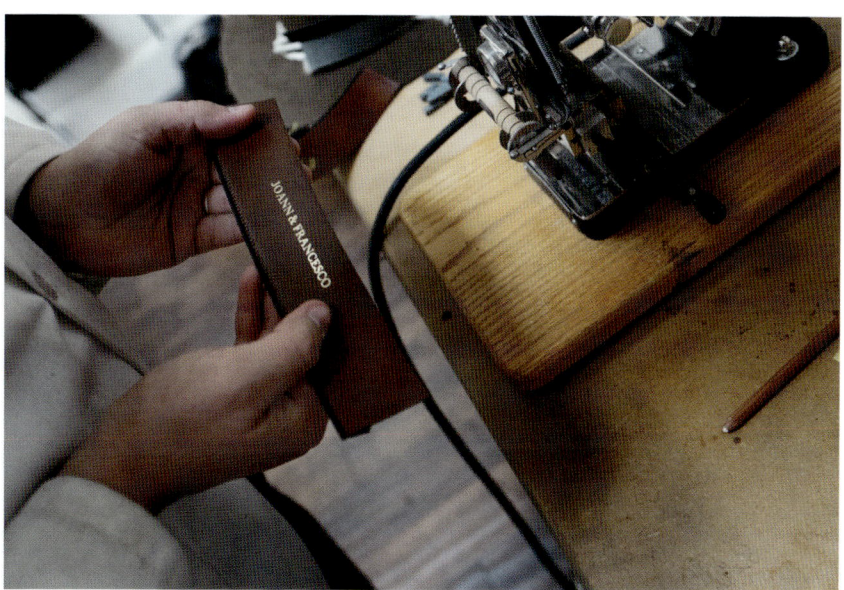

I was working in a small space, so I had to regularly take a step back and assess what I was looking at and what I might be missing. As I asked Cody about his process, I got ideas for photographs that I might not have otherwise considered. As I learned more about him and his way of working, I was led to more images that were not immediately obvious to me.

I was working with a different set of circumstances than those I was accustomed to. On the street, I was used to the unpredictability and chaos of the city. Here, everything had its place and function and could easily be observed and considered. Despite those differences, I had full confidence in my way of seeing and fell back on the same skills and sensibility that I used each and every day in the service of a complete and interesting narrative.

Intentional Post-Processing

When it comes to Lightroom, I have spent countless hours learning to master the numerous controls found in the application. I have learned and practiced a variety of techniques to achieve accurate color and quality sharpening, and to produce the best quality print possible from the resulting files. The application is so flexible and adaptable, I have learned dozens of different ways of achieving a similar outcome. While having such options is invaluable, I have to admit to getting lost in the weeds when it comes to trying to find the perfect method for doing anything in photo editing.

What has been more important in mastering my post-processing is applying the way I see when I create my photographs to what I do when I post-process the files. Rather than just applying some preset or filter equally to each and every image, I have become more thoughtful about what I need the image to look like, whether the destination is a web gallery, Instagram, or a print.

"What has been important in mastering my post-processing is applying the way I see when I create my photographs to what I do when I post-process the files."

Though I initially emulated the techniques and approaches of other photographers, I eventually found my own way of looking, seeing, and editing my photographs. I did not want to rely on someone else's style to create my own.

By evaluating my images based on the visual draws, I think of how I want a viewer to experience the photograph. I need to understand what the subject of the composition is and how the other elements in the frame either lead the viewer to or away from the subject.

It is important to understand that the viewer is drawn to areas in the frame that are brighter than others, areas that possess a greater degree of contrast, sharpness, and color saturation. One or all of these things helps the photographer control where the viewer looks first and where their eyes linger. Though the image straight out of the camera (SOOC) might possess many of these qualities, they could also be enhanced with post-processing.

In this establishing shot of Cody in his workshop, I used his white work jacket to help draw the viewer's eye to him. He is also located in the brightest area of the frame, nicely illuminated by the sunlight coming through his window. The placement of the out-of-focus hat in the foreground is an important storytelling element, and also serves as a point of contrast between softness and sharpness, which again leads the viewer's eye to Cody.

The post-processing that the image received may appear subtle, but I considered how each of those visual elements influenced the viewer's experience of the image. I wanted to reinforce the choices that I had made in composing the image. I not only restored some of the highlight detail in Cody's coat and the back wall, but I also slightly darkened the other areas that had fallen into shadow. I tweaked the contrast and the overall color saturation to achieve the look I was going for.

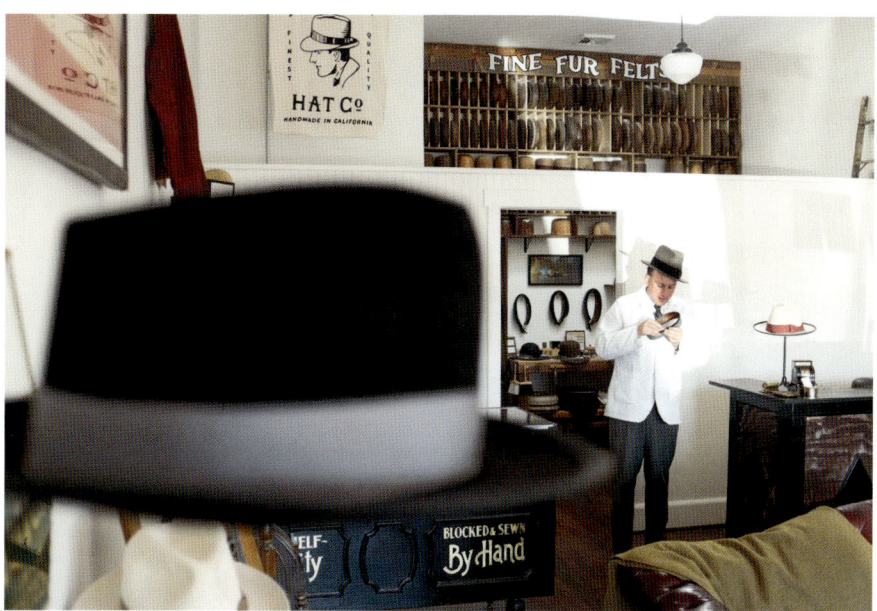

Before

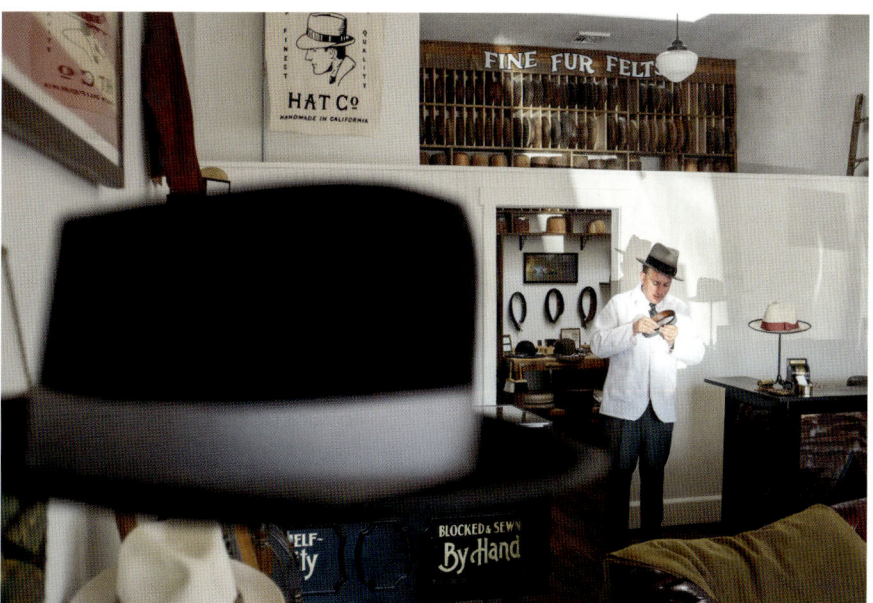

After

The choices I made while composing the photographs made my job in post much easier. If, for example, the blanket draped over the couch in the foreground had been white or bright-red, it would have been a problem. In that case, the blanket would have competed with Cody for the viewer's attention, and I would have needed to change my composition to eliminate the issue. If I didn't, I would have had to crop that element out (which would have completely changed the feel of the photograph) or attempt to change the color or brightness of the blanket (which would have involved a lot more work). I am not a fan of that kind of unnecessary work, especially when I know I could have remedied the problem while making the photograph.

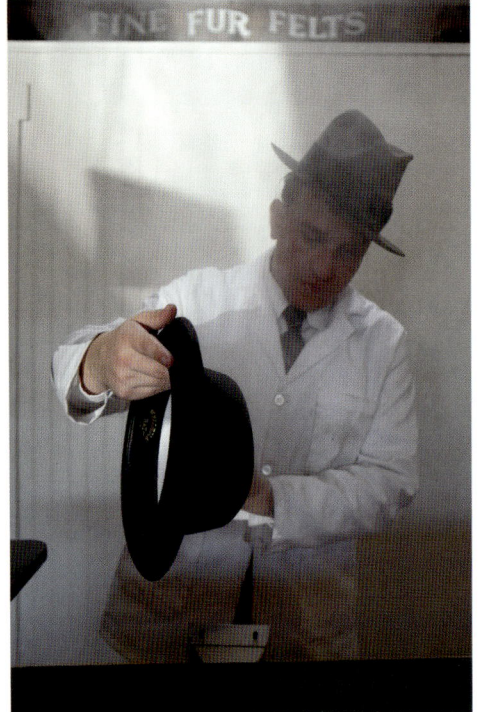

Before

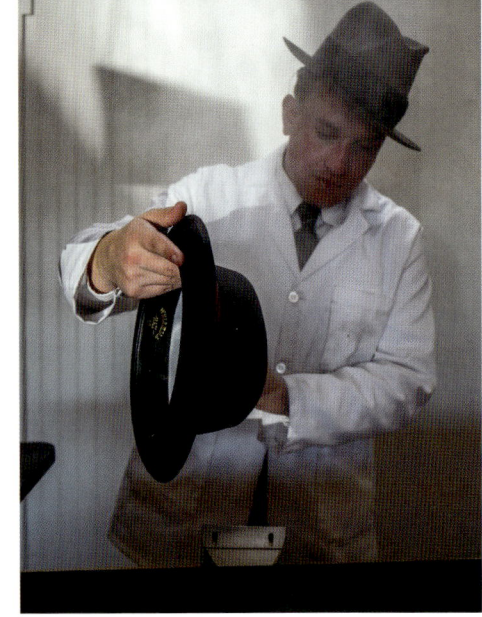

After

Those same considerations came into play when I photographed Cody working with the steamer. I used the same general location and quality of light, but in this frame, I used the light to emphasize his hand. His body and face were relegated to shadow, which was okay because I wanted to draw the viewer's attention to the gesture of Cody's hand with the hat.

By being conscious of all these visual elements while making the photograph, I created not only a well-exposed file, but an image that would eventually require nominal enhancements in post.

Basic Adjustments

Both of the images I just discussed benefited from global adjustments made with the controls in the Basic panel in Lightroom's Develop module, which allows you to adjust things such as exposure, contrast, highlights, shadows, whites, blacks, clarity, vibrance, and saturation. These adjustments influence the look of the entire composition, with some controls, such as highlights and shadows, narrowing the area of influence. This always serves as the starting point for any editing.

I often begin with establishing a black and white point for my file. I do this by holding the Alt/Option key while moving the Blacks and Whites sliders. With the Alt/Option key depressed, I move the Blacks slider until the screen begins to render an area of shadow as black, and then pull the slider back ever so slightly so that only a small portion of the frame registers as black. This establishes the darkest area of the frame. I will then do the same with the Whites slider, which establishes the brightest area of the frame. With the white point, it is important to differentiate between a bright-white area and a specular highlight. A white jacket or coat, for example, is an area where you want to retain detail, whereas a specular highlight will not possess much, if any, detail. If it is a normal white, I will pull back the Whites slider until just before the area goes to black. Once I've done this for both Blacks and Whites, I often see an improvement in contrast.

If needed, I then adjust the Exposure slider until I get the overall brightness that I am looking for. With just those three controls, I often see an improvement in the overall look of the image.

I then use the Shadows and Highlights sliders to bring out or obscure slight detail in the quarter tones. These are tones that are not completely black or white, but that skew toward either end of the tonal range. For example, I will use the Highlights slider to bring out the details in the folds of a white shirt. However, be careful about getting too aggressive with either of these controls, as such adjustments can quickly take on an unnatural look.

The controls in the Presence section at the bottom of the Basic panel— Clarity, Vibrance, and Saturation—can have a big impact on the look of the image, but I tend to be conservative in my application of these adjustments. It is very easy to go overboard with these controls and produce images that look as if they were "Photoshopped," which is something I want to avoid. I do not want to call attention to the fact that I have massaged my images. I want the image itself to speak to the viewer, not the technique that I applied in post.

An extensive explanation of Lightroom is beyond the scope of this book, so I would recommend *The Enthusiast's Guide to Lightroom,* by Rafael Concepcion (Rocky Nook, 2017), for a more exhaustive exploration of this powerful editing software.

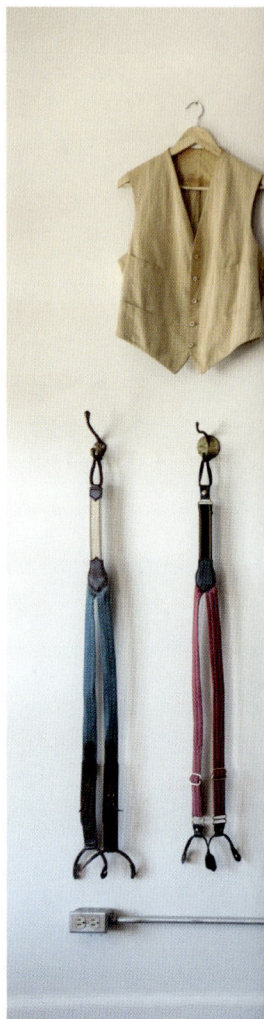

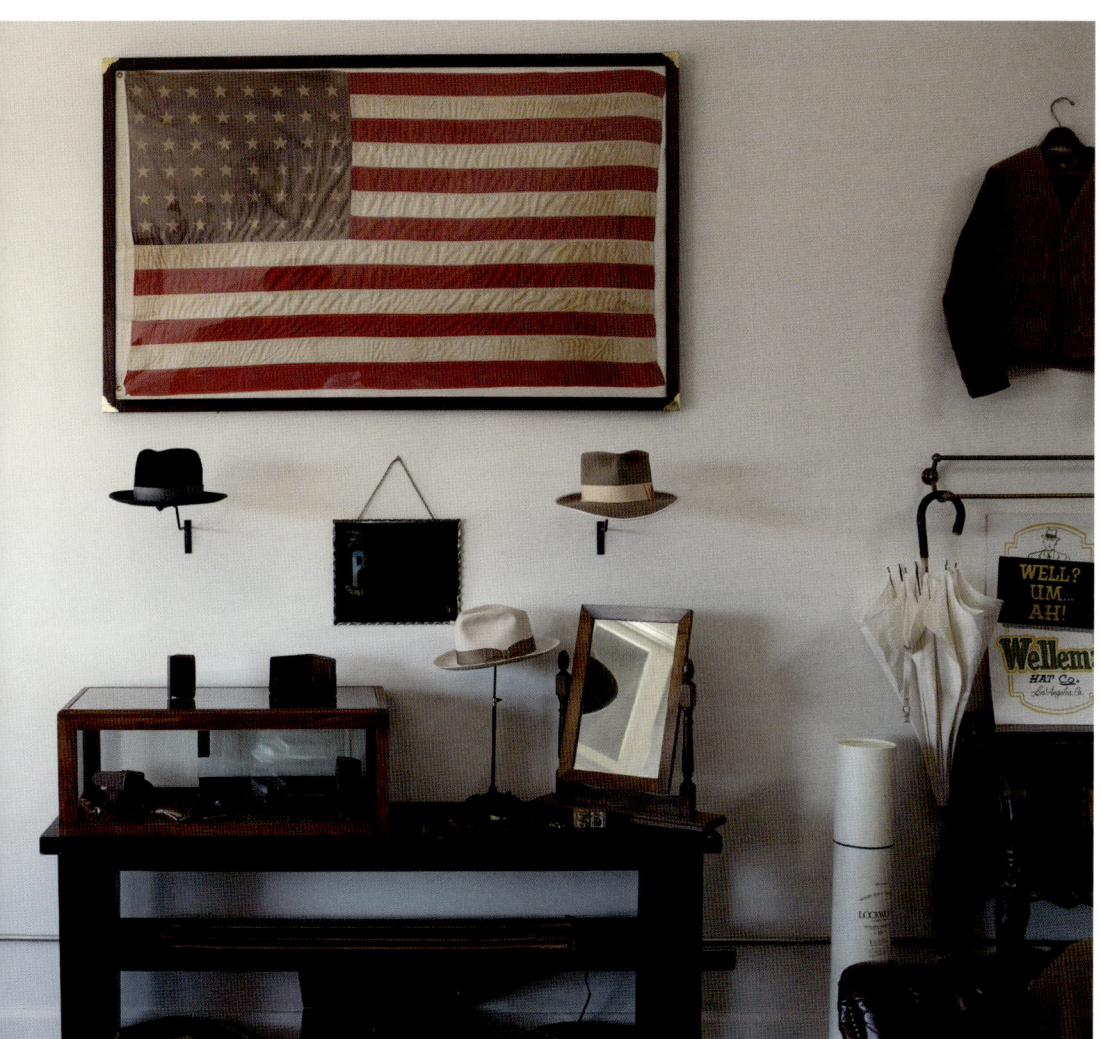

Localized Adjustments

Once I have applied global adjustments, I examine the image to see if it can benefit from more localized or targeted enhancements. I make adjustments like this with controls such as the Adjustment Brush or Radial or Graduated Filters. Once the tool is selected, the interface reveals many of the same sliders that are included in the Basic panel, but now they will affect only those areas targeted by one of the three localized tools.

For example, the Adjustment Brush is a tool I use to apply the technique of dodging and burning. Dodging and burning refers to the old darkroom technique of lightening (dodging) or darkening (burning) certain areas of a photographic print. It is a useful technique for influencing the look of a photograph.

For this photograph of a Wellema promotional card, I darkened the center area, which was appreciably brighter than the rest of the frame. After making my overall adjustments, I used the Adjustment Brush to further tweak the look of the card. I adjusted both the brightness and the clarity to achieve the desired look. I also darkened and slightly desaturated the secondary elements, including the bicycle, to reduce them as potential distractions.

When I consider localized adjustments, I always ask myself how the subject relates to the secondary elements in the composition. In an ideal world, the subject will possess most of the visual draws (brightness, contrast, sharpness, and color saturation). However, that is not always the case, and there may be some element in the background that possesses one or more of those qualities and becomes a distraction. If I was not able to eliminate that element while making the photograph, I can attempt to reduce its influence by adjusting its brightness, contrast, or color saturation.

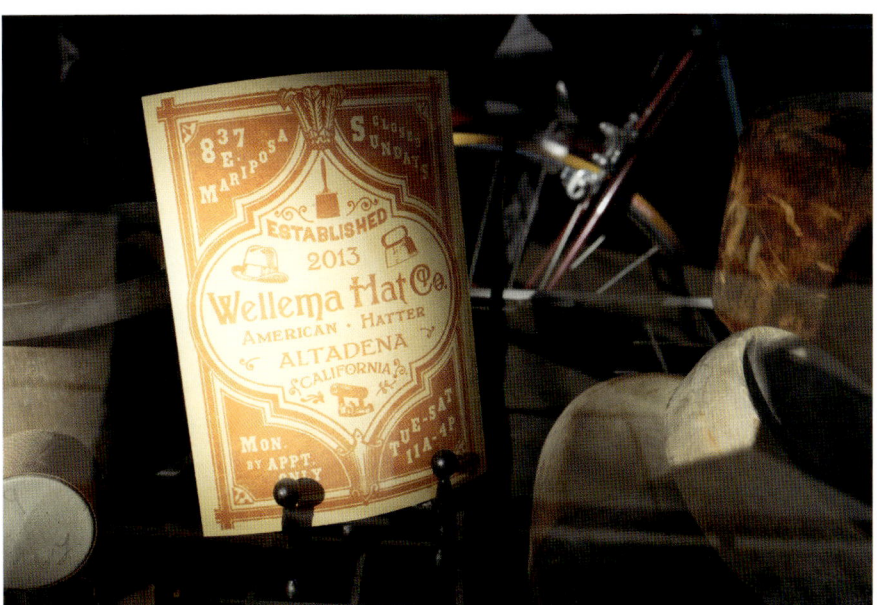

Before

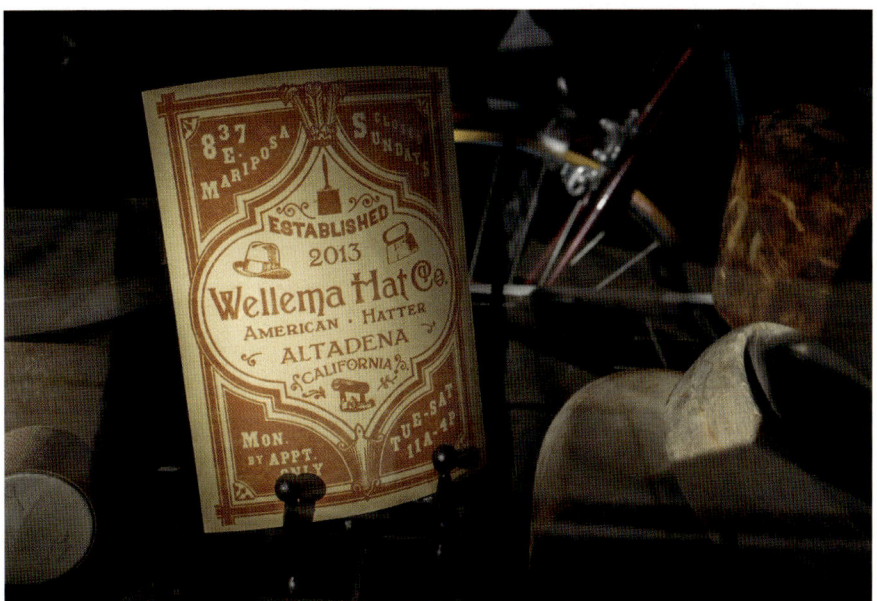

After

For the detail shot of one of Cody's hats (below), I found that the left side of the frame was too bright. It drew my eye away from the heart of the image on the right-hand side. To remedy this, I used the Graduated Filter to reduce the brightness of the left third of the frame. I also reduced the shadow detail and increased the clarity. The resulting contrast helps to draw the eye to the hat.

You will find that you can be much more aggressive with selective dodging and burning of black-and-white images than of color images. With color photographs, you may observe color shifts as well as telltale signs of image manipulation. Black-and-white photographs are much more tolerant of such manipulations.

When evaluating any image, I consider each of the visual draws and see which ones are possessed by either the subject or the secondary elements. The greater the contrast, brightness, color saturation, etc., possessed by the secondary elements, the more I have to consider how those elements may be distracting. If that is the case, I will use both global and selective adjustments to better control the overall look and experience of the photograph.

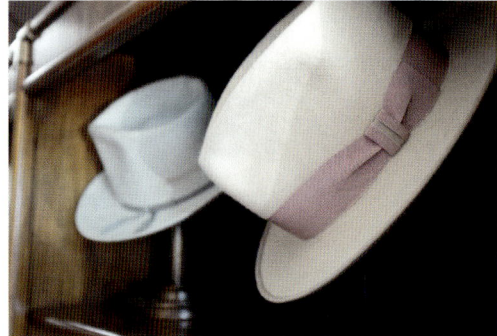

Before

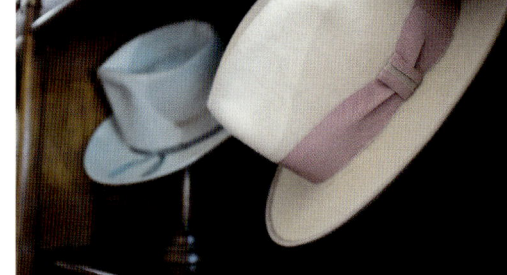

After

Post-process one of your images using the principles discussed in this chapter. Use the concept of the visual draws to determine how you will use your editing tools to emphasize the strengths of your composition.

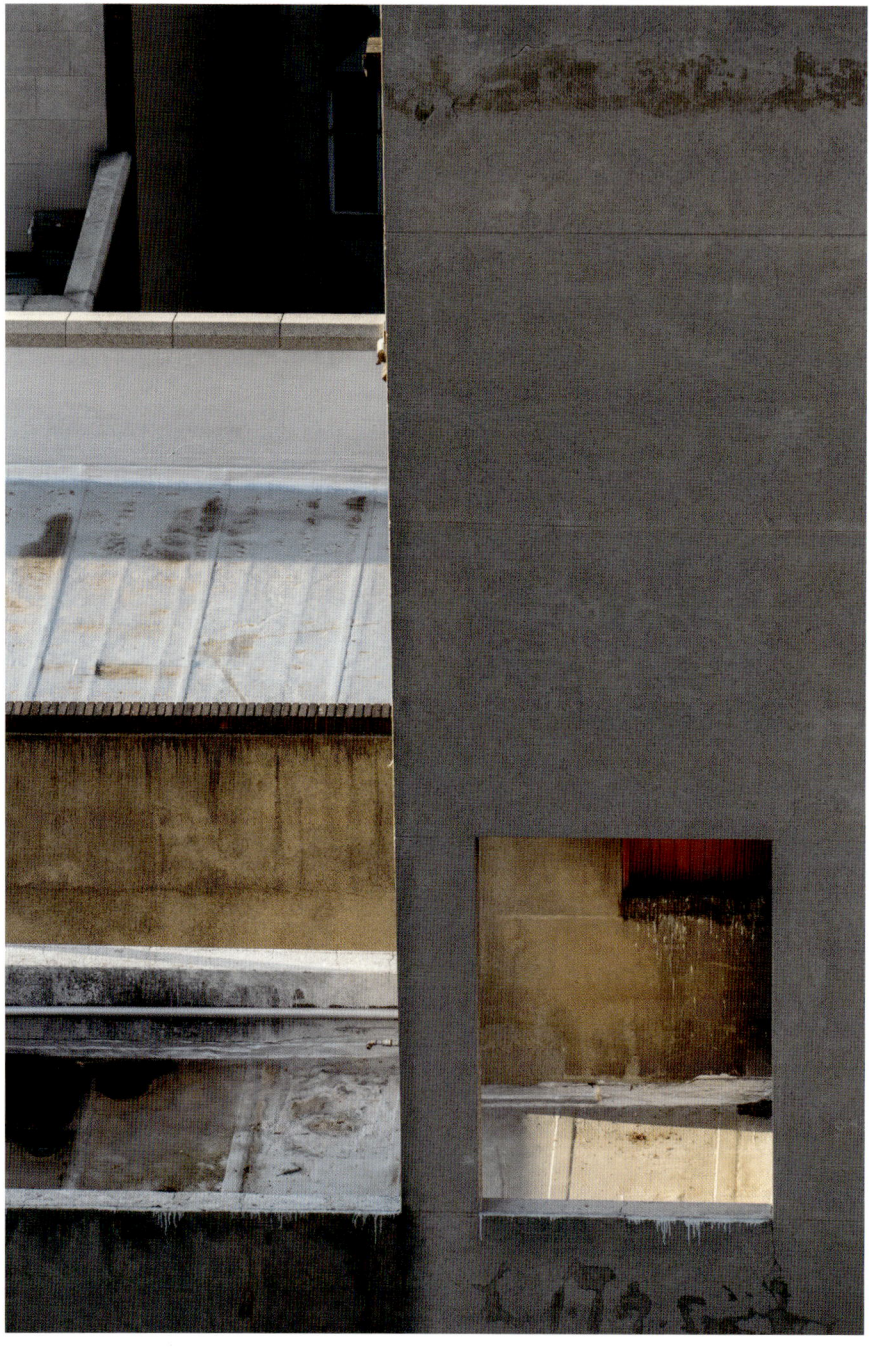

Personal Challenges

I had been invited to Johannesburg, South Africa, to participate in a photographic conference and halfway through my stay there, I was running on fumes. The jet lag was the worst I had ever experienced and no matter how tired I felt at the end of the day, I could not get a decent night's sleep. On several nights I fell asleep and awoke feeling refreshed, only to realize I had fallen asleep just an hour before. Each morning, after very little sleep, I was out of bed preparing for the day's full itinerary.

It was frustrating because I wanted to fully enjoy my first time on the continent. I was surrounded by some amazingly talented photographers. I had the chance to explore and discover South Africa in the company of people who had lived there all their lives. However, there were moments when I felt I was getting through the day by sheer force of will.

On several days we took a group of photographers through downtown Johannesburg. One of those excursions was led by photographer Anton Boseman. Anton is a photographer who not only produces amazing urban landscapes of his beloved city, but has an almost encyclopedic knowledge of the city's architecture and history. He offered us a context for the phases of the city's growth and development through the various styles of architecture.

While demonstrating my personal approach to street photography, I observed how differently Anton saw and experienced the city streets compared to myself. While I often emphasized the interplay of humanity within the city landscape, Anton made the city itself a character in his photographs. Though he was just as attentive to the same visual draws that informed my own photographs, he interpreted the same things in a very different and personal way. His photographs were not just a beautiful document of the city, but a love letter to it as well.

It was fascinating to witness how right after I had taken a street photograph, I found him in the middle of the same street shooting down the canyon of classic buildings. In that moment, I observed the play of light and color, and I caught a glimpse of what and how he saw. We looked at each other and I felt a feeling of acknowledgement pass between us.

As we continued exploring the city, I attempted to reconsider what and how I saw things. I knew I could make good images here as I had in the past, but it seemed that it would be a lost opportunity if I failed to challenge myself to see the world just a little differently. Inspired by Anton and the other photographers I had met, I attempted to do just that.

After some negotiation, we gained access to a rooftop near the center of the city that provided an exceptional view. The dozen or so photographers that were with us fluttered around, snapping away in the late afternoon light.

It was then that I noted a little patch of light that was illuminating a rooftop across the street. Through a rectangular portal in the wall, I saw a sliver of red, along with a textured wall and floor. I grabbed a telephoto zoom and snapped it onto the camera.

I looked at the patterns and shapes created on the adjoining rooftops, and how the light reflected the textures and patterns. I shifted and adjusted my position as much as I could as I continually refined my composition. There were no people in this frame, so I relied completely on my sense of composition and the visual draws to make this as engaging a photograph as I could manage. I knew that the little sliver of red provided a wonderful gesture, but that the rest of the composition had to be strong for the image to not fall apart.

Even after I thought I had the shot, I continued shooting, making further changes until the light changed and the scene became something entirely different.

Though I made many images during that trip that I was happy with, I had a special affinity for this photograph. As simple as it was, it represented how I was inspired by a fellow photographer and how I allowed myself to see the world in a different way.

A Regular Creative Practice

The only way you get better as a photographer is by making photographs. As simple and straight-forward as that statement is, it is easy to forget and can be a difficult thing to actually put into practice.

With our busy work schedules, family obligations, and the everyday demands of life, it can be challenging, if not impossible, to find the time to dedicate to one's passions. However, it is necessary. Because no amount of reading, watching YouTube videos, or chatting about gear ever replaces the gains made by making photographs.

We can spend time on those ancillary activities and feel that we are dedicating time to photography, but that does not mean that we are really improving our skills as photographers. Getting better at anything requires regular and consistent practice. Think of the progress that you would make learning to play a musical instrument if you practiced every day rather than once a month. It is no different when it comes to photography.

But like you, I find it difficult to find time to dedicate to my personal photography. And there are moments when I struggle to dedicate time to photography exclusively, but as experience has shown me, I have to in order to improve.

So over the years I have made the choice to always have a camera with me. Though I do have a camera on my smartphone, I make the conscious choice to have a digital camera over my shoulder at all times. This is my preferred tool of choice. While the camera phone can deliver wonderful results, I want my main tool for creativity to be the means by which I create the majority of photographs.

Making the choice to always have a camera with me results in me constantly being on the hunt for a photograph. Whether I am running around town handling chores or leaving for an appointment, I always have a camera in tow, ready for any opportunity that I discover. As a result, many of the images I produce during the course of the year, and often feature on my Instagram feed, are the result of my everyday wanderings.

Even if I only succeed in producing images for five minutes out of a day, what is really important is that I practiced. Because even though I was only able to make the photographs within a fraction of the time allotted for that day, I was actively seeing most of the time, and that is what is critical for me.

It is the practice of seeing that is the critical skill to develop. When you have a camera on you, you are actively looking at the world and evaluating it for light and shadow, line and shape, color, and gesture. And even though it may not result in you making the photograph, you are learning to see the world in that special way that inevitably improves your way of seeing and your photography.

If you sincerely want to be a better photographer, make the choice to photograph every day.

15 Minutes

No matter how busy your life is, you can always find 15 minutes. Sometimes you spend that time browsing the Internet, turning the pages of a magazine, flipping absently between television channels, daydreaming, or simply staring out of a window. As crazy busy as we all are, there are always minutes of our day that are completely unproductive. Such moments are important because they often provide much-needed stress relief, but they are also a missed opportunity if you are the person who wants to be known as a good photographer.

Hopefully, you discovered the truth of that when you completed one of the assignments in a previous chapter. By practicing this for just one week, you likely found yourself creating images you never would have made otherwise.

I can always find 15 minutes during the course of my day to dedicate to seeing and making photographs. Whether it is part of my lunch break, a casual walk outside the house, or just leaving 15 minutes early for a scheduled appointment, it is time that I can use. Though I love it when I have several continuous hours to dedicate to my photography, I do not allow my inability to do that to prevent me from appreciating and taking advantage of the small moments I do have available. The value of such times is not based on whether I make an exceptional photograph, but rather that I dedicate that time to honing my skills of seeing.

As I began to practice seeing in this way each day, I found my sensitivity to the world around me increasing. Even during moments when I was stuck in traffic on a congested freeway, I noticed the play of light on an adjacent car or a tall building in the distance. While others were stressed being in a traffic jam, I derived a moment of joy at just being able to recognize a wonderful play of light and shadow, even though I was not able to get out of my car to make a photograph of it.

Sometimes those 15 minutes would turn into longer periods of photography, but even if they did not, I felt that those few minutes of my day were put to good use. And as I accumulated photographs over the weeks and months, I saw an accumulation of work that I never would have created had I only considered specific photo outings as productive opportunities to practice my craft.

You also have those 15 minutes available to you; you just have to make the choice to find them. Sometimes you can find the time by choosing to leave early for work or an appointment or when walking the dog. You can find that time by not checking e-mail or browsing the Internet as you walk from your parked car to the restaurant where you are meeting friends. You can find the time while eating breakfast and observing the play of light in your kitchen or dining room. Those 15 minutes are always there for you to leverage. You just have to make the choice to take advantage of them.

Personal Challenges

Some of us are helped by having assignments. Just saying that you are going to make photographs every day is not enough to spur the creative juices and to stay committed to an everyday practice, so having some form of structure becomes important.

I once gave myself an assignment to photograph hands. The images could revolve around a tight shot of hands, hand gestures, or people doing things with their hands. Whatever form it took, the hands had to be at the heart of the composition.

As mundane and ordinary as this might sound, it was quite a challenge to pull off. It was difficult because it was not about making snapshots of hands, but making strong, effective photographs using everything I knew about making a good composition. It was not an opportunity to be lazy. It was quite the contrary—I had to bring my A game for each and every shot.

Making the choice to focus on hands made me sensitive to them throughout the day. I would find interesting subject matter under circumstances that I would not have normally considered for making a photograph. And once I did recognize new subject matter, I had to use my awareness of the visual draws to try and make as good of an image as possible.

Admittedly, I did not always succeed, but I welcomed the opportunity to try. There was something inspiring in recognizing the potential of a scene and trying to give it my all. Regardless of whatever else I was doing that day, I found myself experiencing moments of exhilaration as I attempted to make a good photograph.

During a visit to a doctor to discuss my sciatica, he was using a model of a spine to illustrate the problem I was experiencing. While he did so, I made a photograph of the model and his hand. It was a moment that I normally would not have photographed, but because I had the assignment at the forefront of my mind, I did not hesitate to create the image.

When the nurse took my blood pressure, I made another photograph, which included her hand and my own. The image is oddly framed and slightly blurred because I was holding the camera with one hand while trying to approximate my composition. However, I really like the look and feel of the photograph. It is appreciably different than the more controlled, exacting compositions I normally produce, which is one of the reasons I like it.

Soon after, I was back on the streets and I made a portrait of a man smoking a cigarette (page 300). Again, it is a photograph about the hands, especially the gesture of him reaching for the cigarette firmly clenched in his mouth.

At the end of the week, I had an abundance of photographs, each very different from the others. And while the images might never find their way onto a gallery wall, I was thrilled with the results, not because they were fantastic photographs, but because I had risen to the challenge of seeing differently and seeing creatively.

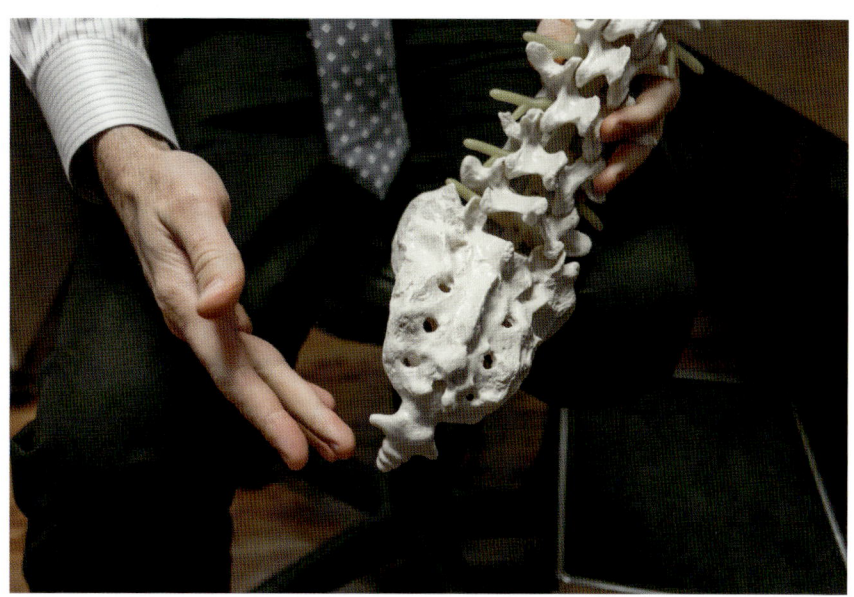

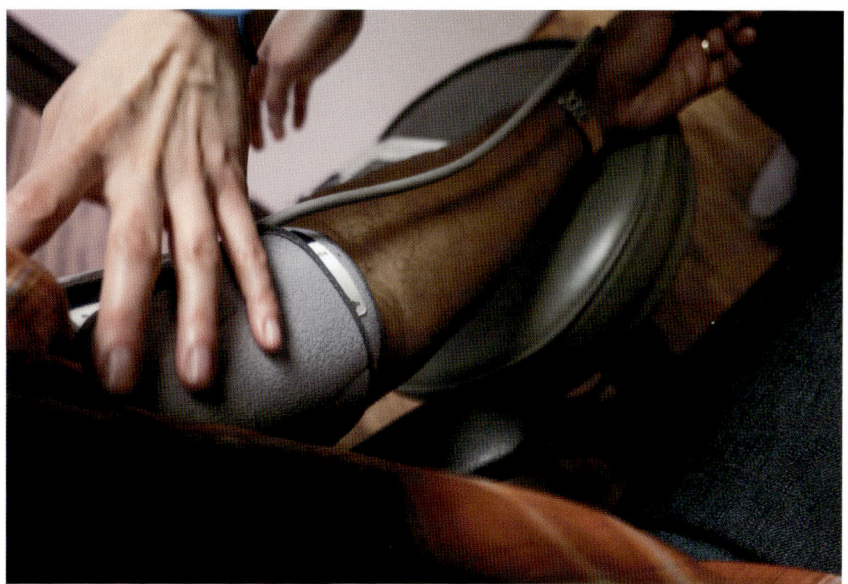

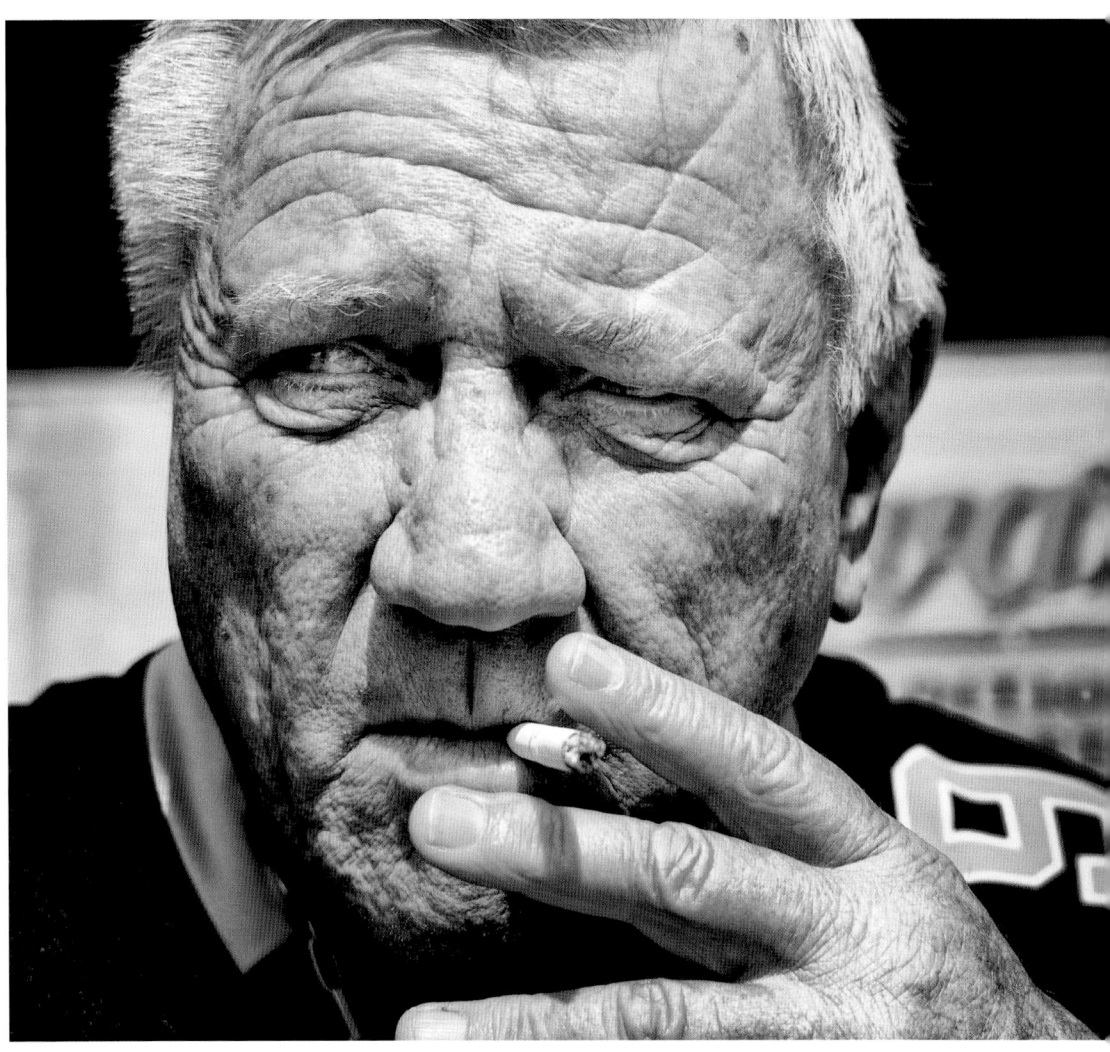

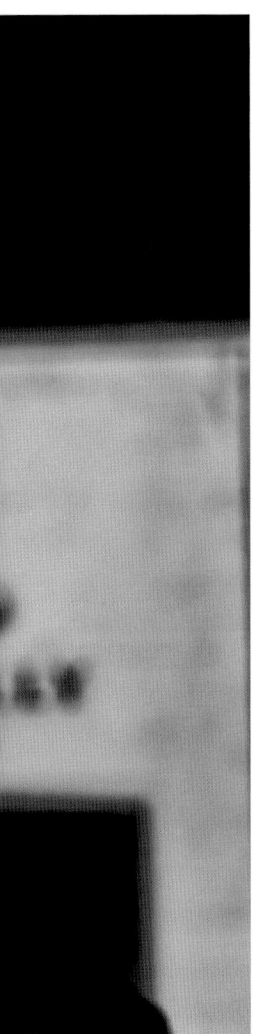

The nature of the assignment you choose is not really as important as just making the choice and time to fulfill it. Whether it is a 365 challenge, 15 minutes a day, or just fulfilling a list of creative challenges, what matters is that you are making the choice to be a photographer and make photographs.

Photo Assignments

Here is a list of photo assignments you can try to help get your creative juices flowing. Use them when you are feeling frustrated with figuring out what to photograph or use them as a launching pad for exploring a particular subject or scene.

You may often find that these assignments help you to begin making photographs, and that you are soon moving away from the assignment and making other kinds of images. That is fine. There are no hard and fast rules here. What is important is how you are seeing. If you begin to struggle, return to the assignment, but you will likely find that when you begin parsing the scene using the visual draws, you will have built enough momentum that the time you have dedicated to photography will fly by.

15 Photographs

Stand in one place and make 15 photographs from where you stand. Do not move from that spot. You can crouch down or use your zoom or change perspective, but you have to stay in place. See how differently you can explore the world around you while staying in one spot.

One Subject

Pick a simple object in your household (a coffee cup, vase, wine bottle) and photograph it until you have produced 36 different photographs of it. Photograph it from different perspectives, using different lenses, or under different qualities of light. Make each photograph as unique as possible.

No Portrait Self-Portrait

Create a series of self-portraits that that do not include an image of your face. Instead, photograph items and things in your life that reveal your personality and your interests. You might include your presence by including your hands, feet, or shadows in the image.

Round the Block

Walk around one block in your neighborhood or near work and find at least a dozen things to photograph. Try to do more than just document those things—try to compose images that make those things interesting and engaging.

Traveling Teddy

Take a small item, such as a teddy bear, small green army man, or action figure, and photograph it in a variety of different environments—the odder, the better. Create images in which the figure is an active presence in the scene, such as having a latte at the local coffeehouse. Have fun and be creative.

Abstract It

Choose an item and produce a series of abstract photographs that do not easily reveal what it is. Include only fragments of the subject in the composition and/or use light and shadow to reveal and obscure certain details. Produce as many images as you can.

Out of Focus

Set your camera to manual focus mode and set your lens to its minimum focus or to infinity, and purposely take out-of-focus photographs. Examine how subjects and scenes appear when they are completely blurred in the frame. Observe how colors and shapes take on a different weight in your compositions.

Don't Look

Snap photographs of things you find interesting without looking through the viewfinder or composing using the camera's LCD. Simply point the camera in the direction of your subjects. Create at least 24 photographs in this way and enjoy the unexpected surprises this provides.

All Vertical

Create images with the camera oriented vertically. No horizontal images allowed. Explore and consider what choices you have to make to make an interesting composition of a subject or scene that you are accustomed to photographing horizontally.

Small Memory Card

Use a small-capacity memory card that limits the number of images you can produce. Try to limit yourself to a few dozen photographs, rather than hundreds or thousands. Avoid deleting images in order to create more space. Just see and photograph more carefully.

At Your Feet

Photograph only things that you find on the ground. Look not only for discarded or lost items, but also examine colors, patterns, and shadows. Use people's feet or shadows to create interesting compositions.

At the Edge

Compose photographs with your main subject positioned at the very edges of your frame rather than at the center. Consider using a limited depth of field to create a contrast between the subject and the background.

Hands Only

Make a portrait series showing only hands. Try to make the images a consistent series by photographing them under similar lighting conditions or with a similar background. Consider whether you want each subject holding something or juxtaposed with something they value.

Morning Routine

Create a series of photographs that reflect your daily morning routine. This could include turning off the alarm clock, brushing your teeth, taking a shower, making coffee, walking the dog, or anything else you do to get ready for the day. Create a series of 15 photographs that capture what life is like for you each morning.

Moods

Create images that evoke a mood (happy, sad, depressed, aroused, etc.). Try to use colors that reflect each mood, and create a total of three different images. Create a triptych of this trio of images and observe how they play off of each other.

These assignments are just a starting point for your creativity. But that is really all that you need. Once you begin, momentum usually takes over and you will soon find yourself exploring your creativity in new and exciting ways. The big challenge is just getting started.

Take on a challenge of producing photographs every day for 15 consecutive days. Find 15 minutes each day to dedicate to your photography. You can leave your choice of subject matter open or find a different focus for each day. Use the culling process to select a "core eight" selection of your best images from the series.

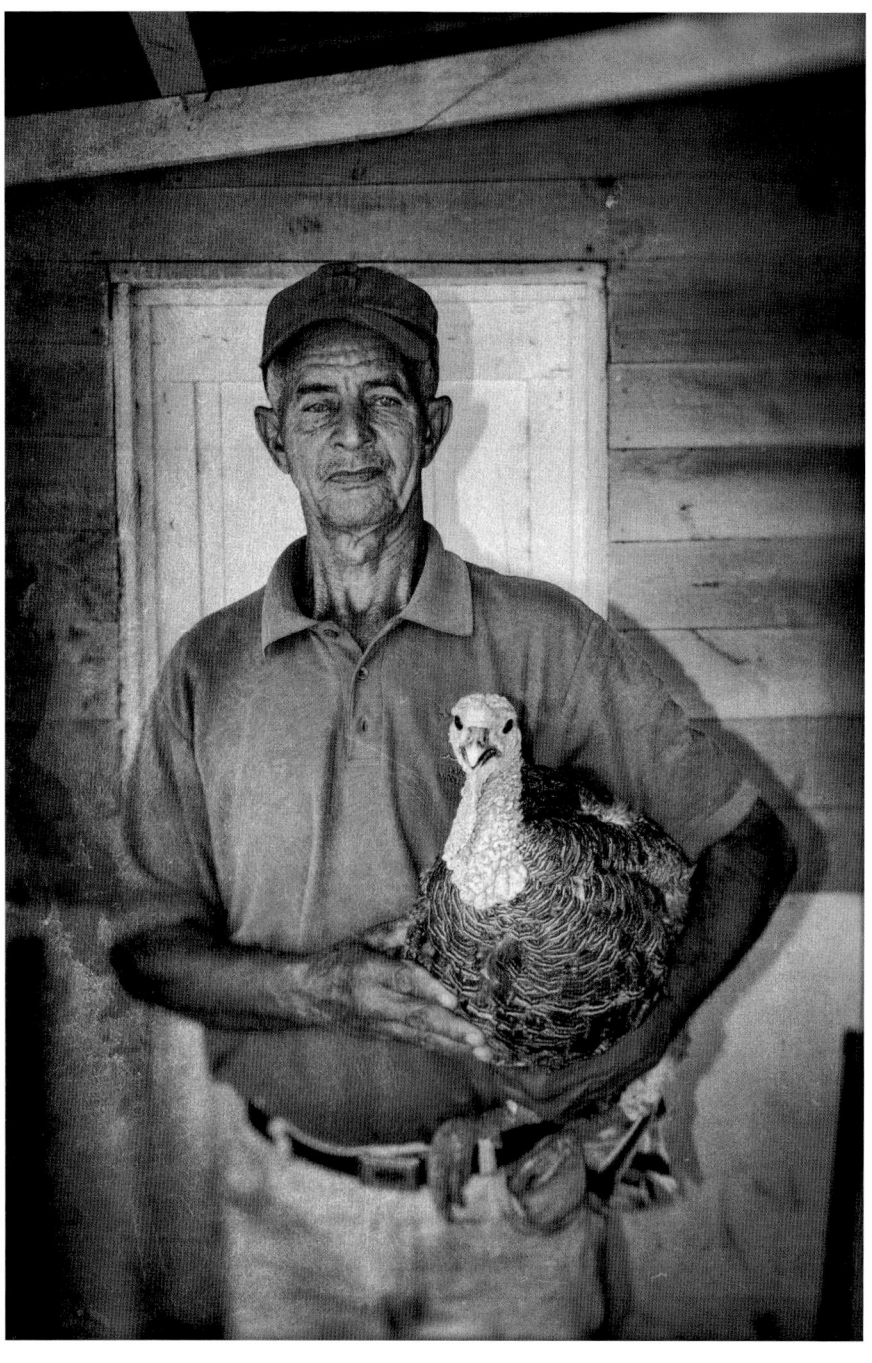

Summary

My wife and I traveled to the Dominican Republic to participate in the remembrances for my father who passed away unexpectedly the year before. My stepmother was planning for a mass to be held in his name, and it would provide a time for each of us to be together as a family.

Just as I had 20 years before when I came to Monte Cristi for the first time as an adult, I had my camera in tow. I made photographs as a way to keep my mind busy because the loss of my father was still a palpable experience for me. As I wandered around the house and the streets of the small town where he grew up, I was constantly aware of him. Ironically, I found myself feeling his presence not when tending to the modest crypt in which he was buried, but in the streets of the first place he had ever called home.

As I walked through the streets making photographs, I imagined how he might have experienced these same locations when he was a boy and when he was a young man. It was easy to imagine because much of the town was made of houses and buildings that looked as they likely had for decades, except for maybe a few coats of new paint.

As if part of a meditative practice, I wandered the streets paying attention to the visual draws of light and shadow, line and shape, color, and gesture. Doing so gave me a way of immersing myself in my surroundings, rather than getting distracted by the many thoughts and feelings that danced around my head. I really wanted to be present and in the moment while here, and this was the means for me to do it.

Later that day my sister took me to a neighbor of my father's who had a pet chicken that she had told me about. She told me that my father had picked up a particular affinity for this bird and had given it to his neighbor as a gift, with the understanding that it was never to be butchered and used for food.

When I arrived at the man's modest home, he gently showed me the bird. He explained that the bird slept with him inside to avoid thieves or stray dogs from claiming him. He told me the story of how he acquired the bird and I could hear in his voice how proud he was to be able to care for this chicken as a way of honoring my father. As I heard from him and from so many others who I would encounter throughout town, my father was not only well respected, but well loved.

I asked permission to make the man's portrait with the bird, which he gladly picked up and took into his arms.

Though I made many images during that particular visit, I am happiest with this simple portrait of this man and his bird. It was a beautiful image to me, and it served as a reminder of the kind man that my father was and the gentleness that he brought into the world, which touched the lives of not only people, but also this very lucky bird.

I was grateful for the moment and for my father who had helped make it possible by allowing me to handle his camera when I was a young boy.

Now as a grown man making a simple photograph, I felt a wave of gratitude sweep over me. In this moment, things both present and past were brought together and I was conscious enough of it all to see and experience it. I recognized it all for the true gift that it was.

Enjoy the Journey

As I write this book, I have been behind a camera for over 40 years. As much as photography is a passion for me, I cannot say that all that time was dedicated to becoming a better photographer. Rather, much of the time involved me just taking pleasure in the act of making photographs.

However, there came a time when I knew that making the occasional good photograph was not enough for me. I wanted to not only make wonderful photographs, but to possess the skill, talent, and experience that allowed me to be more thoughtful about the process than I had been. It was a more difficult task than I had imagined.

Though there were moments of frustration and disappointment, I have come to believe that it was this journey itself that provided me the greatest joy and satisfaction. The conscious choice to become a better photographer has led me on a path where I have learned about who I am and how I see the world. The discovery of the unique way that I experience and capture the world with my camera has led to amazing moments of discovery, joy, and gratitude.

Though publishing magazine articles and books, having exhibits, and speaking in front of hundreds of people have each brought me levels of satisfaction, it is the path that I have traveled to become a better photographer that has made so much of my life so fulfilling.

It may surprise many people that it is not the career achievements that mean the most to me, but rather those quiet and solitary moments when I have walked down a street and seen something marvelous happening in front of me and managed to capture it with my camera. It is those moments that are not only forever etched in my memory, but if I am lucky, are also seen in a finished photograph.

This my hope for you. I hope this book serves to not only make you a better photographer, but that you grow in a way that you see the world and appreciate it and memorialize it. We are among the lucky few who share the passion and have the potential to reveal the world's beauty at both its most epic and its most mundane. Through our photographs, we have the opportunity to reveal what everyone is missing and often takes for granted.

Whether the viewers of your photographs are members of your family or strangers thousands of miles away browsing through your images on a smartphone, there is something special being shared. You are giving voice to the way you, and only you, witness and experience this all-too-brief time on Earth.

Use it well.

Resources

PODCASTS

The Candid Frame Photography Podcast
http://thecandidframe.com

The Martin Bailey Photography Podcast
https://www.martinbaileyphotography.com/podcasts/

Photography Tips from the Top Floor
http://tipsfromthetopfloor.com

Jeff Curto's Camera Position
http://cameraposition.com

On Taking Pictures
http://ontakingpictures.com

Street PX
http://streetpx.com

Hit the Streets with Valérie Jordan
http://valeriejardinphotography.com/podcast/

PetaPixel Photography Podcast with Sharkey James
https://petapixel.com/podcast/

A Small Voice: Conversations with Photographers
https://bensmithphoto.com/asmallvoice/

YOUTUBE CHANNELS

The Art of Photography
https://www.youtube.com/theartofphotography

B&H Video
https://www.youtube.com/user/BHPhotoVideoProAudio/

Adorama TV
https://www.youtube.com/user/adoramaTV

Tony & Chelsea Northrup
https://www.youtube.com/user/VistaClues

Thomas Heaton
https://www.youtube.com/channel/UCfhW84xfA6gEc4hDK9orR1Q

Mango Street
https://www.youtube.com/channel/UC5bp5_6h-ZxkBz6S_33ZUVg

Sean Tucker
https://www.youtube.com/user/seantuckermerge

bigheadtaco
https://www.youtube.com/user/bigheadtaco

Chase Jarvis
https://www.youtube.com/chasejarvis

BLOGS

David duChemin
http://davidduchemin.com/

DP Review
https://www.dpreview.com/

The Phoblographer
https://www.thephoblographer.com/

Petapixel
https://petapixel.com/

The Luminous Landscape
https://luminous-landscape.com/

FujiLove
https://fujilove.com/

Lenscratch
http://lenscratch.com/

Ian MacDonald Photography
https://ianmacdonaldphotography.com/

121 Clicks
http://121clicks.com/

Women in Photography
http://www.womeninphotography.info/

Street Photography Magazine
https://streetphotographymagazine.com/

Dodge & Burn
http://dodgeburnphoto.com/

The Leica Camera Blog
http://blog.leica-camera.com/

Lens – The New York Times
https://www.nytimes.com/section/lens

PHOTOGRAPHIC INSPIRATIONS

Joel Meyerowitz
https://www.joelmeyerowitz.com/

Mary Ellen Mark
http://www.maryellenmark.com/

Stephen Shore
http://stephenshore.net/

Gordon Parks
http://www.gordonparksfoundation.org/

Alex Webb and Rebecca Norris Webb
https://www.webbnorriswebb.co/

Eli Reed
https://www.magnumphotos.com/photographer/eli-reed/

Dan Winters
https://www.danwintersphoto.com/

Mark Seliger
http://markseliger.com/

Maggie Steber
http://www.maggiesteber.com/main.html

Roy DeCarava
http://decarava.org/

Josef Koudelka
https://www.magnumphotos.com/photographer/josef-koudelka/

Hiroshi Sugimoto
https://www.sugimotohiroshi.com/

Alejandro Cegarra
https://www.alecegarra.com/

William Albert Allard
http://www.williamalbertallard.com/

Sam Abell
http://samabell.com/

Arthur Meyerson
http://www.arthurmeyerson.com/

Fred Herzog
https://www.equinoxgallery.com/artists/portfolio/fred-herzog

Index